Interactive Computing Series

Microsoft® Internet Explorer™ 6.0

Brief Edition

Kenneth C. Laudon • Kenneth Rosenblatt

David Langley

Azimuth Interactive, Inc.

McGraw-Hill Irwin

Boston Burr Ridge, IL Dubuque, IA Madison, WI New York San Francisco St. Louis
Bangkok Bogotá Caracas Kuala Lumpur Lisbon London Madrid Mexico City
Milan Montreal New Delhi Santiago Seoul Singapore Sydney Taipei Toronto

McGraw-Hill Higher Education

A Division of The ***McGraw-Hill*** *Companies*

MICROSOFT INTERNET EXPLORER 6.0 BRIEF EDITION
Published by McGraw-Hill/Irwin, an imprint of The McGraw-Hill Companies, Inc., 1221 Avenue of the Americas, New York, NY 10020.

This book is printed on acid-free paper.

1 2 3 4 5 6 7 8 9 0 QPD/QPD 0 9 8 7 6 5 4 3 2 1

ISBN 0-07-247181-6

Publisher: *George Werthman*
Associate editor: *Steven Schuetz*
Developmental editor: *Diana Del Castillo*
Senior marketing manager: *Jeff Parr*
Senior project manager: *Pat Frederickson*
Senior production supervisor: *Michael R. McCormick*
Coordinator, freelance design: *Pam Verros*
Supplement producer: *Mark Mattson*
Senior producer, Media technology: *David Barrick*
Cover design: *JoAnne Schopler*
Interior designer: *Asylum Studios*
Cover photograph: *Bill Brooks/© Masterfile*
Compositor: *Azimuth Interactive, Inc.*
Typeface: *10/12 Times*
Printer: *Quebecor Printing Book Group/Dubuque*

Library of Congress Control Number: 2001012345

www.mhhe.com

Information Technology at McGraw-Hill/Irwin

At McGraw-Hill Higher Education, we publish instructional materials targeted at the higher education market. In an effort to expand the tools of higher learning, we publish texts, lab manuals, study guides, testing materials, software, and multimedia products.

At McGraw-Hill/Irwin (a division of McGraw-Hill Higher Education), we realize that technology has created and will continue to create new mediums for professors and students to use in managing resources and communicating information with one another. We strive to provide the most flexible and complete teaching and learning tools available as well as offer solutions to the changing world of teaching and learning.

MCGRAW-HILL/IRWIN IS DEDICATED TO PROVIDING THE TOOLS FOR TODAY'S INSTRUCTORS AND STUDENTS TO SUCCESSFULLY NAVIGATE THE WORLD OF INFORMATION TECHNOLOGY.

- **Seminar series**—Technology Connection seminar series offered across the country every year demonstrates the latest technology products and encourages collaboration among teaching professionals.

- **Osborne/McGraw-Hill**—This division of The McGraw-Hill Companies is known for its best-selling Internet titles: Harley Hahn's Internet & Web Yellow Pages, and the Internet Complete Reference. Osborne offers an additional resource for certification and has strategic publishing relationships with corporations such as Corel Corporation and America Online. For more information visit Osborne at www.osborne.com.

- **Digital solutions**—McGraw-Hill/Irwin is committed to publishing digital solutions. Taking your course online does not have to be a solitary venture, nor does it have to be a difficult one. We offer several solutions that will allow you to enjoy all the benefits of having course material online. For more information visit www.mhhe.com/solutions/index.mhtml.

- **Packaging options**—For more about our discount options, contact your local McGraw-Hill/Irwin Sales representative at 1-800-338-3987 or visit our Web site at www.mhhe.com/it.

preface

Interactive Computing Series

GOALS/PHILOSOPHY

The ***Interactive Computing Series*** provides you with an illustrated interactive environment for learning software skills using Microsoft Office. The text uses both "hands-on" instruction, supplementary text, and independent exercises to enrich the learning experience.

APPROACH

The ***Interactive Computing Series*** is the visual interactive way to develop and apply software skills. This skills-based approach coupled with its highly visual, two-page spread design allows the student to focus on a single skill without having to turn the page. A Lesson Goal at the beginning of each lesson prepares the student to apply the skills with a real-world focus. The Quiz and Interactivity sections at the end of each lesson measure the student's understanding of the concepts and skills learned in the two-page spreads and reinforce the skills with additional exercises.

ABOUT THE BOOK

The **Interactive Computing Series** offers *two levels* of instruction. Each level builds upon the previous level.

Brief lab manual—covers the basics of the application, contains two to four chapters.

Introductory lab manual—includes the material in the Brief textbook plus two to four additional chapters. The Introductory lab manuals prepare students for the *Microsoft Office User Specialist Proficiency Exam (MOUS Certification).*

Each lesson is divided into a number of Skills. Each **Skill** is first explained at the top of the page in the Concept. Each **Concept** is a concise description of why the Skill is useful and where it is commonly used. Each **Step (Do It!)** contains the instructions on how to complete the Skill. The appearance of the ***MOUS Skill*** icon on a Skill page indicates that the Skill contains instruction in at least one of the required MOUS objectives for the relevant exam. Though the icons appear in the Brief manuals as well as the Introductory manuals, only the Introductory manuals may be used in preparation for MOUS Certification. Some **Interactive Computing Series** texts, such as *Microsoft Internet Explorer 6.0*, are not affiliated with a certification exam.

Figure 1

WD 3.32 | LESSON THREE Advanced Editing

Skill: Each lesson is divided into a number of specific skills

skill Finding and Replacing Text

Concept: A concise description of why the skill is useful and when it is commonly used

concept

The Find command enables you to search a document for individual occurrences of any word, phrase, or other unit of text. The Replace command enables you to replace one or all occurrences of a word that you have found. Together, the Find and Replace commands form powerful editing tools for making many document-wide changes in just seconds.

Do It!: Step-by-step directions show you how to use the skill in a real-world scenario

do it!

Use Find and Replace to spell a word consistently throughout a document.

1. Open student file, wddoit12.doc, and save it as Report12.doc.
2. If necessary, place the insertion point at the beginning of the document. Word will search the document from the insertion point forward.
3. Click Edit, and then click Replace. The Find and Replace dialog box appears with the Replace tab in front and the insertion point in the Find What text box.
4. In the Find What box, type the two words per cent. Click in the Replace With box, and type the one word percent (see Figure 3-37).
5. Click [Replace All] to search the document for all instances of per cent and to replace them with percent. A message box appears to display the results. In this case, one replacement was made (see Figure 3-38). In short documents the Find and Replace procedure takes so little time that you usually cannot cancel it before it ends. However, in longer documents you can cancel a search in progress by pressing [Esc].
6. Click [OK] to close the message box. Click [Close] to close the Find and Replace dialog box.
7. Save and close the document, Report12.doc, with your change.

Hot Tips: Icons introduce helpful hints or trouble-shooting tips

More: Provides in-depth information about the skill and related features

more

Clicking the Replace All button in the Find and Replace dialog box replaces every instance of the text you have placed in the Find What box. To examine and replace a word or phrase manually instead of automatically, start by clicking the Find Next button. If you desire to replace that instance, click the Replace button. Continue checking the document like this, clicking the Find Next button and then, if desired, the Replace button. Keep clicking the pairs of buttons until you have run through the entire document. Unless you absolutely must do otherwise, use the method for shorter documents only.

The first button under the Replace With box usually displays the word More. Click this button when you want to display the the Search Options area of the dialog box. With the area displayed, the More button converts to a Less button. Clicking on the Less button will hide the Search Options area. The Search drop-down list under Search Options determines the direction of the search relative to the insertion point. You can search upward or downward through the document or keep the Word default setting of All to check the whole document, including headers, footers, and footnotes. The Format drop-down list enables you to search criteria for fonts, paragraphs, tabs, and similar items. The Special drop-down list enables you to search for paragraph marks, tab characters, column breaks and related special characters. The No Formatting button removes all formatting criteria from searches. For information on the Search Option activated by the check boxes, consult Table 3-3.

The Find tab of the Find and Replace dialog box matches the Replace tab except it lacks the replace function and only searches documents for items that you specify.

In the book, each skill is described in a two-page graphical spread (Figure 1). The left side of the two-page spread describes the skill, the concept, and the steps needed to perform the skill. The right side of the spread uses screen shots to show you how the screen should look at key stages.

features

Figure 1 (continued)

INTERACTIVE COMPUTING Word XP WD 3.33

Figure 3-37 Find and Replace dialog box

Enter the word or phrase to search for and replace here

Enter the replacement word here

Use check boxes to activate search options

Click to determine direction of search

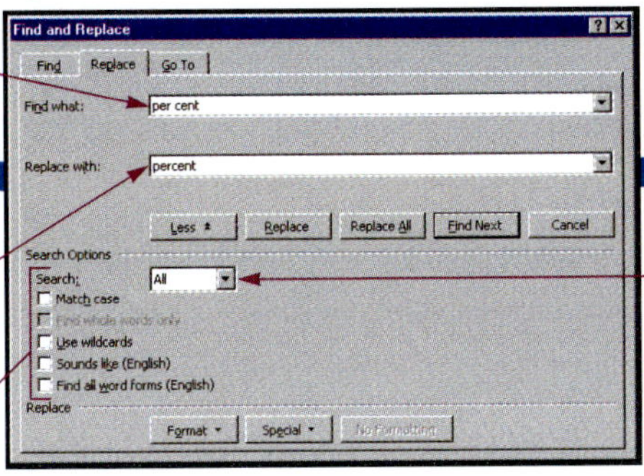

Figure 3-38 Report12.doc, after Find and Replace activity

Find and Replace makes one change in document

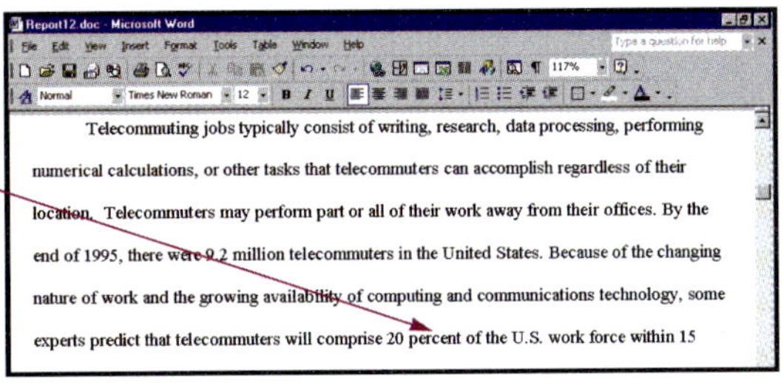

WORD XP

Screen shots: Show you what the screen should look like after following the Do It! steps

Table 3-3 Search Options

Option	Description
Match case	Finds those items in capitals and/or lowercase that exactly match contents of Find What box
Find whole words only	Finds only those items that are whole words, not parts of a larger word
Use wildcards	Searches for wildcards, special characters, or special search operators found in Find What box
Sounds like	Finds words that sound the same as in Find What box but are spelled differently
Find all word forms	Replaces all forms of the text in Find What box with proper forms of the word in the Replace with box; words in both boxes should be the same part of speech

Summary tables: Give you a quick overview of shortcuts, toolbar buttons, and options you can use to complete the skill

Practice

Open student file wdprac3-13.doc and save it as mywdprac3-13.doc. Following the instructions that appear at the beginning of the file, practice using the Find and Replace dialog box to search for and replace text. When you have completed the practice exercise, resave and close mywdprac3-13.doc.

Practice: Allows you to practice the skill with a built-in exercise or directs you to a student file

END-OF-LESSON FEATURES

In the book, the learning in each lesson is reinforced at the end by a Quiz and a skills review called Interactivity, which provides step-by-step exercises and real-world problems for the students to solve independently.

teaching resources

The following is a list of supplemental material available with the Interactive Computing Series:

Skills Assessment

SimNet eXPert (Simulated Network Assessment Product)—SimNet provides a way for you to test students' software skills in a simulated environment. SimNet is available for Microsoft Office 97, Microsoft Office 2000, and Microsoft Office XP. SimNet provides flexibility for you in your course by offering:

- Pre-testing options
- Post-testing options
- Course placement testing
- Diagnostic capabilities to reinforce skills
- Proficiency testing to measure skills
- Web or LAN delivery of tests
- Computer based training materials (New for Office XP)
- MOUS preparation exams
- Learning verification reports
- Spanish Version

Instructor's Resource Kits

The Instructor's Resource Kit provides professors with all of the ancillary material needed to teach a course. McGraw-Hill/Irwin is dedicated to providing instructors with the most effective instruction resources available. Many of these resources are available at our Information Technology Supersite www.mhhe.com/it. Our Instructor's Kits are available on CD-ROM and contain the following:

Diploma by Brownstone—is the most flexible, powerful, and easy-to-use computerized testing system available in higher education. The diploma system allows professors to create an Exam as a printed version, as a LAN-based Online version, and as an Internet version. Diploma includes grade book features, which automate the entire testing process.

Instructor's Manual—Includes:
–Solutions to all lessons and end-of-unit material
–Teaching Tips
–Teaching Strategies
–Additional exercises

PowerPoint Slides—NEW to the *Interactive Computing Series*, all of the figures from the application textbooks are available in PowerPoint slides for presentation purposes.

Student Data Files—To use the *Interactive Computing Series*, students must have Student Data Files to complete practice and test sessions. The instructor and students using this text in classes are granted the right to post the student files on any network or stand-alone computer, or to distribute the files on individual diskettes. The student files may be downloaded from our IT Supersite at www.mhhe.com/it.

Series Web Site—Available at www.mhhe.com/cit/apps/laudon.

Digital Solutions

Pageout—is our Course Web site Development Center. Pageout offers a Syllabus page, Web site address, Online Learning Center Content, online exercises and quizzes, gradebook, discussion board, an area for students to build their own Web pages, and all the features of Pageout Lite. For more information please visit the Pageout Web site at www.mhla.net/pageout.

Digital Solutions (continued)

OLC/Series Web Sites—Online Learning Centers (OLCs)/Series Sites are accessible through our Supersite at www.mhhe.com/it. Our Online Learning Centers/Series Sites provide pedagogical features and supplements for our titles online. Students can point and click their way to key terms, learning objectives, chapter overviews, PowerPoint slides, exercises, and Web links.

The McGraw-Hill Learning Architecture (MHLA)—is a complete course delivery system. MHLA gives professors ownership in the way digital content is presented to the class through online quizzing, student collaboration, course administration, and content management. For a walk-through of MHLA visit the MHLA Web site at www.mhla.net.

Packaging Options—For more about our discount options, contact your local McGraw-Hill/Irwin Sales representative at 1-800-338-3987 or visit our Web site at www.mhhe.com/it.

acknowledgments

The *Interactive Computing Series* is a cooperative effort of many individuals, each contributing to an overall team effort. The Interactive Computing team is composed of instructional designers, writers, multimedia designers, graphic artists, and programmers. Our goal is to provide you and your instructor with the most powerful and enjoyable learning environment using both traditional text and interactive techniques. Interactive Computing is tested rigorously prior to publication.

Our special thanks to George Werthman, our Publisher; Sarah Wood, our Developmental Editor; and Jeffrey Parr, Marketing Director for Computer Information Systems. They have provided exceptional market awareness and understanding, along with enthusiasm and support for the project, and have inspired us all to work closely together. In addition, Steven Schuetz provided valuable technical review of our interactive versions, and Charles Pelto contributed superb quality assurance.

The Azimuth team members who contributed to the *Interactive Computing Series* are:

Ken Rosenblatt (Editorial Director, Writer)
Russell Polo (Technical Director)
Robin Pickering (Developmental Editor, Writer)
David Langley (Writer)
Chris Hahnenberger (Multimedia Designer)

Interactive Computing Series

Microsoft® Internet Explorer™ 6.0

Brief Edition

Contents

Internet Explorer Brief Edition

Internet Explorer continued

LESSON THREE

3

Searching the Web IE 3.1

LESSON FOUR

4

Exploring the Web IE 4.1

Introduction to the Internet

skills

- Introducing the Internet
- Identifying the Features of Internet Explorer
- Opening Internet Explorer
- Exploring the Browser Window
- Customizing the Browser Window
- Changing Your Home Page
- Changing the Way Text Is Displayed
- Controlling the Display of Graphics on a Page
- Printing Material from the Web
- Saving a Web Page
- Activating an E-mail Program from Your Browser
- Checking the Properties of a Web Page
- Using the Help Feature
- Exiting Internet Explorer

The Internet is a worldwide collection of computer networks connecting millions of computers, software programs, databases, and files. You can find, retrieve, view, and send information over the Internet using special software called an Internet browser, like Internet Explorer. The part of the Internet called the World Wide Web (WWW) uses its own protocol and language, enabling interaction between computers and computer users. (A protocol is just a set of conventions by which different computers and other digital devices communicate with one another). The protocols that define the Web are Transmission Control Protocol/Internet Protocol (TCP/IP), Hypertext Transfer Protocol (HTTP), and File Transfer Protocol (FTP). The browser locates specific information on the Web using a unique Internet Protocol, or IP address. Each device connected to the Web, including computers, printers, and routers, has a unique IP address.

The browser uses a port as a communication identifier. Combining a port and an IP Address creates a socket. This socket—known as a Uniform Resource Locator (URL)—identifies specific servers containing data on the Web. Your computer uses this URL to interact with the Web server using a basic client/server model. Users move among pages on the Web using a series of links or hyperlinks that point to specific documents at specific URLs. The links are possible because of the Hypertext Markup Language (HTML) used to create Web pages.

Besides the WWW, other features on the Internet include File Transfer Protocol (FTP), Telnet, and Gopher Services. Many interactive features on the Web also benefit its users, often called surfers. These features include accessing databases and sending electronic mail (E-mail) to people across the globe within seconds. Users can enroll in Newsgroups, or online discussion forums, that enable members to post messages that may be available for public viewing. Users can communicate in real time over the Internet using Internet Conferencing Systems. The software used for conferencing systems allows text, audio, and video conferencing; shares and transports documents; and enables users to work collaboratively with applications. Streaming Media is a technology wherein audio and video content is delivered as a continuous data flow with little wait time before playback begins. The content arrives, is briefly buffered, plays, and is discarded. It is never stored on your computer.

Microsoft Internet Explorer 6.0 is a software application that enables you to use the diverse features of the Web. Using this browser, you can view items for information or entertainment, search for answers to questions, keep in touch with friends and loved ones, and even purchase goods and services.

Lesson Goal:

In this lesson, you will be introduced to the Internet and to Internet Explorer. You will learn to perform basic functions such as saving and printing a Web page. You also will learn to activate an E-mail program from within your browser and how to check the properties of a Web page, in addition to using the Help feature of Internet Explorer 6.0.

skill Introducing the Internet

concept

In 1957, the U.S. government formed the Advanced Research Projects Agency (ARPA), a segment of the Department of Defense responsible for U.S. leadership in science and technology with military applications. In 1969, ARPA established ARPANET, the forerunner of the Internet. ARPANET was a network that connected major computers at the University of California at Los Angeles, the University of California at Santa Barbara, Stanford Research Institute, and the University of Utah. This network grew to include more computers in a couple of years. ARPANET served only computer professionals, engineers, and scientists who knew their way around its complex workings. Throughout the 1970s, developers created the protocols used to transfer information over the Internet.

By the early 1980s, Usenet newsgroups and electronic mail had been invented. Most users were affiliated with universities, but libraries began to connect their catalogs to the Internet too. During the late 1980s, developers created indexes such as Archie and the Wide Area Information Server (WAIS) to keep track of Internet information. To give users an easy-to-use interface to work with, the University of Minnesota created Gopher, a simple menu system for accessing files in 1991.

The Internet was opened for public use in the early 1990s after the development of the World Wide Web (WWW). Ever since then, the Internet has grown rapidly. Tim Berners-Lee, considered the father of the Web, with others at the European Laboratory for Particle Physics, or CERN, invented the hypertext language that makes it possible to connect content on the Web with hyperlinks. By the end of 1992, the first commercial online service provider, Delphi, offered full Internet access to its subscribers. Several other providers followed. In June 1993, the Web boasted just 130 sites. By the next year, the number had risen to nearly 3,000. In the year 2000, the number crossed the 7 million mark.

The World Wide Web is not controlled by any one authority. However, the World Wide Web Consortium (W3C), an international group of industry and university representatives, does monitor the development of Web technology. W3C promotes the Web by developing common protocols for transmitting information over the Internet. The consortium provides information, reference code, and prototype and sample applications to developers and users. It is hosted by organizations in the United States, Europe, and Japan.

The Web works on a client/server model (Figure 1-1). The server is the computer that contains the requested data. It sends information to the computer that requests it, called the client. The transfer of data between the server and the client follows a standardized protocol, or information exchange process. The Web standard is HTTP (Hypertext Transfer Protocol), which allows all kinds of computers to understand and reliably translate hypertext Web files.

Figure 1-1 Model of World Wide Web

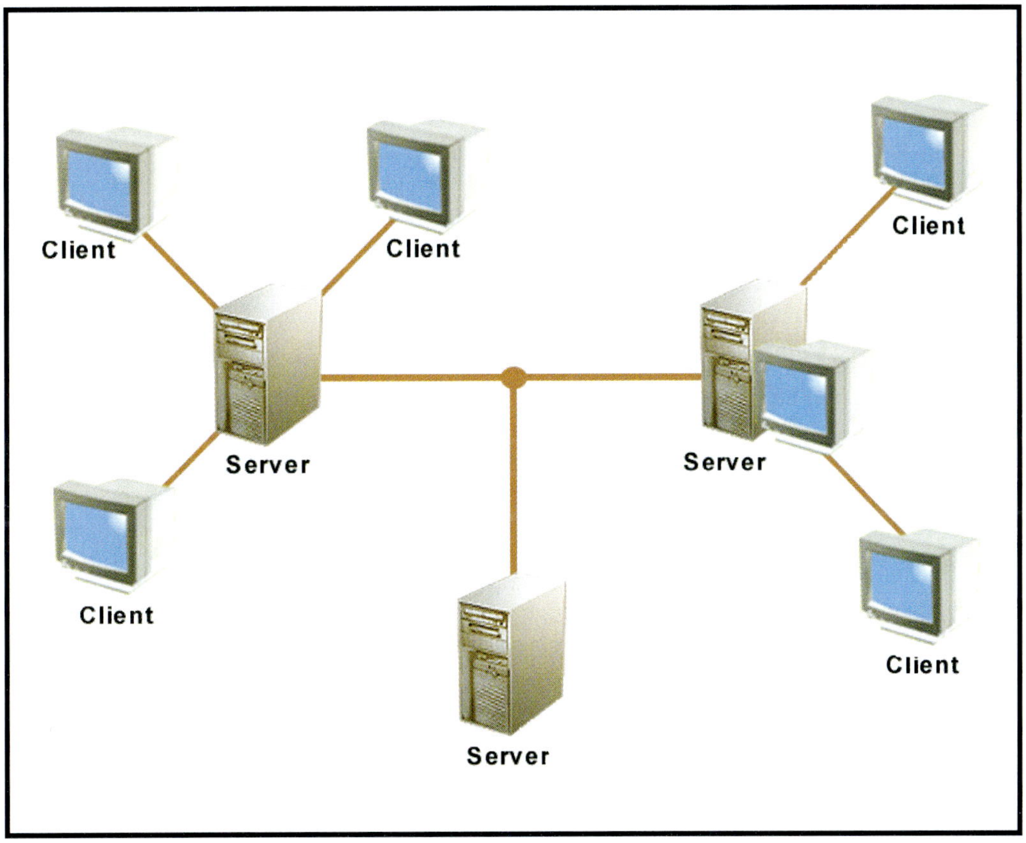

skill Identifying the Features of Internet Explorer

concept

Internet Explorer 6.0 is a set of core technologies in Windows XP. It provides an online experience and a new way of browsing the Internet for users of Windows 98, Windows Millennium Edition, Windows NT Workstation 4.0, and Windows 2000 Professional. Internet Explorer 6.0 will not work on the Windows 95 platform. You must have Windows 98/NT 4.0 SP6a or higher installed on your system to use Internet Explorer 6.0. Internet Explorer 6.0 features a number of enhancements as compared to its predecessors. These enhancements are listed as follows:

- Enhanced Explorer Bars
- Integrated instant messaging
- Media playback
- Automatic picture resizing
- Interface for accessing folders in the computer

One of the enhancements provided by Internet Explorer 6.0 also includes the new P3P privacy standard, which helps in maintaining the privacy of personal information on the Web. This standard lets you set up rules that determine how Web sites use your personal data. This standard is most effective when visiting media sites.

Many of these sites have content such as ads or multimedia that get delivered from a third-party Web site. A third-party may want to track your cookies across the site (a very common feature for ad-serving systems to determine how many and which pages you have viewed on the site). A cookie is simply an HTTP header that consists of a text-only string that gets entered into the memory of a browser. This string contains the domain, path, lifetime, and value of a variable that a Web site sets. If the lifetime of this variable is longer than the time the user spends at that site, then this string is saved to a file for future reference. Cookies pose a hazard to the user's privacy if the user reveals personal information to a Web site and that site stores it in a cookie. Using Internet Explorer 6.0's P3P controls, you will be able to set your browser to block such content. It is a good step towards giving you control over your Web privacy.

The Internet Explorer Administration Kit (IEAK 6) makes it is easier than ever to deploy and support Internet Explorer 6.0 technologies. Version 6 of the IEAK adds control over new features such as the Media bar and auto image resizing.

Outlook Express 6.0 bundled with Internet Explorer 6.0 has a new anti-virus feature that blocks Melissa-like Internet viruses such as the recent Anna Kournikova infection by hindering harmful programming scripts from sending out e-mail to everyone on your contact list.

Internet Explorer 6.0 enables developers to build Web-based applications and develop informative content for users by providing enhanced support for standards-based Internet technologies and improves the ease and speed with which developers can take advantage of these technologies. Improvements to the programming model, such as enhanced DHTML features, further enrich the Windows Web development platform.

The requirements for installation of Internet Explorer 6.0 vary depending on the platform and type of installation (Table 1-1).

more

The Minimal installation only includes the browser. The Typical installation includes the browser, Outlook Express, and Windows Media Player. The Full installation includes everything from the Typical installation plus a host of additional features.

Table 1-1 Requirements for Internet Explorer 6.0

Platform		Windows 98/98 SE/Me/NT 4.0 SP6/2000
Processor		486/66 Mhz
RAM		
	Windows 98/98 SE	16 MB
	WindowsMe/NT/2000	32 MB
	Windows XP	64 MB
Disk space		
	Minimal installation	45 MB
	Typical installation	70 MB
	Full installation	111 MB

skill Opening Internet Explorer

concept

In order to view Web pages, you must first open the browser. There are many ways to open Internet Explorer. This includes using the Start menu, the Quick Launch toolbar, or a desktop shortcut. The Quick Launch toolbar is displayed on the taskbar and makes it easy to open an Internet Explorer window, read your e-mail, or access frequently used programs.

If the Quick Launch bar is not displayed, right-click an empty area on the taskbar, point to Toolbars, and then click Quick Launch.

do it!

Open Internet Explorer using the Start menu.

1. Click Start on the Windows taskbar, point to Programs, and click Internet Explorer on the Programs submenu as shown in Figure 1-2. If you are starting Internet Explorer 6.0 on your computer for the very first time, the browser opens to www.msn.com by default (Figure 1-3). You need to ensure that you are connected to the Internet for the page to be displayed.
2. If you are using a dial-up service and are not on-line yet, the Connect To dialog box displays, prompting you to establish a connection before you can use Internet Explorer.
3. Type in the Username and Password in the respective text boxes and specify the telephone number of your Internet Service Provider (ISP) in the Phone number text box (see Figure 1-4). Ask your instructor for the proper telephone number to enter. Otherwise, use someone else's Internet service to find the proper Access Numbers for your area code at the Web site belonging to your ISP. The ISP's Web site also will provide step-by-step instructions on how to obtain and install the ISP's software on your own computer.
4. Click Connect. If the username and password you have provided are valid and the dial-up number is correct, you will be connected to the Internet and the Connect To dialog box will be closed. Thereafter, you can start viewing Web pages.

more

To create a shortcut on the Quick Launch toolbar in Windows 98, right-click the Internet Explorer command in the Start menu and then click the Create Shortcut command. Once you create it, you can drag the shortcut from the Start menu to the Quick Launch toolbar, where it will become a button displaying the Internet Explorer logo. In the future, you will be able to open the program by clicking the Internet Explorer button on the Quick Launch toolbar. On the other hand, you could use a desktop shortcut to open Internet Explorer. This can be created from the pop-up menu that is displayed on right-clicking the desktop. Point to New and then click the Shortcut command to create a shortcut.

Figure 1-2 Start menu

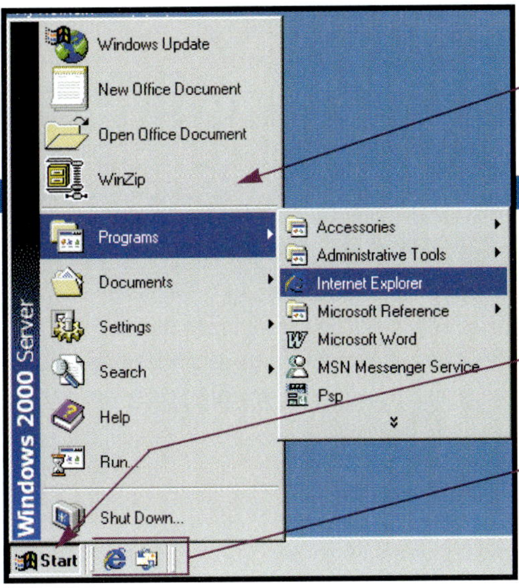

Figure 1-3 Internet Explorer window

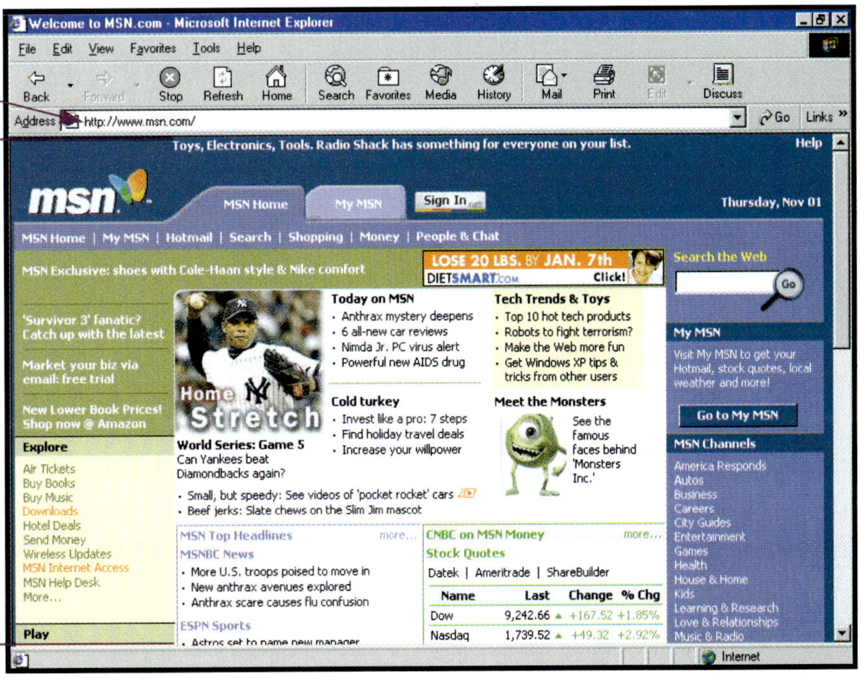

Figure 1-4 Connect To dialog box

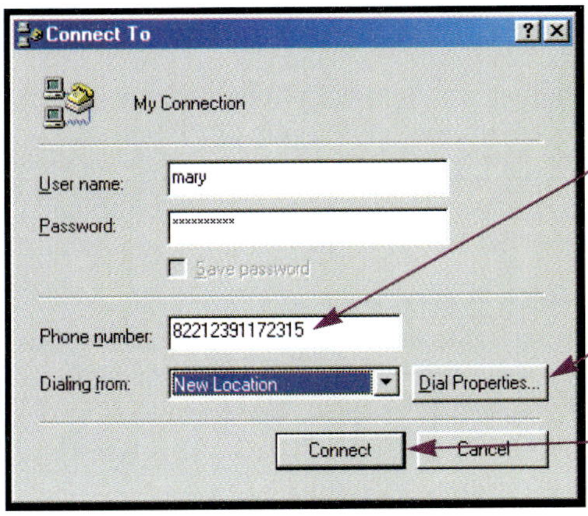

skill Exploring the Browser Window

concept

The window in which Internet Explorer displays Web documents is called the browser window (Figure 1-5). There are many elements in the browser window that enable the user to view Web pages and interact with them. The Window control buttons in the upper right-hand corner of the Internet Explorer window let you minimize, maximize or restore the size of the window, and close the application.

do it!

Guide your pointer over the various parts of the browser window to become familiar with its features.

1. At the top of the program window is the blue Title bar, containing the Internet Explorer program icon, Web site name, Web browser name, and then three Control buttons at the right end of the bar. The Minimize button collapses the program window to its smallest size. The Restore button shrinks the window to something smaller than its largest size (even if only a little). If you click the Restore button, a Maximize button replaces it. Clicking the Maximize button enlarges the program window to its largest size. The Close button shuts down the entire Internet Explorer program and redisplays the Windows desktop, unless another program is active. Placing the mouse pointer over a Control button displays its name in a small, rectangular yellow box, or ScreenTip.
2. Near the top of the window, similar to many other applications, is the Menu bar (File/Edit/View/Favorites/Tools/Help). Click any menu title to reveal a menu of commands. Click another title on the Menu bar to display a different menu of commands. Clicking any command will execute it. To close a menu, move the mouse pointer off of it.
3. An Internet Explorer icon appears at the right end of the Menu bar. A spinning icon signifies that the program is actively seeking or loading information from the Web. A static icon indicates that the activity has stopped.
4. Below the Menu bar is the Standard Buttons toolbar, which allows you single-click access to some of the program's most commonly used functions.
5. Below the Standard Buttons toolbar is the Address bar, where you type in a Web site's URL, or Web address to access the site. It is also where Internet Explorer automatically displays the URL of the sites that you visit. At the right end of the Address Bar is a down-pointing arrow; click the arrow to reveal a menu of sites in your History file (sites you have visited recently). When you use Internet Explorer for the first time, this menu will list only your home page. Click Go to the right of the arrow to access the URL shown in the Address bar. If you prefer using the keyboard, press [Enter] after entering a URL.
6. At the right end of the Address bar is the Links toolbar, containing buttons you can click to visit specific Web sites. The Links toolbar comes with buttons supplied by Microsoft, but you can add your own favorite sites. If the Links toolbar does not display, click View, point to Toolbars, and click Links on the Toolbars submenu. As with other toolbars, an active Links toolbar will display a check mark to the left of its name on the submenu.
7. The Image toolbar displays when you place the mouse pointer over an image of at least 200 x 200 pixels on the Web page (see Figure 1-6). The Image toolbar has a set of buttons that enable you to perform several actions—saving, printing, or e-mailing the image, or accessing the image in the My Pictures folder on your hard drive. To save an image smaller than 200 x 200 pixels, right-click on the image, and click Save. Images will save to the My Pictures folder unless you specify a different location.

more At the base of the browser window is the Status bar. The Status bar gives the following information: (1) Whether the browser is searching for a site, connecting to it, or is done retrieving information. (2) When the mouse is placed over a hyperlink, it displays the URL to which the hyper link is connected even before you click it. (3) In the bottom right-hand corner, the browser window displays the security zone in which a page is located. (4) On networks or in computer labs, it may display the Privacy Report icon, indicating higher privacy controls.

If the Image toolbar does not display when appropriate, click Tools, then click Internet Options to open the Internet Options dialog box. Click the Advanced tab to bring it forward and scroll down to the Multimedia category. Click to add a check mark in the Enable Image Toolbar check box. Click the OK button [OK] to accept the change and to close the dialog box.

Figure 1-5 Exploring the browser window

Figure 1-6 Image toolbar

skill Customizing the Browser Window

concept

You can alter the appearance of the Internet Explorer browser window in certain ways to suit your personal preferences as a user. For example, you can change the order in which buttons are placed on the Standard Buttons toolbar or even remove them from the toolbar, especially if you rarely or never use them. You can fully display the Links bar or any other partially hidden toolbar by clicking and dragging it, placing it above or below other toolbars as desired. You also can hide toolbars to see a larger browser window, if you prefer, then redisplay those toolbars later if you want to use them. You also can display. more, or hide several Explorer bars, which are explained in later Lessons. (The Explorer bars are the Search, Favorites, Media, History, and Folders bars.) None of these alterations will, however, affect the functioning of the browser itself.

do it!

Customize the browser window.

1. To alter the order in which the Standard Buttons toolbar buttons are displayed, right-click anywhere on the Standard Buttons toolbar, click the Customize command in the pop-up menu, which is displayed. (It does not matter which of the buttons you right-click.) Alternatively, click View on the Menu bar, point to Toolbars, and point to the Customize command on the submenu (Figure 1-7). Click the Customize command, and the Customize Toolbar dialog box is displayed.
2. Select the Home button [Home] (scroll, if needed, to find it) from the Current toolbar buttons list box (see Figure 1-8). Holding down your left mouse button, drag the icon and place it above the [Stop] button. (As you drag, a small arrow is displayed to show you where the icon will be placed when you release the mouse button.) Let go of the mouse button when the arrow is in the new position where you want the button. The Home button should now appear between the Forward and Stop buttons in the dialog box. Alternately, you can select the Home button with a single click, then click the Move Up [Move Up] or Move Down button [Move Down] until the Home button is placed where you want it.
3. Click [Close] to close the Customize Toolbar dialog box. You will see that the Standard Buttons toolbar on your browser window reflects the change you have made. You can open the Customize Toolbar dialog box and click a button that you want to remove from the Current toolbar buttons list, and then click [<- Remove]. To add a button from the list of Available toolbar buttons on the left, select it and click [Add ->], or drag the icon from one list to the other (Figure 1-8), then close the dialog box.
4. To move the Links bar, click and hold on the word Links in the Internet Explorer window. Your mouse pointer will change to a four-way arrow ✥. Drag the Links bar down so it appears from right to left across the program window, just below the Address bar and just above the browser window, as shown in Figure 1-9. (You can drag the Links toolbar anywhere you want in relation to the other toolbars: above the Menu bar, above the Standard Buttons toolbar, or even to the right of either.) If you cannot display the four-way arrow ✥ or move a toolbar, click View, point to Toolbars, and click the Lock the Toolbars command on the Toolbars submenu to remove the check mark next to it. After moving a toolbar as desired, you can reclick View, point to Toolbars, and click the Lock the Toolbars command to reapply the check mark so the toolbars are locked. Unlocked toolbars will display a vertical ridge at their left end, and locked toolbars will not.

(continued on IE 1.12)

Figure 1-7 Toolbars pop-up menu

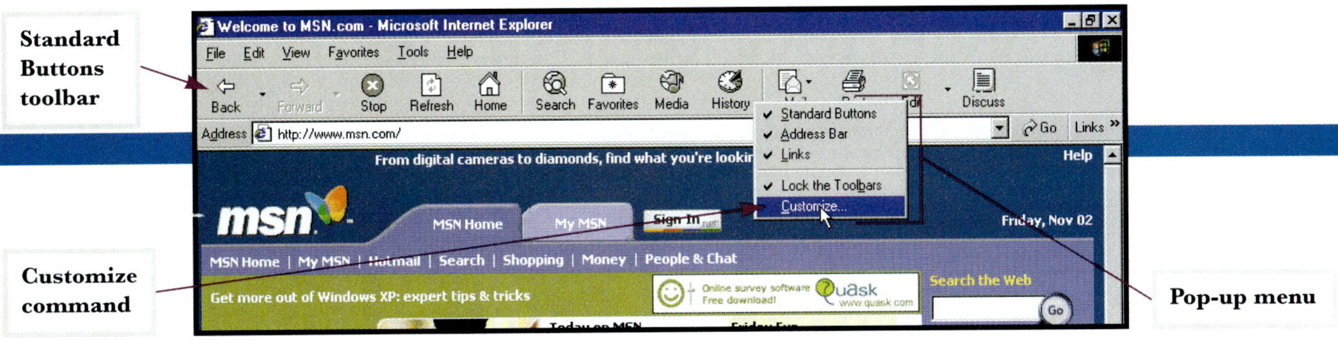

Figure 1-8 Customize Toolbar dialog box

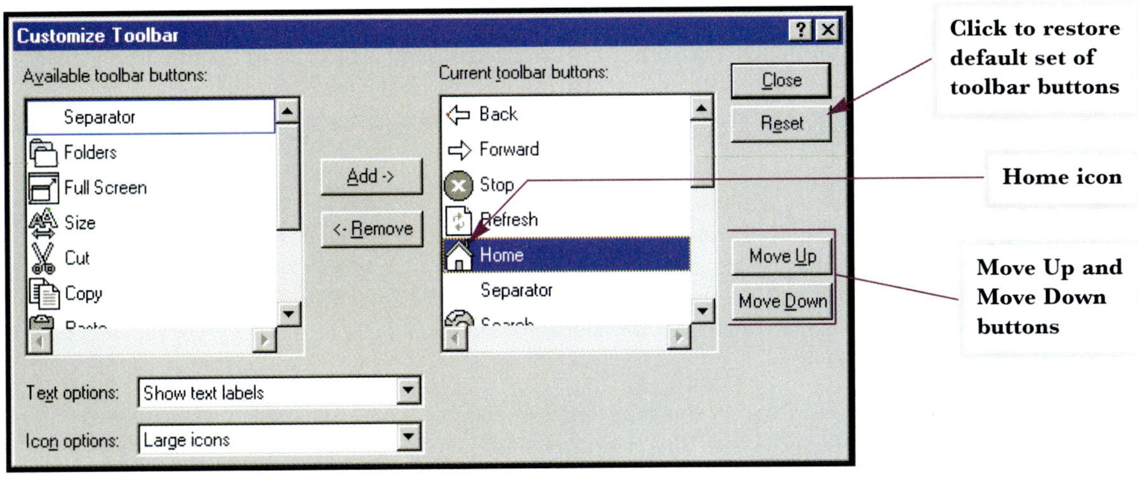

Figure 1-9 Repositioned Links bar

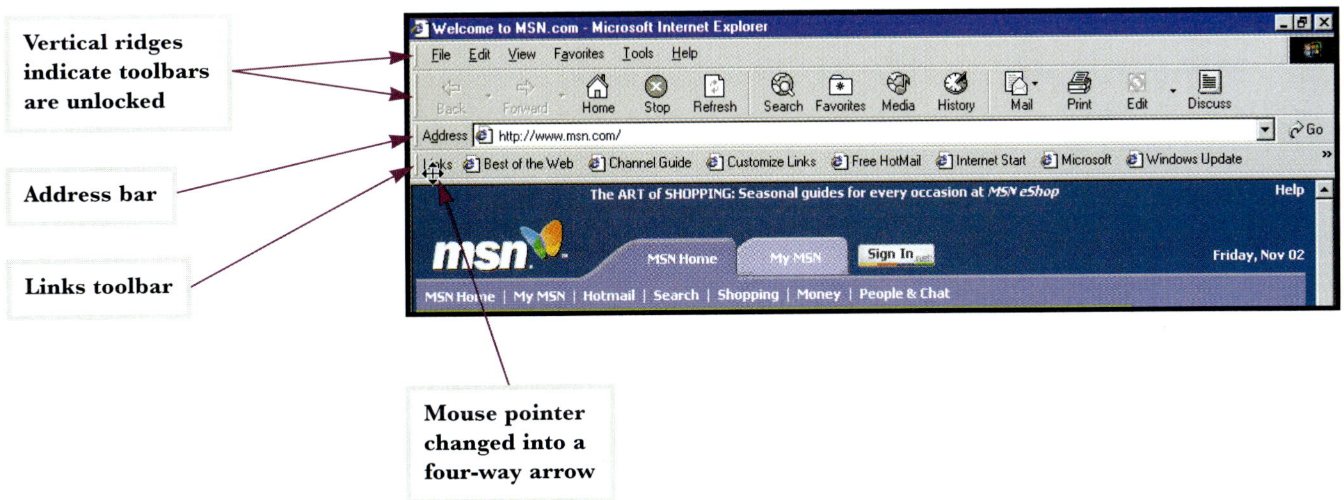

skill Customizing the Browser Window (continued)

do it!

5. To hide the Address toolbar, click View, point to Toolbars, and then click Address Bar on the Toolbars submenu. This action will hide the toolbar in the Internet Explorer program window and close the submenu. To restore the toolbar, go to the same submenu and click its name again (Figure 1-10).

6. You will learn about various Explorer bars later. However, at this learning stage you may want to turn on the Tip of the Day, or daily advice provided by Microsoft on using basic features and tools in Internet Explorer. Click View, point to Explorer Bar, and click Tip of the Day on the submenu. The tip will display in a narrow pane at the bottom of the browser window, just above the Status bar (see Figure 1-11). To close the Tip pane, return to the Explorer Bar submenu and reclick Tip of the Day.

more

The Customize Toolbar dialog box also allows you to select whether text labels for each of the buttons will be displayed underneath them, to the right, or not at all. It also enables you to select large or small icons. It may be best to use the default settings for a while until you gain familiarity with Internet Explorer and your own use patterns. Rearrange your buttons and toolbars to maximize your efficiency, not just for visual appeal. Note also that the display of text labels for buttons of the toolbar can be altered using the Text Options list box on the Customize Toolbar dialog box.

Below the Tip of the Day on the Explorer Bar submenu is the Discuss command, which when clicked will replace the Tip of the Day with the Web Discussions toolbar. This toolbar enables you to attach comments to Web pages or to documents that you can open with a browser. These comments, stored on a separate discussion server, enable Web page and Web document reviewers to read and reply to each other reviewer's comments. This cooperative activity is designed to help Web site owners and site designers to improve Web sites in response to users' comments and concerns. Be aware, however, that because of security considerations the vast majority of completed Web sites and Web documents do not authorize discussions.

Figure 1-10 Hiding toolbars

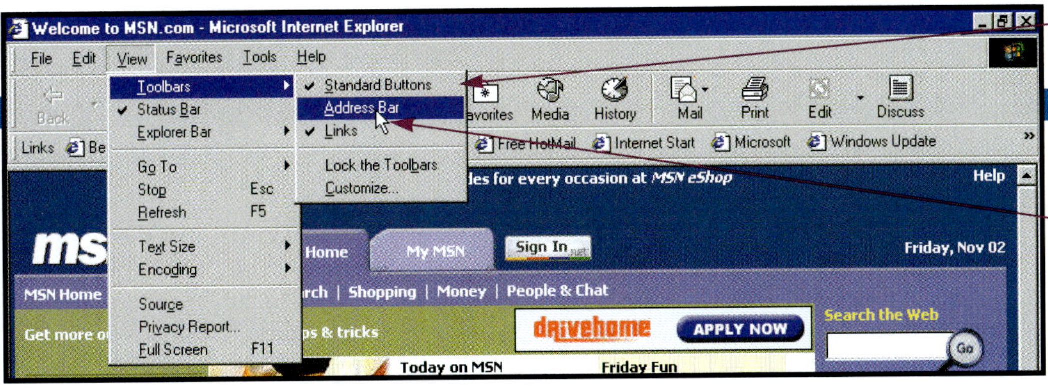

Figure 1-11 The Tip of the Day

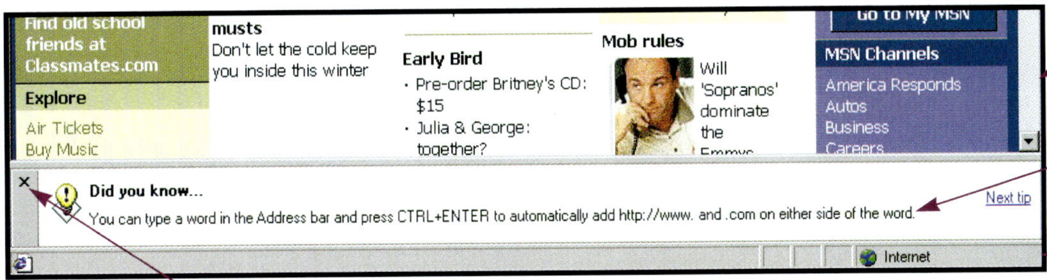

Practice

Move Home two positions after the Refresh on the Standard Buttons toolbar. Then restore the button to its previous position on the toolbar.

skill Changing Your Home Page

concept

A Home page is the default page which is displayed when the browser is opened. Even when users have opened up a different Web page, they can access the Home page at any time by clicking [Home] on the Standard Buttons toolbar. In addition to setting a Web-page that you frequently visit as your Home page, you may consider adding it to the Favorites folder by opening the Favorites menu and clicking the Add to Favorites command. This way the link to the Web page is saved and can be accessed by clicking the Favorites button on the Standard Buttons toolbar.

When Internet Explorer is first installed, the Home page is set to the Microsoft Network's Web site by default. However, this setting can be changed to point to a different page.

do it!

Change the browser Home page setting to a different page.

1. Click Tools on the Menu bar, then click the Internet Options command. The Internet Options dialog box (Figure 1-12) is displayed with the General tab activated. In the Home page section of the tab, the current home page address is highlighted in the Address text box. To change the home page, simply type a new address.
2. Type http://www.loc.gov in the Address text box. This will be the address of your new Home page. If at some time you wanted to make the Microsoft Network site your Home page again, you would just click [Use Default].
3. Click [OK] to confirm the new settings and close the dialog box.
4. Click the Home button the next time you start the browser and the Home page of the Library of Congress will be the page your browser displays (Figure 1-13).

more

Your Home page can be any site you choose. If you want Internet Explorer to open to a blank screen each time you start the program, click [Use Blank] in the Internet Options dialog box. If you know the URL of a particular page, type it in the Address text box. If you were browsing a page before opening the Internet Options dialog box and want to make that page your home page from now on, click [Use Current].

If you frequently do research, you may set an Internet search engine site, a database on a specific topic, or even the Library of Congress Web site as your Home page. If your extended family keeps in touch using a Web page, you may want Internet Explorer to open to that page so you can see news and photos of your loved ones. Many people choose the Web pages of newspapers, news services, or weather information services as their home pages.

On the other hand, you may set the portal on which you have your e-mail account also as your home page, so that you can check your e-mail first thing when you start surfing.

The term home page is also used to refer to the main page of a Web site. This Home page can be accessed by clicking the Home link on the Web page(s) of the Web site. The page displayed in Figure 1-13 is called a Home page because it is the main page in the Library of Congress Web site.

Figure 1-12 Changing the Home page

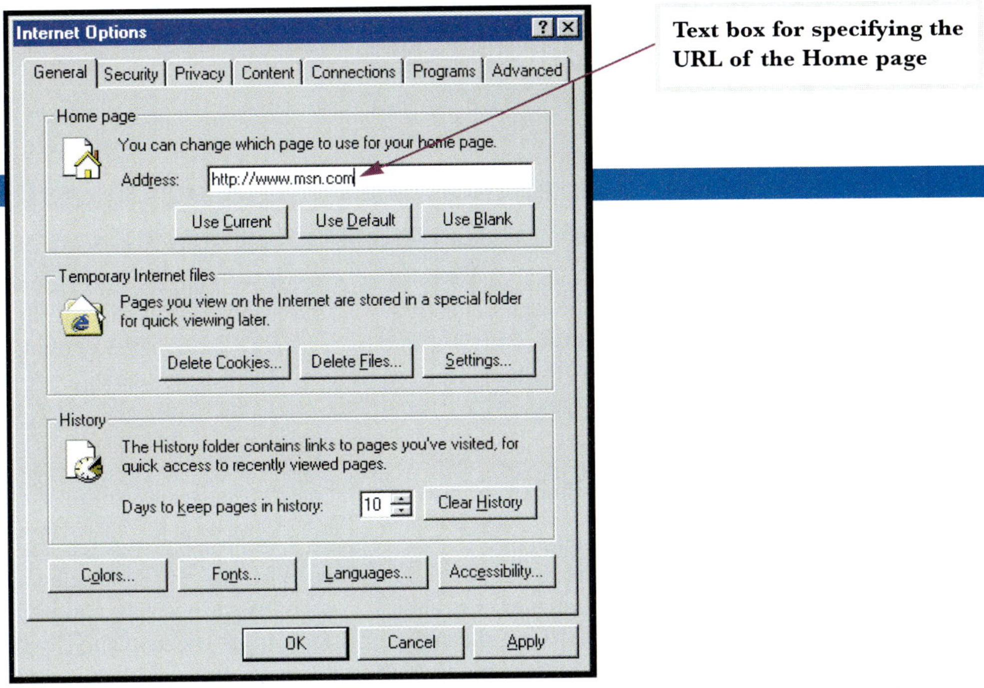

Figure 1-13 Library of Congress Home page

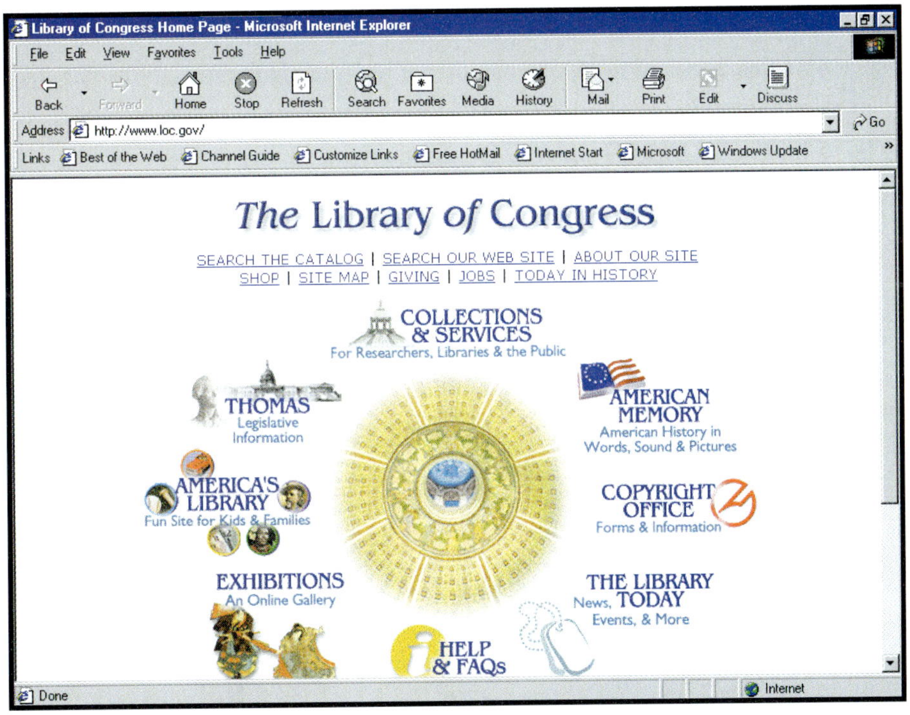

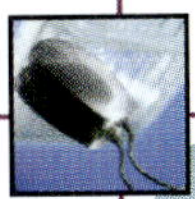

Practice

Change your Home page to the New York Times site, www.nytimes.com. Click the Home button to see if you have done it correctly. Then, change your Home page back to the default Microsoft site and click the Home button again.

skill Changing the Way Text Is Displayed

concept

Text constitutes a major portion of most Web pages. The properties of text such as font size, font color, etc. can be altered. You may find the font size of the text too small for comfort, and hence wish to view it in a larger size. Additionally, certain Web sites tend to use very bright colors for text, and you may wish to change the color to suit your taste.

do it!

Change the size of the text and the background color of the Web page you are viewing.

1. Double-click in the text box of the Address bar to select the entire Web address currently appearing there. Go to the Library of Congress Home Page by typing www.loc.gov and then pressing [Enter]. Click View on the Menu bar, and point to the Text Size command. A submenu listing the different size options will appear. The bullet on the left side of the submenu marks the current font size (Figure 1-14).
2. Click the Largest command on the submenu. The text on the page will increase in size.
3. Return to the Text Size submenu and change the text size back to Medium.
4. Click Tools on the Menu bar, then click Internet Options to display the Internet Options dialog box.
5. Click Accessibility... (Figure 1-15). In the Accessibility dialog box that is displayed (Figure 1-16), add a check mark to the the Ignore colors specified on Web pages check box. Click OK to close the Accessibility dialog box. Adding a check mark to this box enables you to override the settings for the text and background colors that Web page authors have applied to their Web pages.

(continued on IE 1.18)

Figure 1-14 Increasing the text size

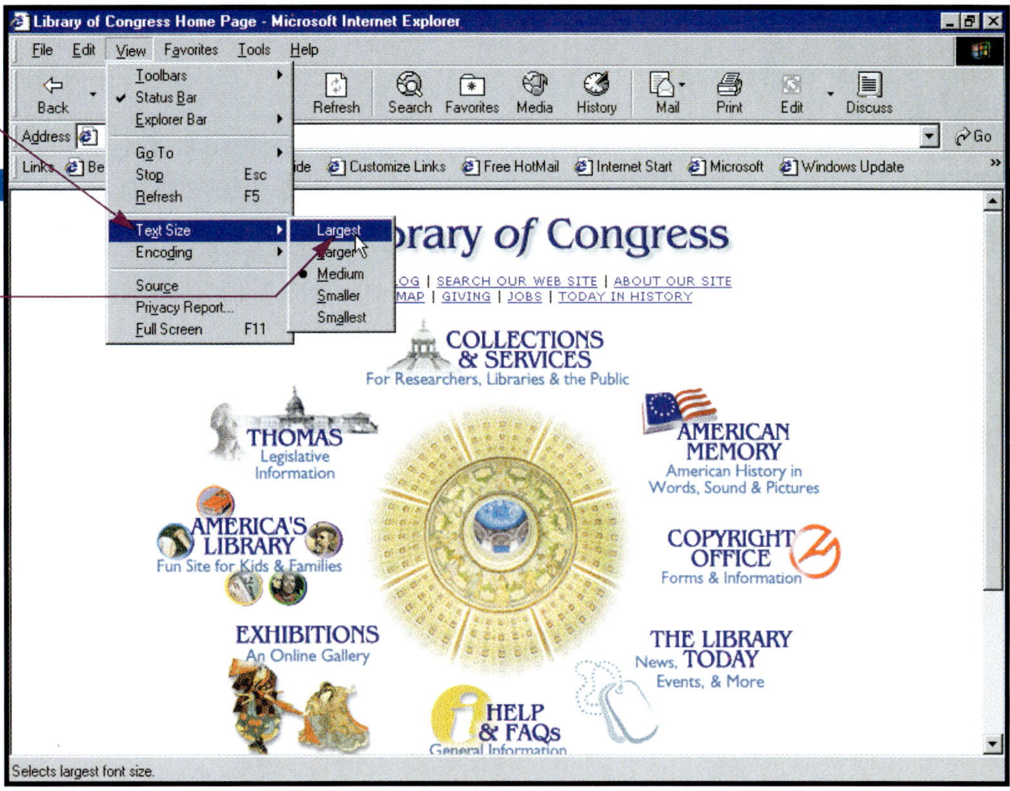

Figure 1-15 Internet Options dialog box

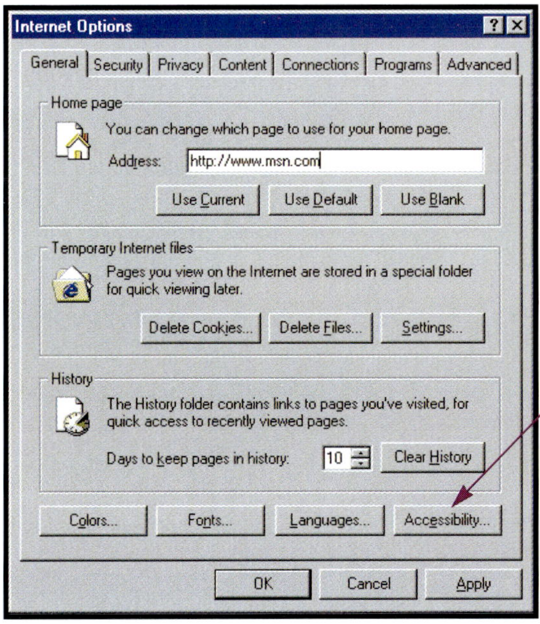

Accessibility button

Figure 1-16 Accessibility dialog box

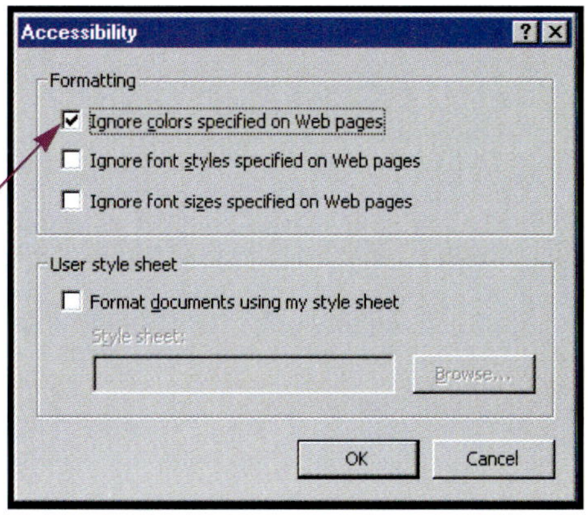

Check box for ignoring the colors on the Web page

skill Changing the Way Text Is Displayed (continued)

do it!

6. In the Internet Options dialog box, click Colors... to open the Colors dialog box. The Colors dialog box will be displayed.
7. Clear the Use Windows colors check box. The Text and Background color buttons will become active.
8. Click the Background button to display the Colors palette (Figure 1-17).
9. Click the yellow color square in the second row of the Basic colors palette to select it and then click OK. The Background color button now displays the color you selected (Figure 1-17). Avoid very bright colors, but at the same time maintain adequate contrast for text visibility.
10. Click OK in the Colors dialog box, and again in the Internet Options dialog box. The Library of Congress Home page is shown with its new background color in Figure 1-18. In the Practice exercise on IE 1.19, you will restore the original background setting of the Web page.

more

Different colors can be used for hyperlinks, in order to show the difference between visited and fresh links. A different color can also be set as hover color, which shows up when the mouse is placed over the link. In order to set the hover color, add a check mark to the Use hover color check box in the Colors dialog box, then click the Hover button and select a color from the colors palette.

Figure 1-17 Choosing background color

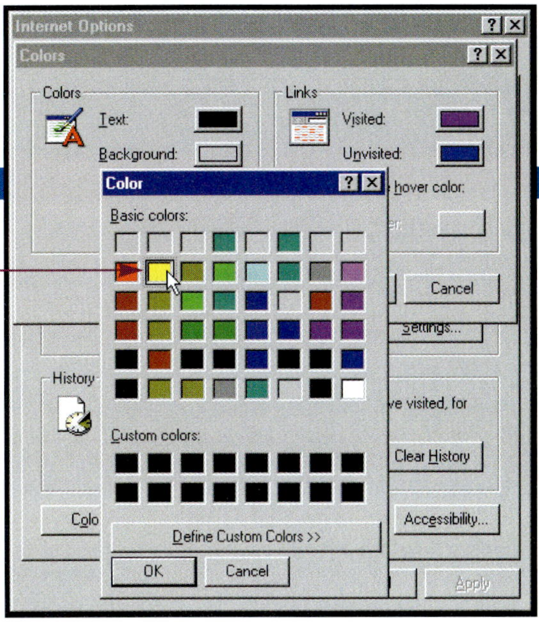

Color chosen for the Web page background

Figure 1-18 Web page with new background

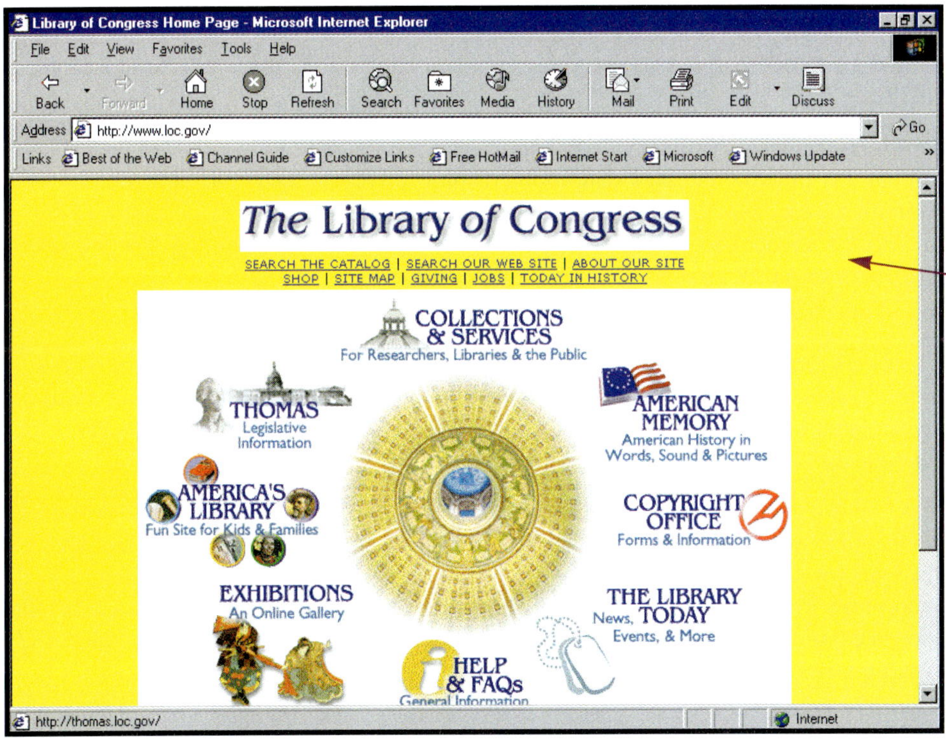

New background in the Web page

Practice

Change the Web page you are viewing so that it displays small green text on a red background. Then restore the color of your browser and accessibility settings to their defaults by changing the browser settings to use Windows colors and colors specified on Web pages.

skill Controlling the Display of Graphics on a Page

concept

Although pictures add visual appeal to the Web pages, there could be times when you wish to see only the text content of a page. This happens most often when your Internet connection is slow or the page is very large, and you want to eliminate steps and access the text as quickly as possible. In order to achieve this, you can specify that only text is to be displayed on a page and not the pictures.

do it!

Turn off the display of pictures on a Web page.

1. Click Tools on the Menu bar, then click Internet Options to display the Internet Options dialog box.
2. Click the Advanced tab (Figure 1-19) in the Internet Options dialog box.
3. Scroll down to the Multimedia section and clear the Show Pictures check box.
4. Click Apply to confirm the new settings and then click OK to close the Internet Options dialog box.
5. Click Refresh on the Standard Buttons toolbar. The current page will be reloaded into your browser, but this time the pictures will not be displayed (Figure 1-20). As long as you retain these settings, all subsequent pages will load without pictures. To restore the original settings, go back to the Advanced tab in the Internet Options dialog box and select the Show Pictures check box.

more

When display of pictures is turned off on a Web page, icons are displayed instead of the pictures. If you right-click such an icon and click Show Picture from the pop-up menu, then that picture is displayed to the user. Thus, only the picture you have selected will load. The Advanced tab in the Internet Options dialog box gives you similar control over the display of animations, video clips, and sounds.

Internet Explorer 6.0 has the automatic picture resizing feature for pictures that are too large to display in the browser window. The pictures are automatically resized so that they fit within the dimensions of the browser window. In addition, if you navigate to pictures that fit within the browser window and then you change the window dimensions, Internet Explorer automatically adjusts the pictures to fit the new window size. To prevent image distortion, Internet Explorer adjusts both the picture height and width, even if only a single dimension needs adjusting. The Image Toolbar allows you to quickly and easily save pictures, e-mail pictures, and print pictures that you find on Web pages.

Figure 1-19 Turning off the display of pictures on a Web page

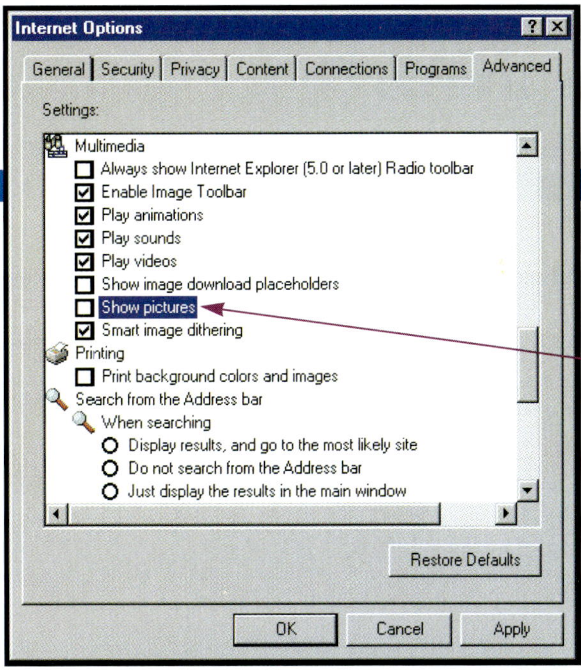

Figure 1-20 Web page without pictures

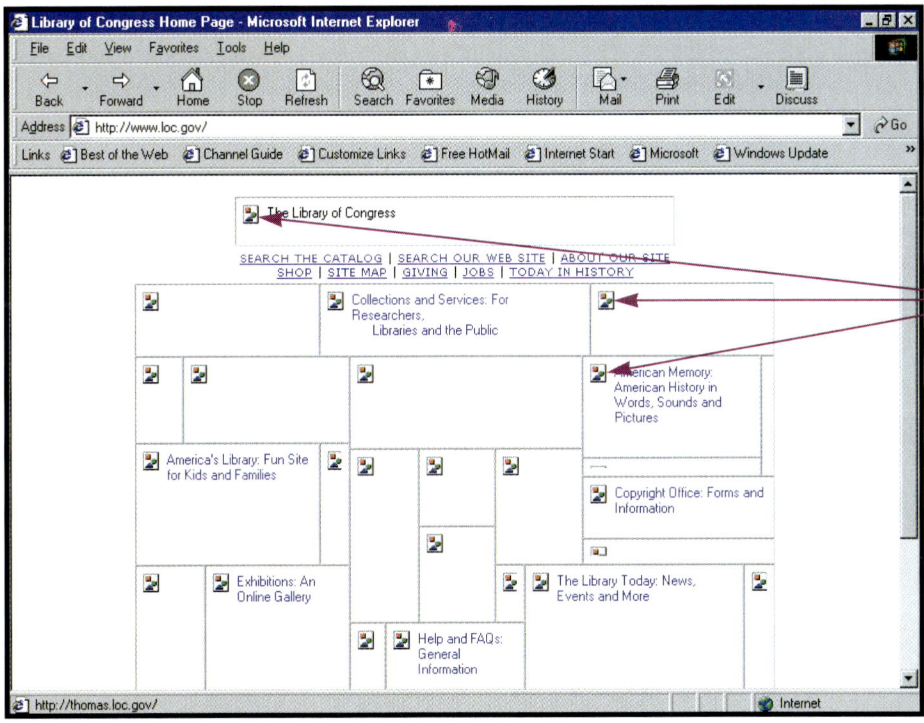

Practice

Go to the National Park Service home page (www.nps.gov). Turn off the display of pictures on this page. Visit other Web pages (e.g., www.expedia.com, www.msnbc.com, or www.travelocity.com) while the display of pictures is still turned off. Finally, turn on the display of pictures again and refresh the last Web page you have visited to see the difference.

skill Printing Material from the Web

concept

When you come across a Web site that is rich in text, and you do not wish to sit glued to your computer screen for hours reading it, you could take a printed copy of the same. If you have a printer that is connected to your computer, you can print entire Web pages or even parts of Web pages. The options that are available on the Print dialog box would depend on the kind of operating system you are using. For instance, the option for printing frames on a Web page is available in the main dialog box in Windows 98, whereas on a Windows 2000 platform, you would have to click the Options tab to invoke the same option.

do it!

Print the entire contents of a Web page.

1. Double-click in the text box of the Address bar to select the entire Web address currently appearing there. Then type www.nps.gov. Press [Enter] and wait until the complete page is displayed.
2. Click File on the Menu bar, and then click the Print command. The Print dialog box, shown in Figure 1-21, is displayed if you are working on the Windows 98 platform. This dialog box may vary depending upon the operating system you are using.
3. The Print dialog box provides several options for printing a page. To print the whole Web page, make sure that the All option button is activated in the Print range section. Also make sure the printer you wish to use is displayed in the Select Printer box in the top section of the dialog box.
4. Click Print to print the page.
5. After you have printed a page for the first time this way and verified that the settings are the way you want them, you can do your next printing job merely by clicking Print on the Standard Buttons toolbar. Any time you wish to change the settings page range, number of copies, or any other parameter, you will have to return to the Print dialog box to make the required changes.

more

The text to be printed can be selected in many ways. The Print range section of the Print dialog box, can be used to specify a range of pages to print. Another option is to select the text on the Web page and then print only that text by activating the Selection option button in the Print range section. Multiple copies can be printed automatically by specifying the required number in the Number of Copies spin box.

Some Web pages are presented in a format called frames, which divides the page into different areas that scroll and change independently from each other. If the page you are printing uses frames, a segment of the Print dialog box labeled Print frames is available (Figure 1-22), giving you the chance to decide what will be printed: all the frames as they appear on the screen, all the frames one after the other, or only the selected frame. The selected frame is the one in which you last clicked your mouse or performed an operation.

In a color printer, color printing can be turned off by clicking the Properties button in the Print dialog box and activating a simple option such as Print in Grayscale or Black and White. Select the Collate check box in the Print dialog box to print the complete document before printing the next copy of any multi-page document.

Figure 1-21 Print dialog box

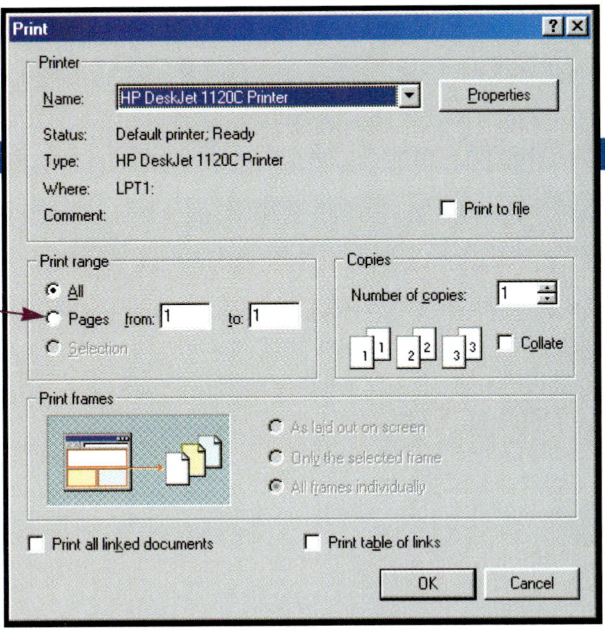

Option for specifying the range of pages to be printed

Figure 1-22 Printing frames

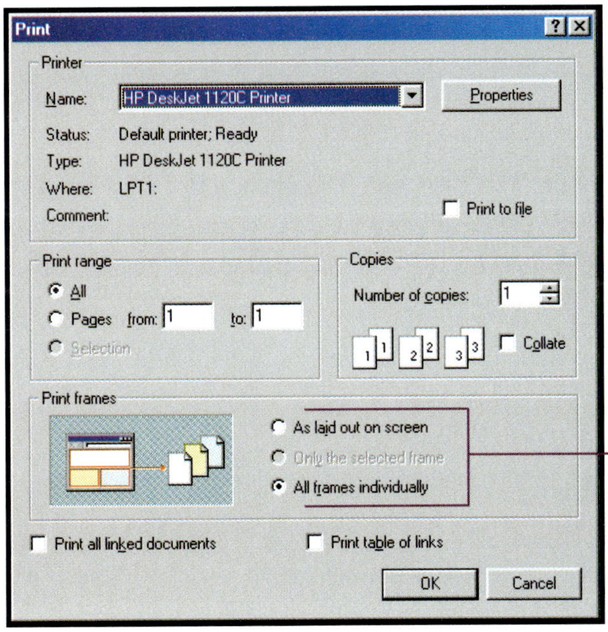

Options for printing frames

Practice

Go to any site of your choice. (For example, you will find sports news at www.cnnsi.com, Habitat for Humanity International at www.habitat.org, the National Science Foundation at www.nsf.gov, Poets and Writers Online at www.pw.org, and the Smithsonian Institution at www.si.edu). Then, select a paragraph of text and print it.

skill Saving a Web Page

concept

While surfing the Web, you may come across important information that you would like to peruse later. In this case, you can save a copy of the Web page. When you save a Web page, in addition to a HTML file, a folder containing the image files and other accessory files used on the Web page is also saved on your machine. In order to save a Web page, you first have to open the page in the browser window before saving it.

do it!

Save a Web page in a folder on the hard drive of your computer.

1. Go the Library of Congress Home Page (www.loc.gov).
2. Click File on the Menu bar and then click the Save As command (Figure 1-23). The Save Web Page dialog box is displayed.
3. The Save in list box allows you to select the folder where the Web page will be saved. The default location is the My Documents folder on your hard drive. If you want to select a different storage location, click the arrow in the Save in list box. A list of all the top level locations available to you will appear. If you click one of these locations, its contents will appear in the window below the Save in list box. To select a lower level folder as your Save in location, double-click it in the contents window.
4. Select the Web Page, complete option from the Save as type list.
5. The default file name for a Web page is the name that appears in the title bar of the browser window. The Save Web Page dialog box should look similar to Figure 1-24.
6. Once the file name, file type, and destination folder are displayed as you want them, click Save. The page will be saved to your hard drive.

more

Four options appear in the Save as type list box.

- Web Page, complete will save everything on the page, including text, pictures, hyperlinks and the layout in which they were presented on the Web.
- Web Archive, single file for e-mail will save a snapshot of the current Web page so that it can be displayed or e-mailed as a single file later.
- Web Page, HTML only will save the HyperText Markup Language information on the Web page, but not the pictures or other files to which the HTML page refers.
- Text File will save the text content of the page and nothing else.

Internet Explorer automatically saves the contents of pages you have viewed recently in a location called Temporary Internet Files, mainly for the purpose of reloading them more quickly when you return to them. The Save options described above give you a greater range of options, however, in how you save Web material and how you use what you have saved.

more

If you are in the habit of saving files from the Web, you may want to create a folder especially for that purpose. That way you will avoid cluttering the My Documents folder, which is also the default folder for saved files from many other applications.

Figure 1-23 Using the Save As command

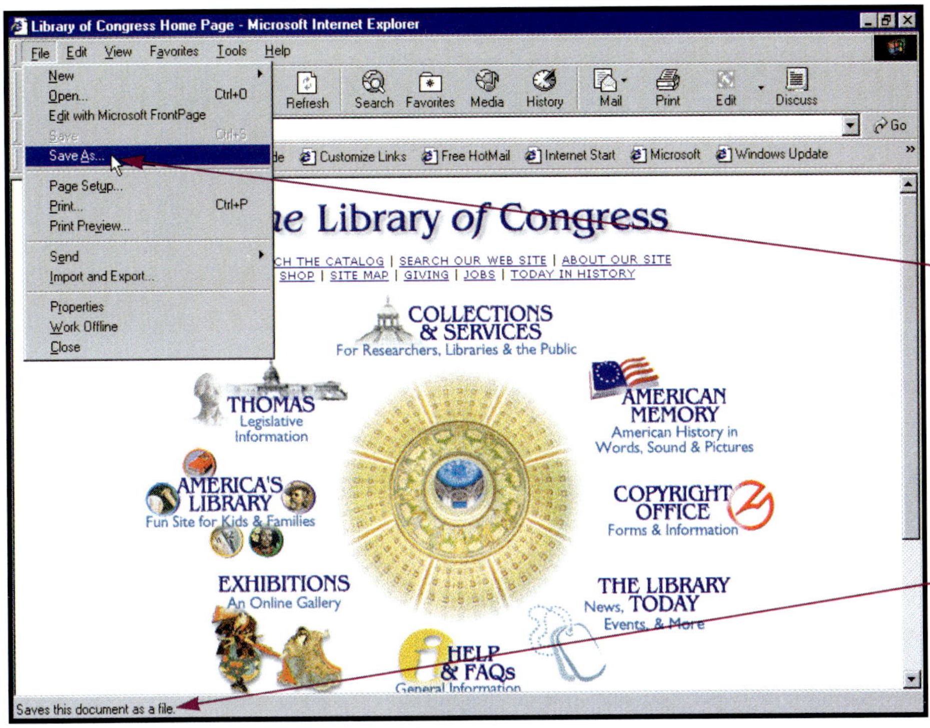

Click Save As command to save a Web page

Description of selected command appears in Status bar

Figure 1-24 Save Web Page dialog box

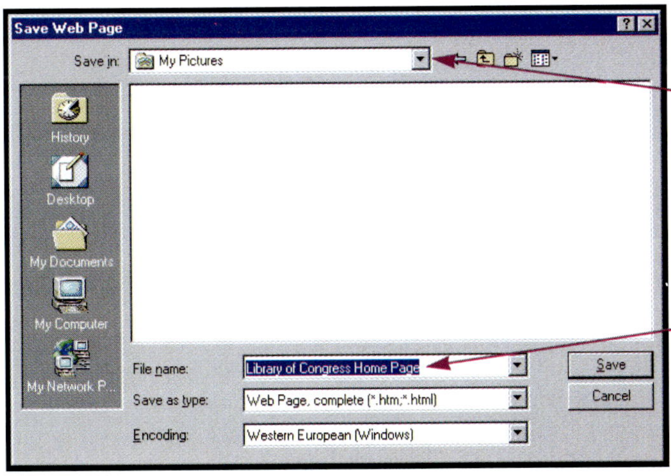

Click arrow to display drop-down list for selecting destination for saving Web page

Text box for specifying file name for the saved Web page

Practice

Go to www.msn.com and save the Home page to the desktop of your computer.

skill Activating an E-mail Program from Your Browser

concept

You can access your e-mail program from within Internet Explorer. When you click a mailto: hyperlink on a Web page, Internet Explorer will open an addressed message composition window in the e-mail software you have specified in the Programs tab. You can send e-mail, initiate a computer-to-telephone call, or view properties of your Outlook or Windows Address Book contacts without quitting Internet Explorer. This is useful when you spend a considerable number of hours surfing the Net and would also like to check your e-mail at regular intervals.

do it!

Select an e-mail program to access from Internet Explorer.

1. Click Tools in the Menu bar and click the Internet Options command. The Internet Options dialog box is displayed.
2. Click the Programs tab to activate it. The Programs tab, shown in Figure 1-25, allows you to specify which program you will use for each of the Internet services.
3. Click the arrow at the right end of the E-mail list box labeled to view a list of the mail programs that are available to you. Options may include Microsoft Outlook, Hotmail, Outlook Express, Windows Messaging, or others. Select the program you want to use by clicking it.
4. Click Apply to change the settings.
5. Click OK to confirm your choice and close the Internet Options dialog box. This preference will remain in effect until you change it.
6. To activate your selected e-mail program from Internet Explorer, click Mail on the Standard Buttons toolbar. A drop-down menu is displayed.
7. Click the Read Mail command (or the command that relates to the task you wish to complete) on the menu. Your chosen e-mail application will open. Internet Explorer will remain open, but will go to the background.
8. Click File in the Menu bar and then click the Exit command to close your e-mail program.

more

If your Internet connection is not active when you open the e-mail program, you may receive a prompt to establish the connection as shown in Figure 1-26. If your e-mail program and Internet Explorer use the same Internet connection, both applications can send and receive data as part of the same session, and you can leave both open and toggle back and forth between them. When multiple application programs are running in Windows, you can toggle between them using the key combination [Alt]+[Tab].

Figure 1-25 Programs tab

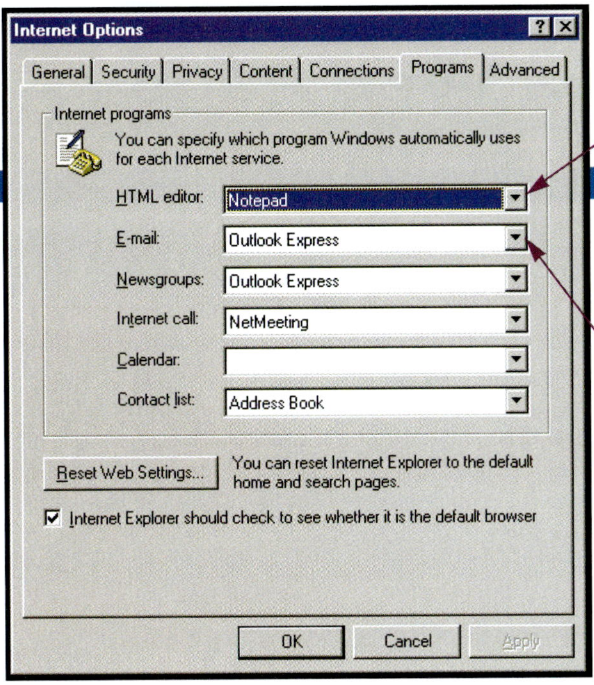

Figure 1-26 Prompt to establish Internet connection

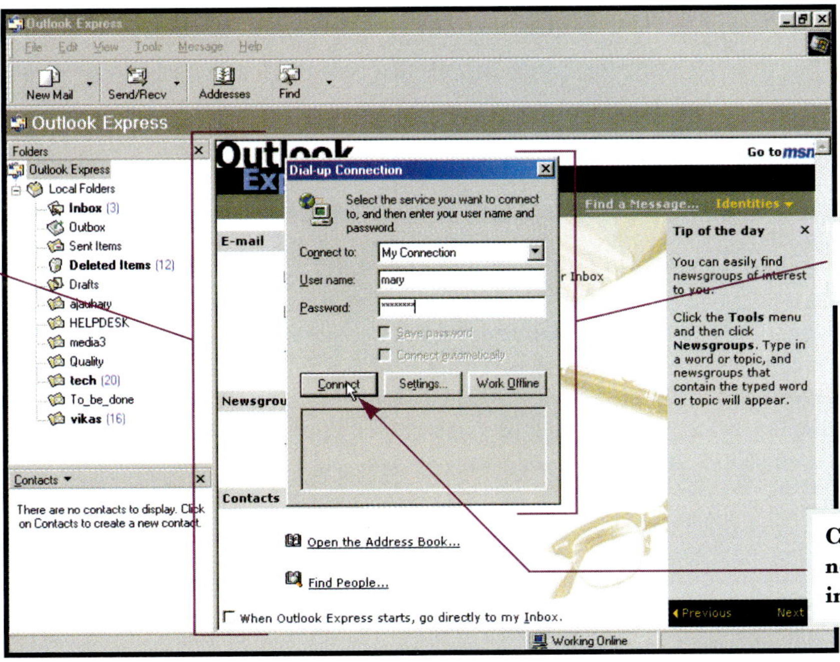

Practice

Set Outlook Express as your preferred e-mail program.

skill Checking the Properties of a Web Page

concept

Every Web page has certain properties such as its title, URL, file size, and date of creation. At times you may need to know this information, especially if you have saved a Web page to a disk, are working offline, and want to check where the material you are viewing originated or when it was posted. Digital information is generally measured in bytes: 1,024 bytes = 1 kilobyte; 1,024 kilobytes = 1 megabyte; 1,024 megabytes = 1 gigabyte; and 1,024 gigabytes = 1 terabyte. The smallest unit of code is a bit, eight of which equal one byte. Each character of text—such as a letter, number, symbol, or space—requires a byte of memory. Graphics generally are several hundred bytes to several kilobytes in size, document files can be several kilobytes or more, and audio-visual files on the Web easily can run scores of megabytes.

do it!

View the properties of the page you are viewing.

1. Click File in the Menu bar, then click the Properties command. The Properties dialog box is displayed as shown in Figure 1-27.
2. The General tab in the Properties dialog box lists the various properties of the Web page, including protocol, document type, Internet address, file size, date created, and date modified. Review these properties to become familiar with the way in which they are expressed.
3. Click OK to close the Properties dialog box.

more

The Certificates button in the Properties dialog box relates to a security feature of Internet Explorer. Clicking this button displays the Certificate Information message box (Figure 1-28). If the Web page does not have have any certificates associated with it, then the certificate information dialog box displays the message This type of document does not have a security certificate. Certain Web sites have files attached to them called certificates, which attest to who created the site and other facts. This can be useful in evaluating the safety or validity of the content on a site. Some document types do not have certificates. After reviewing a Certificate Information dialog box, simply click the OK button OK to close the dialog box and to return to the Properties dialog box.

Figure 1-27 Properties dialog box

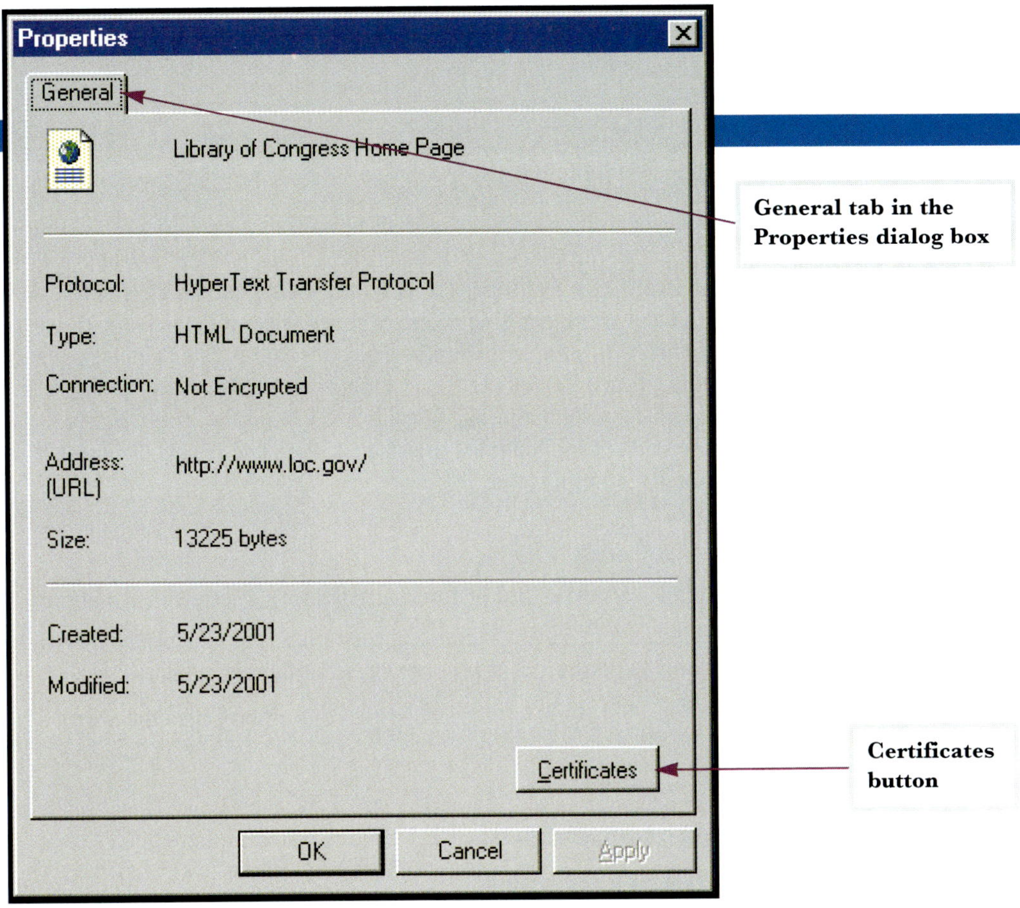

Figure 1-28 Certificate Information message box

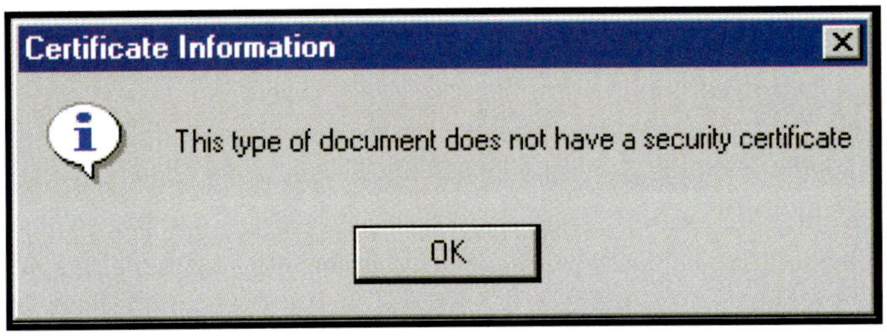

skill Using the Help Feature

concept

Internet Explorer includes a Help feature that provides information on the functions and features in Internet Explorer. It also gives step-by-step instructions on how to perform the tasks in the application. It opens as a window that can be kept active while you follow its instructions.You can select one of three ways to search for the information you need: the Contents tab, a list of general topics; the Index tab, which provides an alphabetical list of specific functions; or the Search tab, which allows you to enter a question or phrase that Help will try to match. Click Help on the Menu bar and then click the Tip of the Day command. This displays a message at the base of the Explorer Window about useful shortcuts in Internet Explorer.

do it!

Open the Help facility of Internet Explorer; use it to learn about a feature of Internet Explorer.

1. Click Help on the Menu bar, then click the Contents and Index command. The Help window is displayed. If you are opening the Help facility for the first time on the computer, the Contents tab will open by default. If necessary, click the Maximize button near the top right corner of the Help window to make the Help window fill the entire program window.
2. If necessary, click the Index tab. Type the phrase home page in the text box near the top of the tab (Figure 1-29). A list of topics that alphabetically match what you have typed is displayed in the box below the text box. In the lower text box, the selection pointer rests on the words that match the phrase you typed. Notice that there are two subtopics under the topic home page.
3. Double-click the changing subtopic under the home page topic. The subtopic now appears selected in the left pane, and the title and text of the subtopic appear in the right pane (Figure 1-30). If you press [Enter] instead of double-clicking, an advisory box will appear (Figure 1-31), telling you to select one of the subentries in the list. To access the subentries, click the OK button OK in the advisory box.
4. Read the Help file, and then click ✕ to close the Help window.

more

If a Help topic has no subtopics, simply press [Enter], and its title and text will appear in the right pane. If a topic has subtopics, but they do not appear as in Step 2, pressing [Enter] will display the Topics Found dialog box. Double-click the desired subtopic in the dialog box, and its title and text will display.

By accessing the Contents tab, you can click on Help categories such as Getting Started with Internet Explorer, Finding the Web Pages You Want, and so on. Under each category you will find one or more Help topics related to that category. Under the category Finding the Web Pages You Want, for example, you will find the topic Changing your home page, which you discovered in this Skill via the Index tab. By accessing the Search tab, you can enter basic questions or phrases in an upper text box. After you press [Enter], the Help facility will search for a list of Help topics that potentially relate to what you asked, then display them in the lower box. For example, if you type change background color on the Search tab, it will display a list of related topics, including Changing Web page fonts and background colors, a Skill that you already studied in this Lesson.

Finally, Internet Explorer 6.0 has a Favorites tab in the Help window. You can add Help topics displayed in the right window to the Favorites section by clicking the Add button Add in the Favorites tab. The Remove button in the Favorites tab Remove is used to remove the Help topic from the Favorites section.

Figure 1-29 Index tab

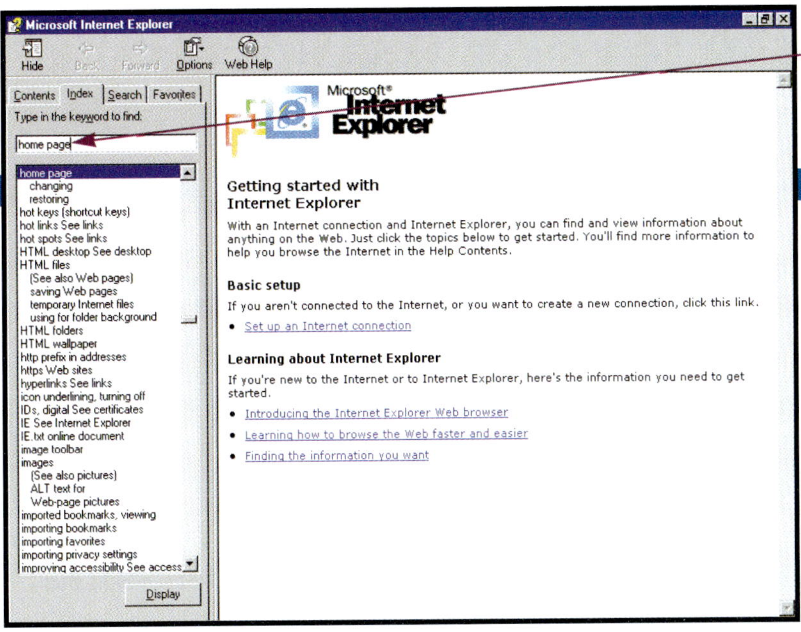

Text box for typing the desired keywords

Figure 1-30 Change home page Help topic

Subtopic appears selected in lower text box of left pane

Title and text of selected subtopic appear in right pane

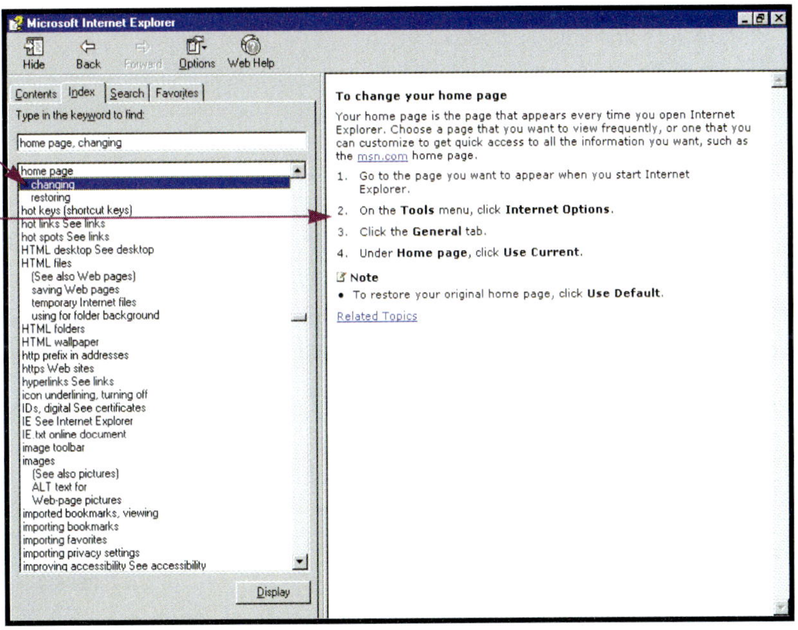

Figure 1-31 Advisory box

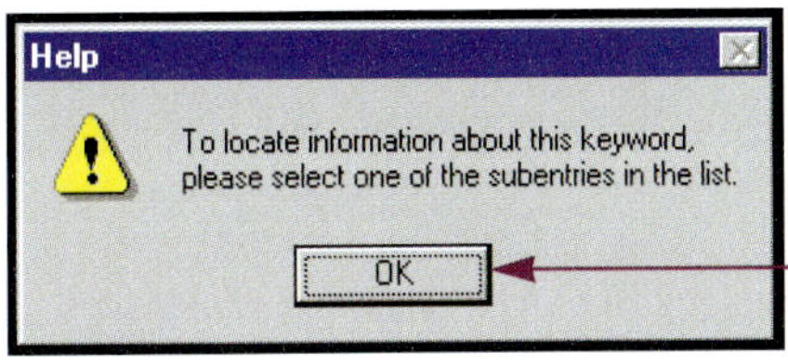

Click to return to list of Help topics and subtopics

Practice

Use the Index tab in Microsoft Internet Explorer Help window to find information on the Refresh button.

skill Exiting Internet Explorer

concept

When you are finished viewing files on the World Wide Web, you should close Internet Explorer and make sure your Internet connection is terminated properly. If you want to work in another application, you do not have to close Internet Explorer. Simply open the other application and Internet Explorer will go to the background. You can return to it later and your session will not have been interrupted.

do it!

Close the Internet Explorer application.

1. There are two common ways to close Internet Explorer. One way is to click File on the Menu bar and then click the Close command (Figure 1-32).
2. Alternatively, click the Close button in the upper-right corner of the Internet Explorer application window (Figure 1-32).

more

Users familiar with word processors, spreadsheets, and other applications may be accustomed to the need to save and close a document before exiting the application. In Microsoft Word, for example, if you attempt to close the application with an unsaved file open, you will be prompted to save the file first. In Internet Explorer, however, there is no need to save or close the page you are viewing before exiting the application. You may wish to save the page you are viewing, but Internet Explorer will not prompt you to do so. When you exit Internet Explorer, therefore, the page you are viewing will disappear. Most Web pages will still be available on the Web the next time you connect, though their content may have changed.

You also have to ensure that your Internet connection is closed properly, unless you intend to keep the session open and use an e-mail program or other application. Some Internet Service Providers' systems will require you to logoff, while others will let you merely hang up. Closing Internet Explorer without closing the Internet connection will bring up a prompt asking if you want to disconnect. If you are in a business or educational setting and connect to the Internet through a Local Area Network (LAN), you may be able to open and close Internet Explorer without a logon or logoff procedure. Some organizations use a LAN to install their own logon systems so that they can monitor Internet usage.

Figure 1-32 Closing Internet Explorer

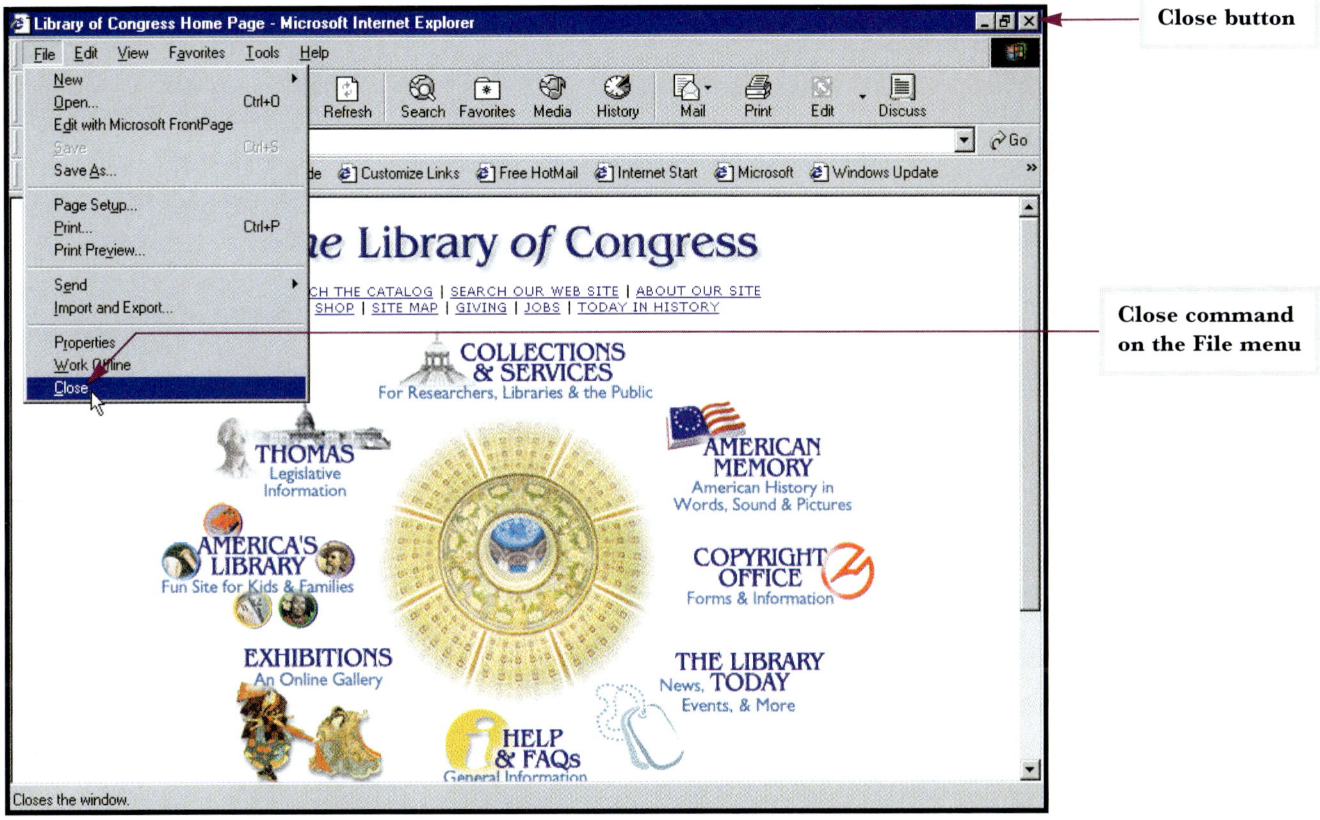

Practice

Open Internet Explorer and then practice the different ways to close the application.

shortcuts

Function	Button/Mouse	Menu	Keyboard
Open Internet Explorer		Click Start, point to Programs, then click Internet Explorer	
Return to Home page		Click View, point to Go To, then click Home Page	[Alt]+[Home]
Print current Web page		Click File, then click Print	[Ctrl]+[P]
Stop downloading a page		Click View, then click Stop	[Esc]
Save current Web page		Click File, then click Save As (only to update a page you have already saved)	[Ctrl]+[S]
Open mail program		Click Tools, then point to Mail & News, then click Read Mail	
Open Help window		Click Help, then click Contents and Index	[F1]
Exit Internet Explorer		Click File, then click Close	[Alt]+[F4]

quiz

A. Identify Key Features

Name the items indicated by callouts in Figure 1-33 and state their functions.

Figure 1-33 Elements of the Explorer Window

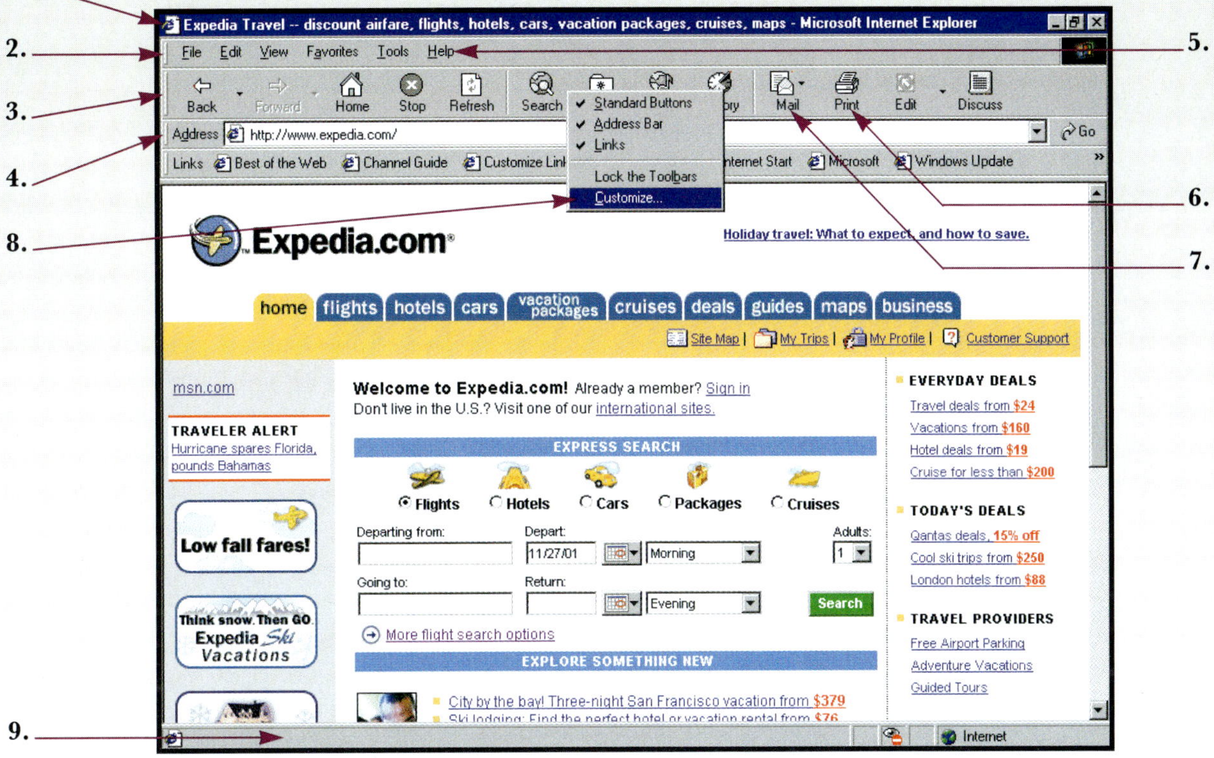

B. Select the Best Answer

10. Menu that gives you access to the Internet Options dialog box

11. Image, object, or text that connects you to another Web page when clicked

12. Page that is automatically displayed when you start Internet Explorer

13. Huge collection of hyperlinked documents you can read with Internet Explorer

14. Menu that gives you access to directions on using Internet Explorer

15. Global computer network made up of smaller networks linked together

16. Location of the Home, Print, and other useful buttons

17. Protocol used to transfer data over the Web

18. Part of the browser window that gives the URL of the current page

a. Help

b. Hyperlink

c. Standard Buttons toolbar

d. Tools

e. Address bar

f. HTTP

g. Internet

h. Home page

i. World Wide Web

quiz (continued)

C. Complete the Statement

19. The address of a document on the Internet is also known as its:

a. HTML

b. URL

c. WWW

d. ARPA

20. When you start Internet Explorer, you will see:

a. Your Home page

b. The Help screen

c. Only text

d. Only pictures

21. The Internet Explorer icon in the upper-right corner of the window spins when the program is:

a. Downloading a Web page

b. Seeking or loading information

c. Saving a Web page

d. Printing a Web page

22. To change the size of the text on a Web page, you should open the:

a. Text Size dialog box

b. Tools menu

c. View menu

d. File menu

23. When you save a page, you can use the Save Web Page dialog box to alter its:

a. URL

b. Name

c. Size

d. Certificate

24. To speed the loading of a Web page, you can:

a. Toggle to a higher data transfer rate

b. Turn off the display of pictures

c. Select a smaller text size

d. Reduce the size of the Internet Explorer window

25. To access an alphabetical list of Help topics, use the:

a. Index tab

b. Contents tab

c. Search tab

d. Advanced tab

26. You can choose your preferred e-mail program by going to the Internet Options dialog box's:

a. Accessibility section

b. Advanced tab

c. General tab

d. Programs tab

interactivity

Build Your Skills

1. Open Internet Explorer and customize the browser window:
   a. Launch Internet Explorer from the Start menu.
   b. Move the Home button to place it between the Refresh and Search button on the Standard Buttons toolbar.
   c. Move the Address bar below the Standard Buttons toolbar.
   d. Move the Links bar so it is a small bar just to the right of the Go command on the Address bar.
   e. Undo the actions in Steps (b) through (d), then use the Reset button in the Customize Toolbar dialog box to return all of the toolbars to their default positions.

2. Assign a new page to serve as the Home page of your browser:
   a. Change the Home page to http://www.altavista.com.
   b. Click the Home button to visit your new home page.

3. Change the way a page is displayed and print a copy of it:
   a. Change the text size on your new Home page to Smallest.
   b. Change the background color of display to light green.
   c. Set your browser to repress the display of pictures.
   d. Click Refresh, and then print a copy of the entire page.
   e. Restore all of the options you just changed to their previous settings.

4. Save a Web page to your hard drive and then note the properties of the page to check the file size:
   a. Open the Save Web Page dialog box.
   b. Save the complete page in your My Documents folder with the name Altavista.
   c. Open the Properties dialog box for the current page.
   d. Note the properties of the saved page.
   e. Close the Properties dialog box.

interactivity (continued)

Build Your Skills (continued)

5. Use the Help facility of Internet Explorer:

   a. Open the Microsoft Internet Explorer Help window.

   b. Use the Index tab to get help on keyboard shortcuts.

   c. Locate information on setting up an Internet connection on the Contents tab.

   d. Close the Help window.

6. Terminate your work session:

   a. Reset the Home page to the default setting.

   b. Exit Internet Explorer.

   c. If necessary, close your Internet connection.

Problem Solving Exercises

1. You work in a small real estate office. Since the World Wide Web has taken on an important role in your industry, with property listings widely available on many sites, everyone in your office has been given an Internet connection and the Internet Explorer Web browser. You are the most experienced user of the software, and your boss would like you to configure everyone's browser with a standard setup. Make the following changes to your browser: arrange the Standard Buttons toolbar so that the buttons are in alphabetical order; change the Home page to http://realestate.lycos.com; set the text size of the browser to Larger. Then, visit the new home page, print a paper copy of it, and save the page to your hard drive using the default page name.

2. You have just finished converting from another Web browser to Internet Explorer. Since you are somewhat experienced at browsing the Web, you already have some preferences as to how your browser is configured. Make these changes to your browser setup: If necessary, click View and point to Toolbars, then add check marks to all toolbars to ensure that they are displayed. Move the Address bar below the Links toolbar; move the Home button to the very beginning of the Standard Buttons toolbar; set your text size to Smallest; set Hotmail as your default e-mail program. Then exit Internet Explorer.

3. You would like to prepare a document to distribute throughout your company that details some of the important features of Internet Explorer. Before writing the document, you need to do some research. Use the Contents tab in Internet Explorer's Help to read all the help files listed under the heading Getting Started with Internet Explorer. Next, switch to the Index tab and examine help files for the following topics: adding toolbars, browser terminology, Content Advisor, security zones, and multiple browsers. Finally, switch to the Favorites tab and add the topic To turn on Content Advisor and set limits to the list of favorites.

4. As a research analyst, you spend hours every day studying pages of text on the Web. Therefore, you want to maximize the amount of space available for text in your browser window. Start by removing the Standard Buttons toolbar and the Links toolbar from view. Then set the browser's text size to Smallest, and turn off the option that allows pictures to be displayed. Finally, change your Home page to http://www.dol.gov, visit the page, print it, and save it to your hard drive.

Browsing the Web

skills

- Accessing a Page by Typing Its URL
- Accessing a Page Using Links
- Going Back and Forward
- Stopping the Loading of a Page
- Refreshing a Page
- Creating a Desktop Shortcut to a Page
- Copying Text from a Page
- Saving an Image from a Page
- Exploring the AutoComplete Feature
- Customizing AutoComplete
- Using the History Function
- Modifying the History of Your Browser
- E-mailing a Web Page

In its simplest form, browsing the Web requires only that you type the address of a Web site into a text box in Internet Explorer called the Address bar. Of course, there are many other ways to access Web sites, and we will visit them all in this lesson. You can also save organized lists of your favorite sites and search for Web sites. After accessing the Web page that you are looking for, you can also e-mail the page to a friend.

Internet Explorer offers several easy and intuitive ways to navigate the practically limitless content of the Web. If you know the address or URL of a Web site, you can enter it directly in the Address bar of Internet Explorer. You can access a page that you did not know existed, by following a hyperlink from another page. Or, you can set a shortcut on your desktop that will allow you to go directly to a particular page with a click of your mouse.

A very convenient feature of Internet Explorer is that it stores the last several locations you have visited during a Web session. If you follow a trail from one site to another, you can retrace your steps without having to keep notes or remember a long string of URLs.

Lesson Goal:

In this lesson, you will explore the different ways of accessing the content in Web pages. In addition, you will examine the different ways to take information from the Web and use it for your own purposes, including saving pictures, copying text, and e-mailing URLs and Web pages to your friends or colleagues.

skill Accessing a Page by Typing Its URL

concept

Each page on the World Wide Web is identified by a unique address called a Uniform Resource Locator (URL). Locating a page by its URL requires you to type its URL in the Address bar every time you wish to access the page. A URL is typically composed of four parts—protocol name, location of the site, name of the organization, and the type of the organization. For instance, in the URL http://www.microsoft.com/, the four parts are:

- http: is the protocol name (a protocol is a set of rules and standards that enable computers to exchange information).
- www is the server designation, in this case a server on the World Wide Web.
- microsoft is the name of the organization that maintains the site and is indicated by the third parameter.
- .com identifies the type of organization. For instance, Microsoft is a commercial organization.

Before starting Lesson 2, set the toolbars in their default locations. Click View, point to Toolbars, and click Customize to open the Customize Toolbar dialog box. Click the Reset button [Reset], then click the Close button [Close] to apply the default settings.

do it!

Use the Address bar to visit the Web site of the U.S. National Park Service.

1. Double-click the desktop shortcut of Internet Explorer to open the browser. If your computer has the Active Desktop feature turned on, you can single-click the desktop shortcut to start Internet Explorer. Double-clicking in this case may start two separate sessions of the application.
2. Click in the Address bar to select the existing URL.
3. Type the URL http://www.nps.gov to replace the selected URL (Figure 2-1).
4. Press [Enter] or click [Go] on the Address bar. The Web page for National Park Service will be displayed (Figure 2-2). If you type only msn in the Address bar instead of www.msn.com, and then press [Enter], Internet Explorer will add "www" at the beginning and ".com" at the end for you. If pressing [Enter] alone does not work for you, press [Ctrl]+[Enter].

more

Typing the URL of a Web page is the simplest method of accessing that page. Most sites use the HyperText Transfer Protocol (HTTP) and hence the addresses of Web pages of these sites are prefixed with http://. Some sites however use a different protocol such as File Transfer Protocol (FTP). The site addresses of these sites have the prefix ftp://.

Depending on who owns a Web site, there are different categories of domains in the World Wide Web (WWW). These categories are identified by a three-letter suffix to the domain name. For instance, the .gov suffix in the National Park Service's URL represents a government organization. The other common categories are as follows:

- .org for nonprofit organizations
- .net for networking organizations
- .edu for educational institutions
- .mil for military services
- .int for organizations established by international treaty

more While surfing the Web, you will also see domain names with .net suffixes for Internet related sites, and suffixes that indicate the country in which a Web server is located such as .in for India. Web pages would be displayed in your browser window only if your Internet connection is functioning properly.

Figure 2-1 National Park Service home page

URL entered in the Address bar

Figure 2-2 Web page for www.nps.gov

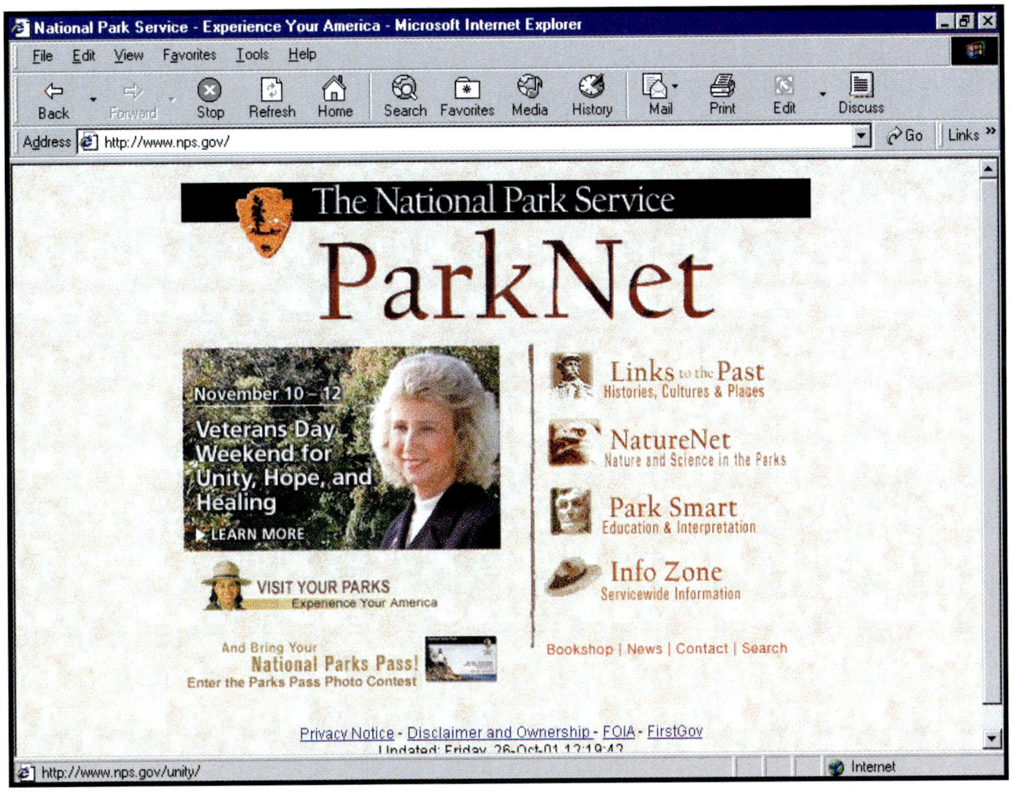

Practice

Practice accessing a few different Web sites by typing in their URLs and then pressing [Enter]. For example, you can find Harvard University at www.harvard.edu, find Motown Records at www.motown.com, find The Carter Center at www.cartercenter.org, find the Poetry.net Web site at www.poetry.net, and find the Permanent Missions to the United Nations at www.un.int.

skill Accessing a Page Using Links

concept

Web pages are written in a platform-independent language called HyperText Markup Language or HTML, which is a set of codes, or tags, that tell your browser how to display the Web pages that appear on your screen. HTML documents consist of the text that will be displayed on the page, formatting instructions, and references to other files such as graphics that will be displayed on the page. HTML is responsible for the hyperlink feature of the World Wide Web. Hyperlinks are sections of a Web page that link to another Web page on WWW. Hyperlinks exempt users from the need to remember the addresses of Web pages. Hyperlinks allow you to navigate from any one place on the Web to any other without having to follow a linear path.

do it!

Use a hyperlink to move to another Web page featuring information about National Parks from the National Park Service home page.

1. Position your mouse pointer over the text Visit Your Parks, as shown in Figure 2-3. Notice that the mouse pointer changes from an arrow to a hand with a pointing finger, called a Link Select pointer, and a ScreenTip is displayed. The URL to which the hyperlink is directed, http://www.nps.gov/parks.html, is displayed in the status bar at the bottom of the browser window.
2. Click the mouse just once while the Link Select pointer is over the Visit Your Parks hyperlink in the National Park Service page. Internet Explorer will connect to the hyperlinked page, National Park Guide, and the page will load into the browser window (Figure 2-4). Although Visit Your Parks is the largest text on the page, the page itself is named National Park Guide, as shown in the Title bar. Note that the contents of the Address bar have changed to reflect the new page. Apart from linking to a different file, a hyperlink may also link to a different section on the same Web page. Note also that, whereas sometimes you must double-click to start a program or perform a similar action, when accessing a hyperlink you need to click only once.
3. Position your mouse pointer over the text National Parks Reservations, near the lower right area of the National Park Guide page. (With the mouse pointer hovering over the Reservations hyperlink, an explanatory pane may appear, indicating that you can use the upcoming page to make campground and tour reservations.) Click the text hyperlink to move to the Reservations page.

more

A Web page can have two kinds of hyperlinks, graphic and plain text. Pages that contain many hyperlinks often include the most important ones in two locations: first, scattered throughout the page wherever the page designer places them in context, and second, in a list at the bottom or along the side of the page.

Figure 2-3 Identifying a hyperlink

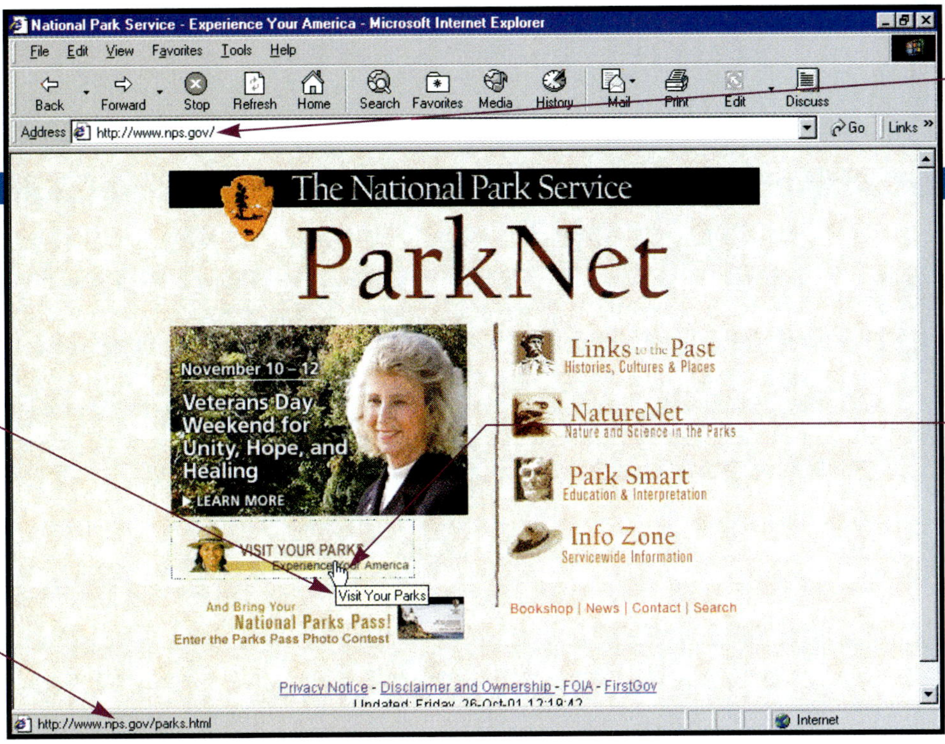

Figure 2-4 Showing the hyperlinked page

skill Going Back and Forward

concept

Many times while surfing the Web, you may have come across a situation where you have had to revisit a particular Web page. In order to do this, you need not remember the URL of the Web page. The Back button on the Standard Buttons toolbar takes you to the Web page you had accessed immediately before the current page. Once the previous Web page has been displayed and you have obtained the information you wanted, you may wish to go back to the original page from where you had accessed this page. The Forward button on the Standard Buttons toolbar can be used to go back to the page.

do it!

Move back to a page you viewed earlier, and then navigate forward to the page from which you have just returned.

1. Make sure the Web page from the end of the previous Skill, US National Parks Reservation Service, still appears in your Web browser. Click on the Standard Buttons toolbar.
2. You will return to the National Park Guide page. The text in a hyperlink on most Web pages is displayed in a different color if you have already visited the link.
3. Click on the Standard Buttons toolbar. The US National Parks Reservation Service is displayed again. If you right-click a non-link area of a Web page, a pop-up menu is displayed that includes the Back and Forward commands.

more

Notice that there is a small arrow to the right of . Clicking it will display a list of all the most recently visited pages in a single browsing session (Figure 2-5). This way, if you want to go more than one page back along the trail you have followed, you can do it in one step without having to click Back repeatedly. As with the Back button, has an accompanying arrow (Figure 2-6) that provides a menu of recently viewed pages (in the other direction, this time), allowing you to skip ahead several pages.

Once you have gone forward and then back, you can go back and forth in both directions and see the same pages. However, if you go back, and then select a different hyperlink than the one you clicked originally, the path that had been stored in the Forward list is replaced by the new page you accessed.

If, at any time, you have moved all the way back to the first Web page at which you started moving forward, the Back button will appear dimmed, since you have no earlier pages to visit. Conversely, if you have moved all the way forward to the last page that you visited in a sequence, then the Forward button will be dimmed.

Figure 2-5 Back list

Links in the Back list

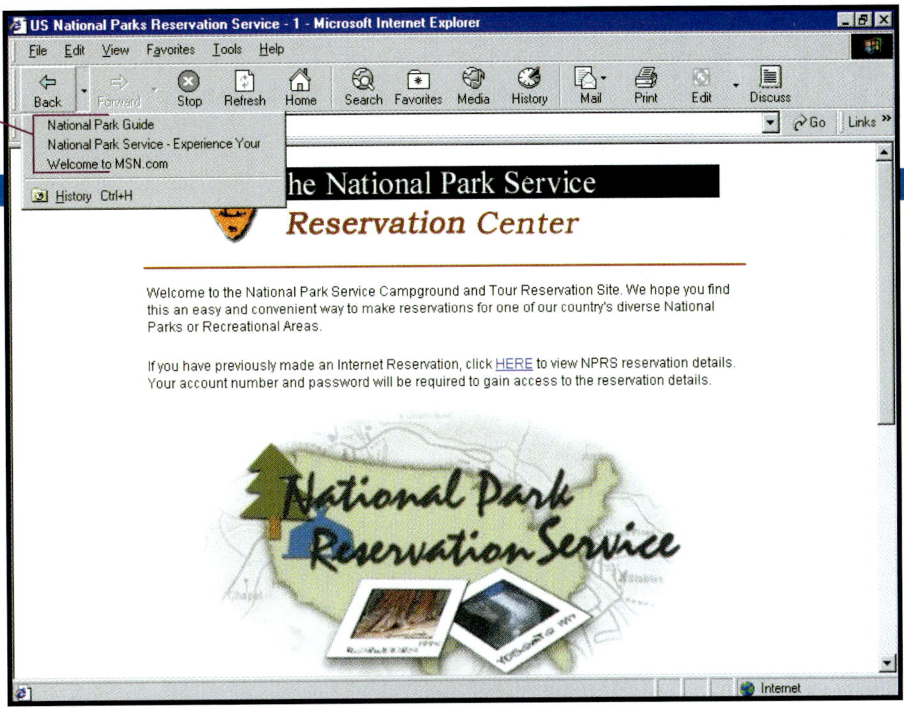

Figure 2-6 Forward list

Links in the Forward list

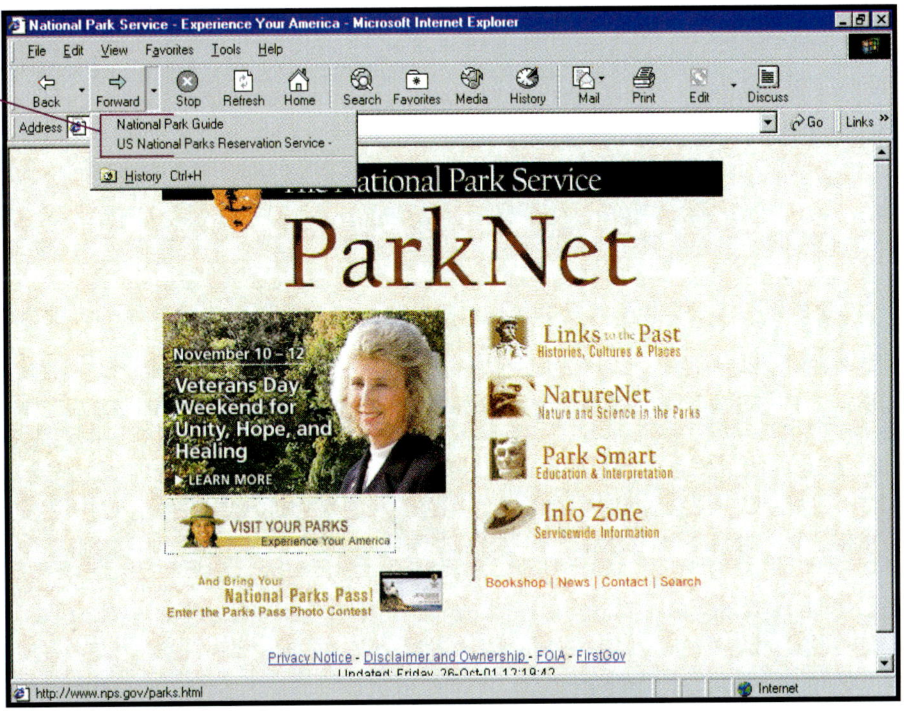

Practice

Follow a hyperlink on the National Park Guide page, and then navigate back from the new page to the National Park Service page. Finally, move forward to the National Park Guide page again.

skill Stopping the Loading of a Page

concept

Sometimes when a page is in the process of loading, you will want to cancel the operation. You may have clicked the wrong hyperlink by mistake, or perhaps the loading is taking too long and you do not wish to continue. You can also utilize this when you have already received the text of a page and do not need to wait for the graphics to load.

When you click a hyperlink on a Web page and then cancel the loading of the page, the hyperlink changes color as if you had viewed the aborted page. The aborted page will however not register for either the Back or Forward commands. Therefore, if you change your mind and want to view it, you will have to click the hyperlink again or type its URL.

do it!

Stop the loading of a page before it is completed.

1. Open the Library of Congress Home Page by typing the URL www.loc.gov in the Address bar.
2. Click the Stop button on the Standard Buttons toolbar. If you clicked Stop early enough, the requested page will not even be displayed in the browser window, and the home page will remain active. If you clicked Stop after a slight delay, the Action Canceled message will be displayed (Figure 2-7) and the requested page will not be displayed. If you clicked the Stop button later than that, portions of the requested page may be displayed (Figure 2-8). Click the Back button to return to the National Park Service home page, if the latter is true. Pressing [Esc] is equivalent to clicking the Stop button on the Standard Buttons toolbar.

more

At different stages of downloading of a Web page, appropriate messages are displayed in the status bar of the browser. After you click a hyperlink or type the URL of a Web page, Internet Explorer will start looking for the page, and the logo in the upper-right corner of the window for your browser will become animated. During this time, the status bar flashes the messages—"Web site found. Waiting for reply…" and "Connecting to the site" followed by the address of the Web site. After this, the requested page displays and the components of the page download. Finally, after all the components have downloaded, the "Done" message displays in the Status bar. (Sometimes, the "Done" message will display prematurely before all page components have downloaded.) After the page has finished downloading, it will be displayed in the browser's viewing area.

An especially long delay in loading the Web page, along with a Status bar message that reads "Connecting to site…" and the name of the site, means Internet Explorer cannot find the site. Eventually the application will display a message indicating that the file you are looking for cannot be displayed. If the download takes too long, use the Stop button to interrupt the attempt to connect to the Web page.

Although the more popular way to stop downloading of a Web page is to click the Stop button on the Standard Buttons toolbar, the same can also be achieved through the View menu.

Figure 2-7 Downloading stopped at an early stage

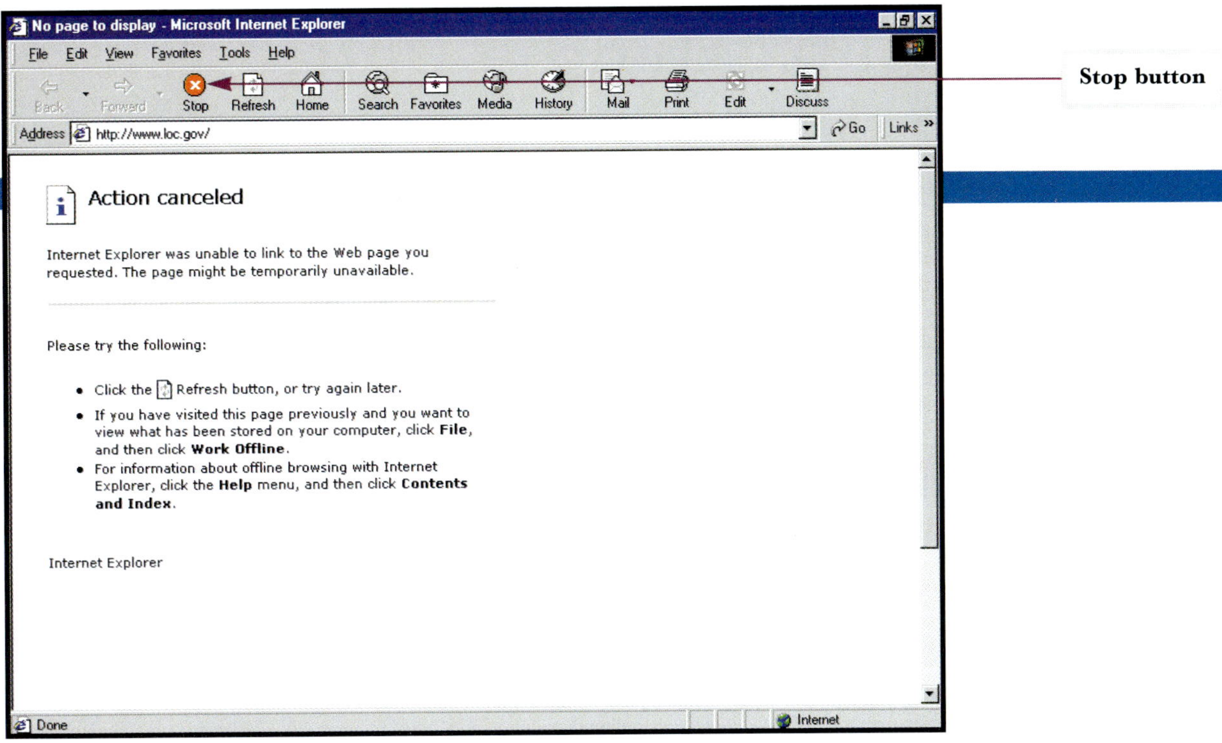

Figure 2-8 Partially downloaded Web page

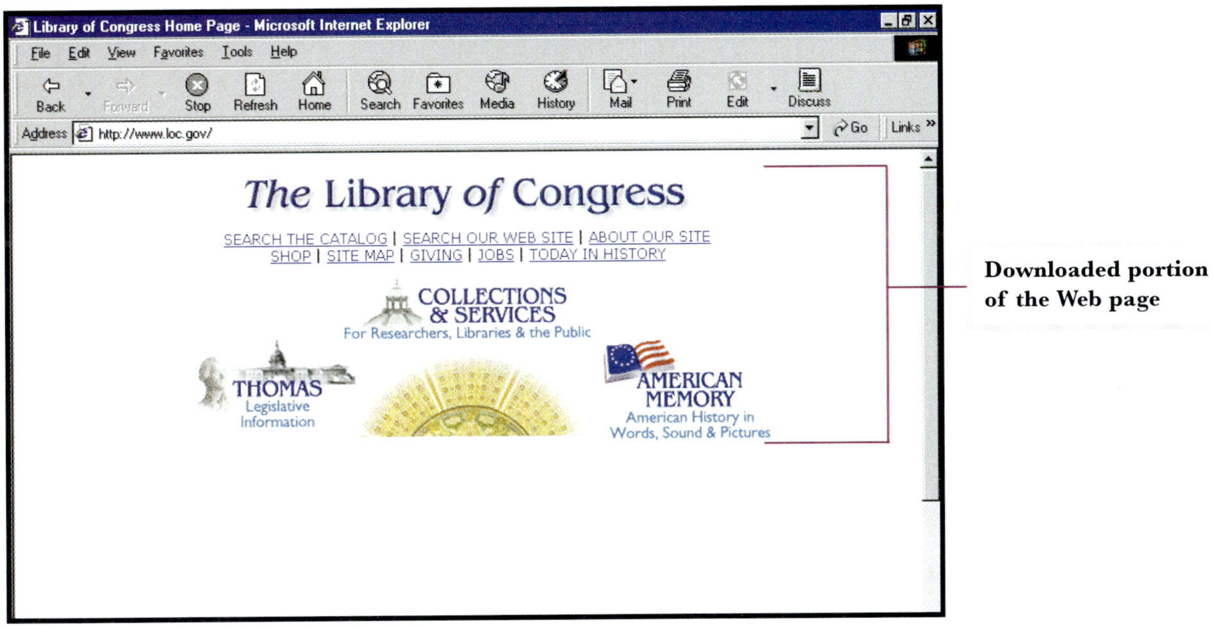

Practice

Click a hyperlink on the current page and stop it from loading before it is displayed in the browser window.

skill Refreshing a Page

concept

Sometimes, a Web page may not load correctly. In such cases, you can reload—or refresh—a Web page that is currently being viewed by using the Refresh button on the Standard Buttons toolbar. You also may want to load a fresh copy of a Web page when the content of the page has changed since you originally requested it (for example, a Web page with a stock ticker or a similar page that has constantly changing content).

do it!

Refresh a page in your browser window.

1. While still on the National Park Service page, click Refresh on the Standard Buttons toolbar, as shown in Figure 2-9. The page will reload from its Web server. Any items that have been edited since the page was last loaded will now be updated.

more

Refreshing is a simple operation that might not seem very valuable at first glance, but it does have several uses. Sometimes an error in transmission will cause some of a page's content to load improperly or not at all. The button gives the page a second chance to load correctly. Of course, pages that suffer from faulty authoring or contain features that are not compatible with your browser will not load correctly no matter how many times you refresh them.

There are also many pages whose content changes often. For example, if your home page is a news service, you might leave the page open all day while you work with other applications, and then check in on the news page every few hours. Clicking the Refresh button will load any new news items that the editors of the page may have added. Some sites feature live "Webcams" that display frequently updated real-time views of scenes from around the world (Figure 2-10). There are even sites that keep running scores during sporting events and update their live coverage several times a minute! The Refresh button helps you make the most of sites such as these. Some Webcams and live data pages are programmed to refresh themselves after a set time such as 60 seconds. In some cases, you can increase the frequency of updates by refreshing the page manually.

Figure 2-9 Standard Buttons toolbar

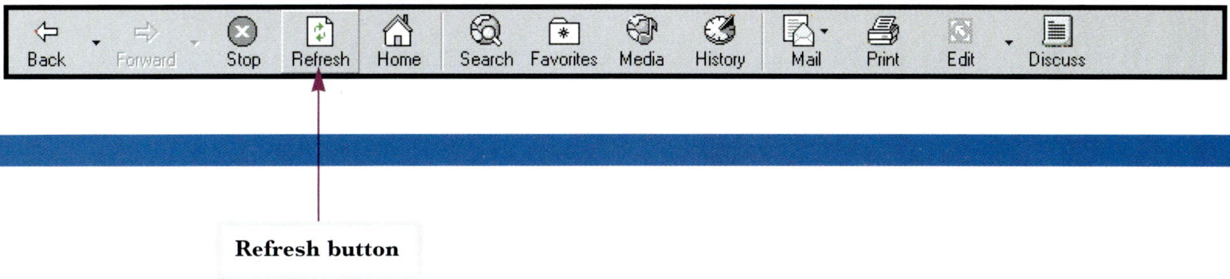

Figure 2-10 Example of a Webcam

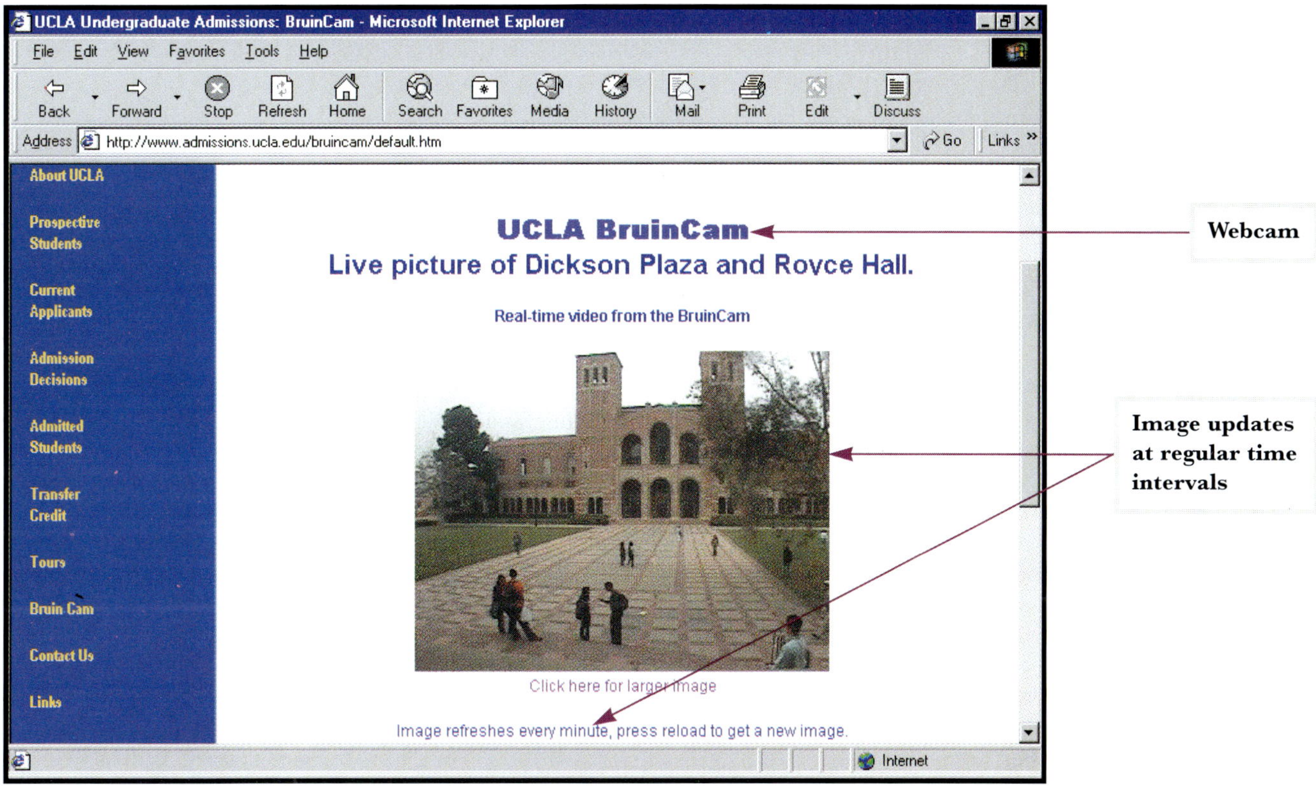

Practice

Type www.nps.gov in the Address bar and stop the loading of the page when half the page has been loaded. Then, use the refresh feature to view the entire page.

skill Creating a Desktop Shortcut to a Page

concept

The combination of Internet Explorer and the Windows operating system provides a unique way to access a Web page. This method is very direct. You can view the page without first starting your browser. This method involves creating a shortcut to the Web page on the desktop. This shortcut is then used in much the same way as a shortcut to any other Windows application. Double-clicking the icon would access the Web page if you are connected to the Internet.

do it!

Create a desktop shortcut to a Web page.

1. Open the Library of Congress (www.loc.gov) page.
2. Click File on the Menu bar.
3. Point to Send and click the Shortcut To Desktop command (Figure 2-11).
4. Minimize Internet Explorer and all the other active applications so that you can see your desktop. The desktop shows the shortcut icon to the specified page (Figure 2-12). The next time you start your computer, if your Internet connection is active and you double-click this icon, Internet Explorer will launch automatically and the Library of Congress Home Page will be displayed. If you double-click the shortcut icon in the midst of your browsing session, the targeted page will be displayed immediately.

more

The shortcut is not a saved file of the page; it is merely a saved command that directs your computer to the Web page whose shortcut it represents.

If you create a shortcut to a page and the URL of that page changes, the shortcut will no longer be valid. You can create a new shortcut or edit the existing one. You can change the icon or URL, or assign a shortcut key to the shortcut of the Web page you create on the desktop. To change the icon, right-click the icon and select the Properties command from the pop-up menu. The Properties dialog box for the Web page is displayed. Click Change Icon... . The Change Icon dialog box is displayed (Figure 2-13). Select an icon of your choice from the Current icon list and click OK to close the Change Icon dialog box. Then, click OK to close the Properties dialog box. To remove a desktop shortcut, right-click it and select the Delete command from the pop-up menu that is displayed. This action will send the shortcut to the Recycle Bin.

Figure 2-11 Creating a desktop shortcut of a Web page

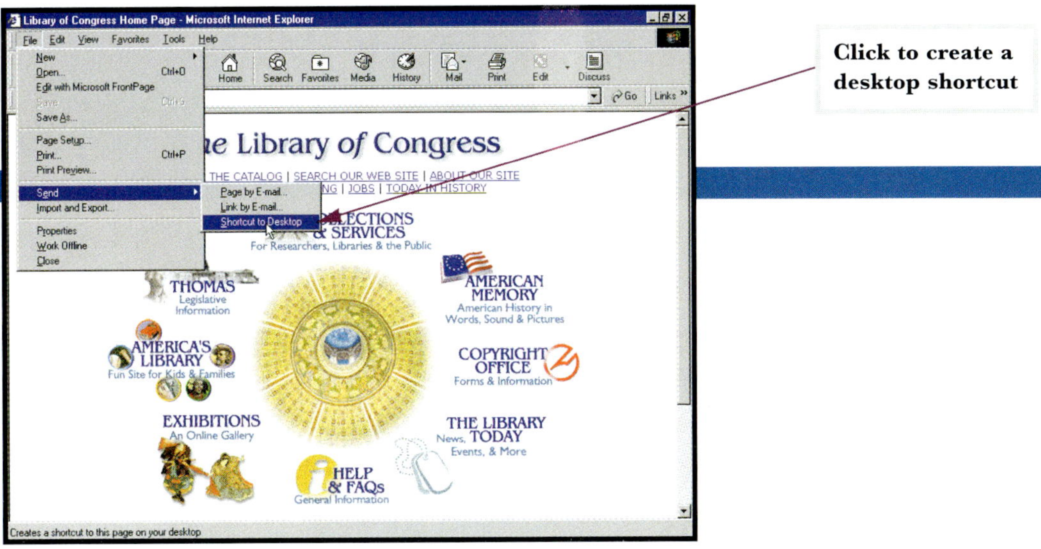

Figure 2-12 Web page shortcut on desktop

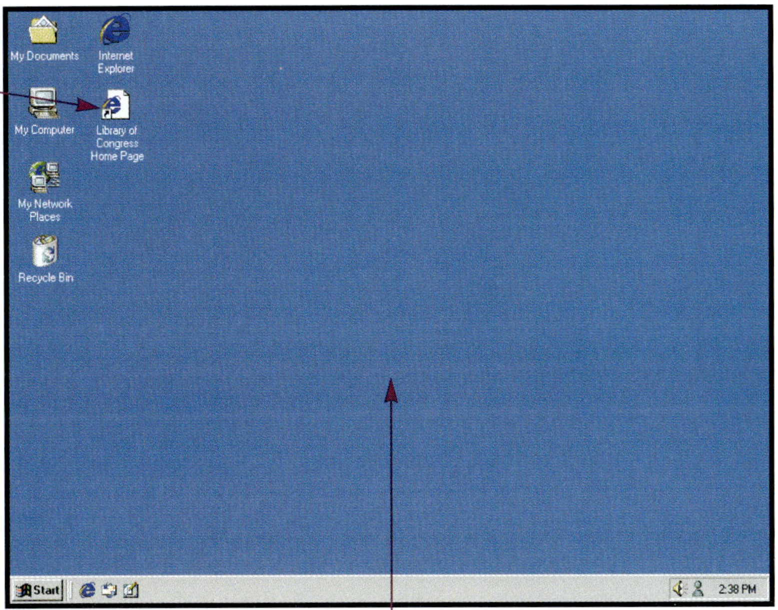

Figure 2-13 Change Icon dialog box

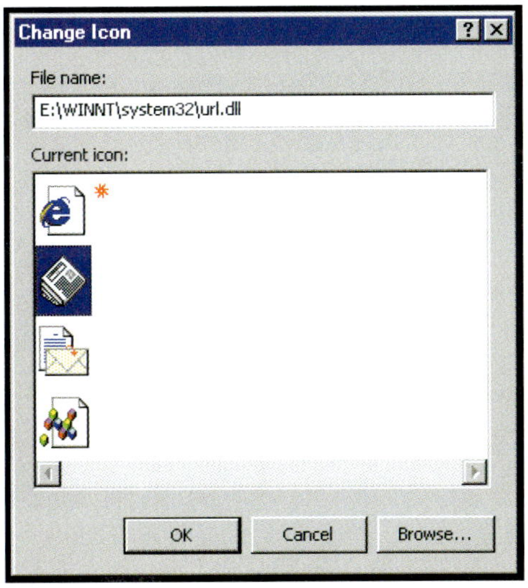

Practice

Create a shortcut to the National Park Service home page (www.nps.gov) on your desktop, close Internet Explorer and then access the page through the shortcut that you have just created.

skill Copying Text from a Page

concept

Sometimes you may come across very little information in a Web page that is useful to you. In such cases, rather than save the entire Web page as a file, it would be ideal to save just the relevant text. This can be done by copying the text from the page and pasting it in a document. This document can then be saved for later use.

do it!

Copy an important message pertaining to reservations for the Park Service from the Reservation Service page and paste it in another application.

1. Open the home page of the National Park Service (www.nps.gov), and click the Visit Your Parks hyperlink.
2. You will be taken to the National Park Guide page. Click the National Park Reservations hyperlink.
3. In the US National Parks Reservation Service page, scroll down to the Important Messages section. Then click, hold, and drag your mouse across the bulleted list (do not include the heading) to select the text (Figure 2-14).
4. Click Edit on the Menu bar, then click the Copy command. The selected text has now been copied to the Windows Clipboard, which is a segment of your computer memory that is used to hold small amounts of data temporarily for transfer within or between applications.
5. Click Start on the taskbar, point to Programs, point to Accessories, and then click WordPad. WordPad is the built-in word processor for the Windows operating system (you may also use Microsoft Word for this step).
6. Click Edit on the Menu bar, then click the Paste command. The text you copied from the Web page is inserted into the document (Figure 2-15). Save this document and then close the application. Occasionally, the text that you paste into a document may be cluttered with lines and/or boxes that did not appear on the Web page. To avoid bringing such clutter into the document, copy and paste your text into the Notepad program, which also appears on the Accessories submenu of Windows. Then copy and past the text from Notepad into your word processing program.

more

The above example is a common use of the Copy command. You can also copy text by right-clicking the selected text. A pop-up menu will be displayed that includes the Copy command. This pop-up menu also permits you to print the selected text or add the remaining text on the page to the selection (Select All). Note, however, that the Select All command will copy not only the text but also the graphics on the Web page.

The copy-paste feature comes in handy when you are looking through large text files from which you want to retrieve only certain amounts of data, such as apartment listings, want ads, or event schedules. Data that you copy to the Clipboard will remain there until you copy something else or shut down your computer. You can paste the same piece of data from the Clipboard multiple times.

Once you have pasted the copied text into another application, you can manipulate it just as easily as if you had typed it yourself. For example, if you pasted the text from the National Park Service Web page into Microsoft Word or another word processor, you could change its font type or size, rearrange where the text lines break, add text, or delete parts of copied text.

Figure 2-14 Selected text on a Web page

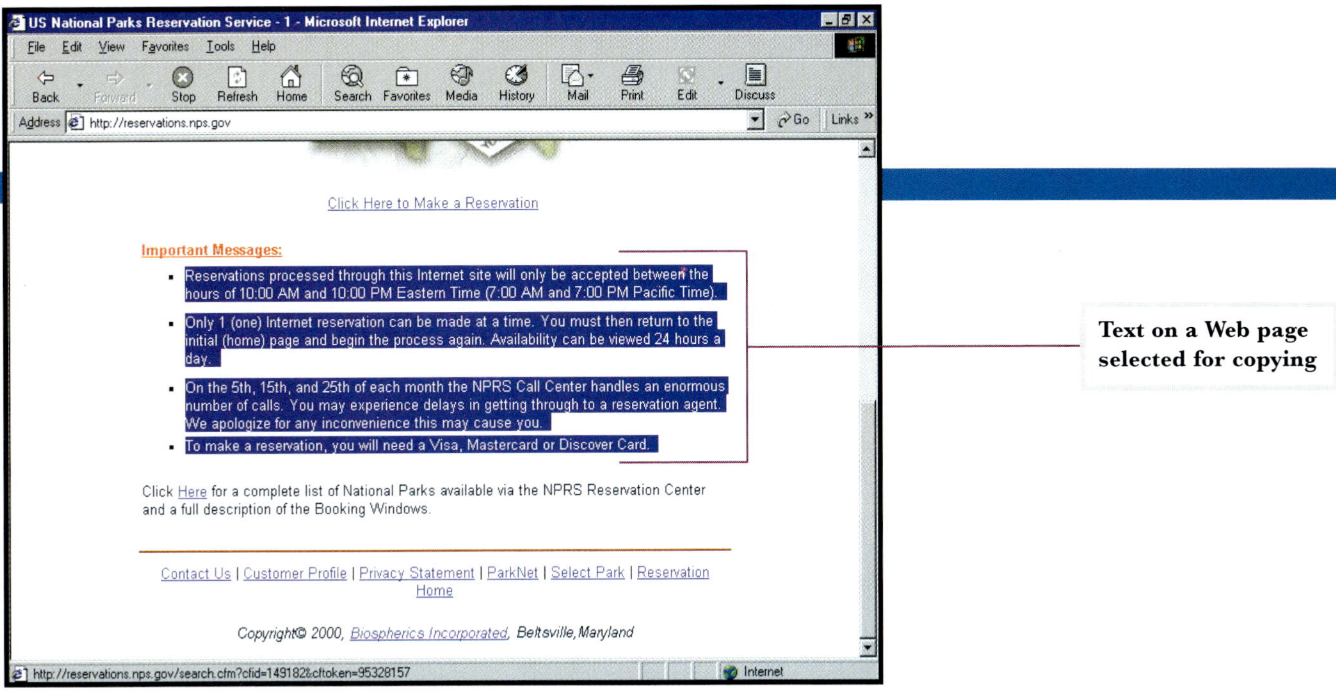

Figure 2-15 Copied text pasted into WordPad

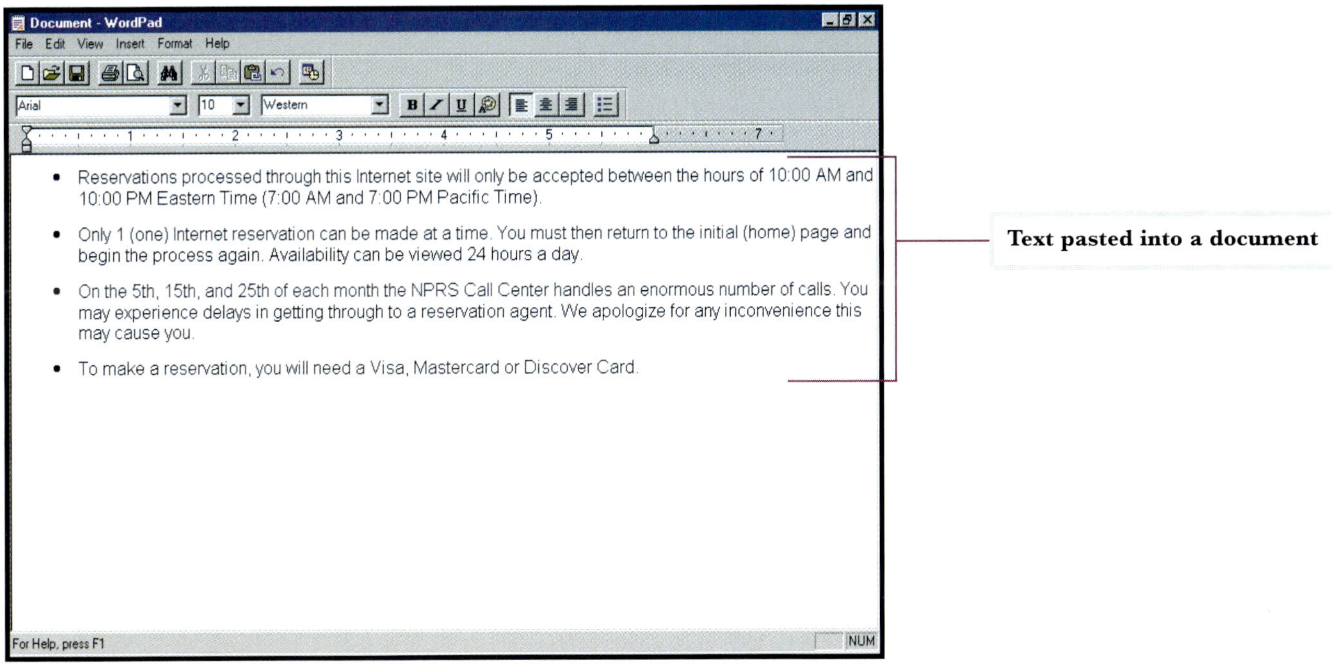

Practice

Click the Contact Us hyperlink near the bottom of the National Parks Reservation Service page. Copy the Contact Phone Numbers and paste them into a word processing document.

skill Saving an Image from a Page

concept

The images displayed on Web pages are actually individual files that you can save to the hard drive of your computer without saving the entire Web page. You can keep the picture files for later viewing, for use in other documents, or even to decorate your desktop. Internet Explorer provides the Image toolbar to help you to manipulate these images as you choose. You can save the image or even e-mail it to your friend. Despite the ease of copying text and images from the Web, remember that copyright protection may apply to the material. Do not misuse items you find on the Web.

do it!

Save the image from the National Park Guide Web page using the Image toolbar.

1. Be sure that the National Park Guide Web page (www.nps.gov/parks.html) appears on your screen.
2. Move the mouse pointer over the main image on the Web page. The Image toolbar is displayed (Figure 2-16) with four buttons for performing various operations on the image—namely, saving, printing, mailing, and working with the My Pictures folder.
3. Click the Save button on the Image toolbar to save the image.
4. The Save Picture dialog box is displayed allowing you to decide where to save the image and what to name it (Figure 2-17). The My Pictures folder is selected in the Save in list box by default.
5. The File name list box already contains the name that the creator gave to the image file (in this case it is vyp_main_photo1 for the image on Visit Your Parks page), but you can replace it with a name of your choice, such as Visit_Parks_Photo.gif. The dialog box gives you the option to save this image as either a GIF or BMP file. You specify the file type in the Save as type list box. If you are merely going to view the picture later, it is usually best to save it in the same format as it already exists. If you plan to use the file in another application, that application may require or recommend the use of a different file type.
6. Click the Save button Save to save a copy of the image file to your disk and to close the dialog box.

more

When you right-click an image hyperlink, a pop-up menu is displayed. The pop-up menu contains the Save Picture As command and the Set As Wallpaper command. Wallpaper is a Windows feature that allows you to display an image as part of your desktop. The image on the desktop is displayed the moment you start Windows, and will stay there until you decide to remove it. Clicking the Set As Wallpaper command will set the image as your desktop wallpaper. It will automatically remove any other image that you had previously set as wallpaper. The Print Target and Save Target As commands will be active if the image you right-clicked is a hyperlink. The target is the page to which the hyperlink would send you if you clicked it, and these operations will be performed without leaving the current page.

Figure 2-16 Image toolbar

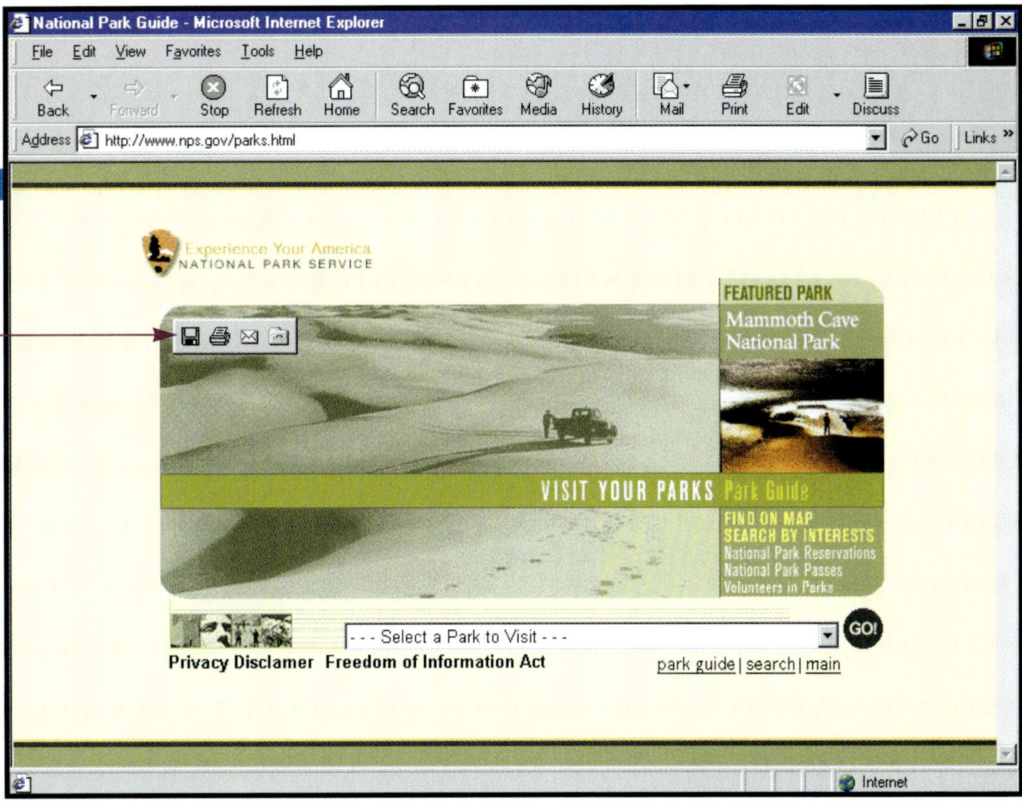

Figure 2-17 Save Picture dialog box

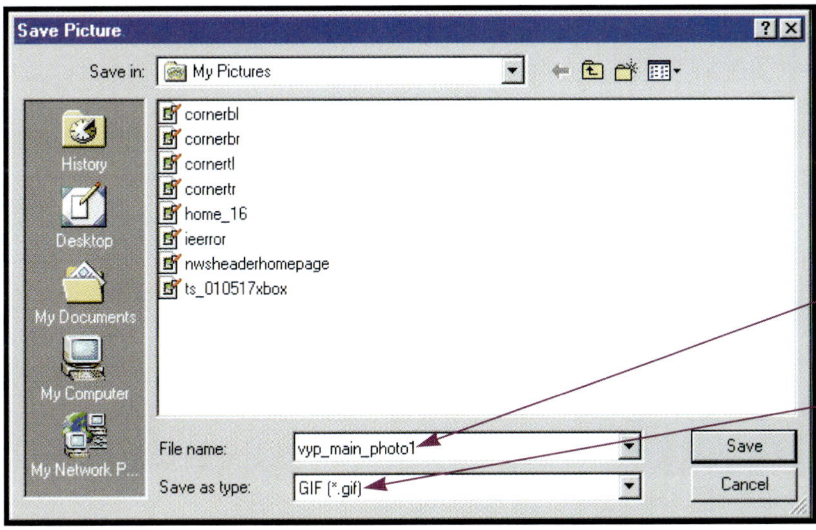

Practice

Find a picture of another national park on the National Park Service Web site and save it in the My Pictures folder. (Remember: For pictures at least 200 x 200 pixels in size, open the Save Picture dialog box by clicking the Save icon on the Image Toolbar. For smaller pictures, simply right-click on them and select the Save Picture As option on the pop-up menu that appears.)

skill Exploring the AutoComplete Feature

concept

Internet Explorer contains a convenient feature called AutoComplete that stores previous entries of URLs you have typed in the Address bar and suggests matches for you. AutoComplete can also be used optionally to complete user names and passwords in forms. The AutoComplete feature can be activated by changing the browser settings.

do it!

Allow AutoComplete to help you type the address of the National Park Service page.

1. Click the URL currently displayed in the Address bar to select it.
2. Type www.nps.gov to replace the current URL. A list is displayed about the time you type the n in nps (Figure 2-18). The list will include all of the recently entered URLs that match what you have typed so far. If you continue to type, the AutoComplete options will be narrowed down to match your entry exactly. When the AutoComplete list is displayed, you can use the down arrow key on the keyboard to select the URL you want to access. Once the correct URL is selected, press [Enter] to load the page.
3. Click http://www.nps.gov in the AutoComplete list (Figure 2-19). Your browser will take you to the page immediately. If none of the options that the list presents is the one you had in mind, just keep typing in the Address bar and enter the URL in the usual fashion.

more

AutoComplete works in other ways as well. If you have a frequently visited Web page that accepts form data—in other words, information like your name and address that you type in—AutoComplete will finish your entries in much the same way. Because some data you enter may be sensitive, such as passwords or credit card numbers, the data AutoComplete uses to finish your typing is encrypted on your hard drive. The menu options AutoComplete produces are not sent out over the Web; only the selection you choose and deliberately enter in a text box goes out over the Web.

Because AutoComplete works without your having to do anything, it is not as much a skill as just a feature that you should be aware of. In the next Skill, we will examine ways to control the AutoComplete function, including turning it off.

Figure 2-18 AutoComplete list

AutoComplete list (your list may vary)

Address bar

Figure 2-19 Selecting a URL

Click desired URL from the AutoComplete list to display its Web page in the browser window

Practice

Use the AutoComplete feature to go to http://www.msn.com.

skill Customizing AutoComplete

concept

AutoComplete lists possible matches from the entries you have typed before. This feature can be customized to suit individual preferences. This involves modifying specific aspects of the feature or disabling it altogether. You can selectively disable it or enable it for user names and passwords. This comes in handy when you do not want your browser to remember the passwords you use on the Web, as this would mean anybody accessing your computer would be able to access those sites.

do it!

Turn off the use of AutoComplete for user names and passwords on forms.

1. Click Tools on the Menu bar and then click the Internet Options command. The Internet Options dialog box is displayed.
2. Click the Content tab to activate the Content tab page, as shown in Figure 2-20.
3. Click [AutoComplete...] in the Personal information section of the Content tab. The AutoComplete Settings dialog box, shown in Figure 2-21, is displayed.
4. Clear the User names and passwords on forms check box (if it is already cleared, leave it that way).
5. Click [OK] to confirm the settings and close the AutoComplete Settings dialog box.
6. Click [OK] to close the Internet Options dialog box.

more

Until you change the settings again, AutoComplete will not function when you are filling in your name or password on a form on a Web site. You can use the same procedure to disable AutoComplete for typing URLs in the Address bar or for typing any information into Web based forms.

The AutoComplete Settings box also gives you the option of clearing the "history"—in other words, AutoComplete's stored list of form entries and/or passwords. The history list of URLs for entry in the Address bar is a separate record with other uses, as we will examine in the next section. In Web forms, when typing information such as user names and passwords, you can remove an item from the list of suggestions by clicking the item and then pressing the [Delete] key.

Figure 2-20 Content tab

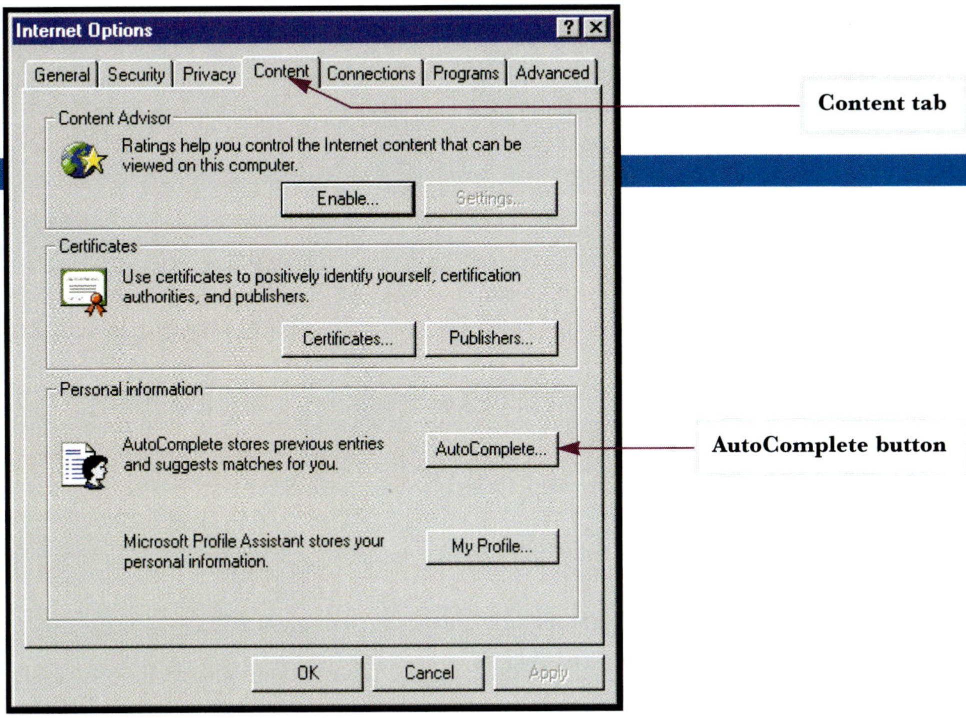

Figure 2-21 AutoComplete Settings dialog box

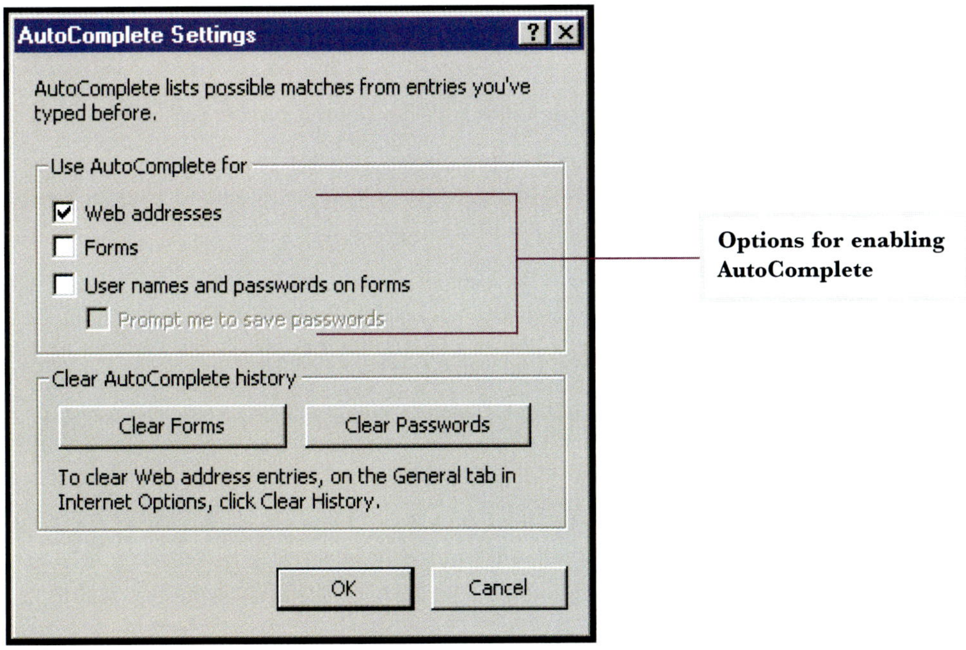

Practice

Enable AutoComplete for user names and passwords on forms.

skill Using the History Function

concept

Internet Explorer will store the URLs of Web sites you have visited recently, even after you have turned off your computer. This list of recently viewed sites is called history. History can be used to return to a site you have seen in the last several days. This is very useful when over a period of a few days you frequent a few selected sites. This feature also saves you the trouble of remembering URLs of Web sites that you have visited and are sure to visit again. Since, any page you visit is automatically saved in the history folder, you do not have much control over this feature. However, you can still customize a few aspects such as the number of days for which the history has to be maintained.

do it!

Access a recently visited page using the History function.

1. Click the History button on the Standard Buttons toolbar. The browser window will be split into two panels. The contents of your browser window slide to the right panel to make room for the History bar in the left panel (Figure 2-22). This bar lists the active links you can click to revisit the pages you have already visited in the past few Skills. The drop-down arrow on the right end of the Address bar functions as an abbreviated way to access the History list. Click it and all the recently visited sites will be listed chronologically.
2. Click any of the Web pages displayed in the History bar to load that page into the right panel of the browser window (Figure 2-23).
3. Click the History button on the Standard Buttons toolbar to close the History bar when you are finished using it.

more

The History function of the Internet Explorer application used in this Skill was set at only one day of memory. However, as the next Lesson teaches, the default number of days for the History function is ten days and you can modify the History of your browser. Additionally, the History bar normally is organized by days. When the History function is set for multiple days, you can click another day to see sites you visited on that day. Within each day are folders that contain all of the pages visited from a particular domain or site. Click the folder icons to show and hide their contents.

If you wish to organize the contents of the History bar in a different way, click View in the upper-left corner of the bar. You can choose to have your recent Web pages listed by date, by site name, by frequency of your visits, or by the order in which you visited them on the current day. The Web pages in History are saved in a History folder which is a part of operating system folders.

Figure 2-22 Using History bar links

History button on the Standard Buttons toolbar

History bar organized by date (then alphabetically)

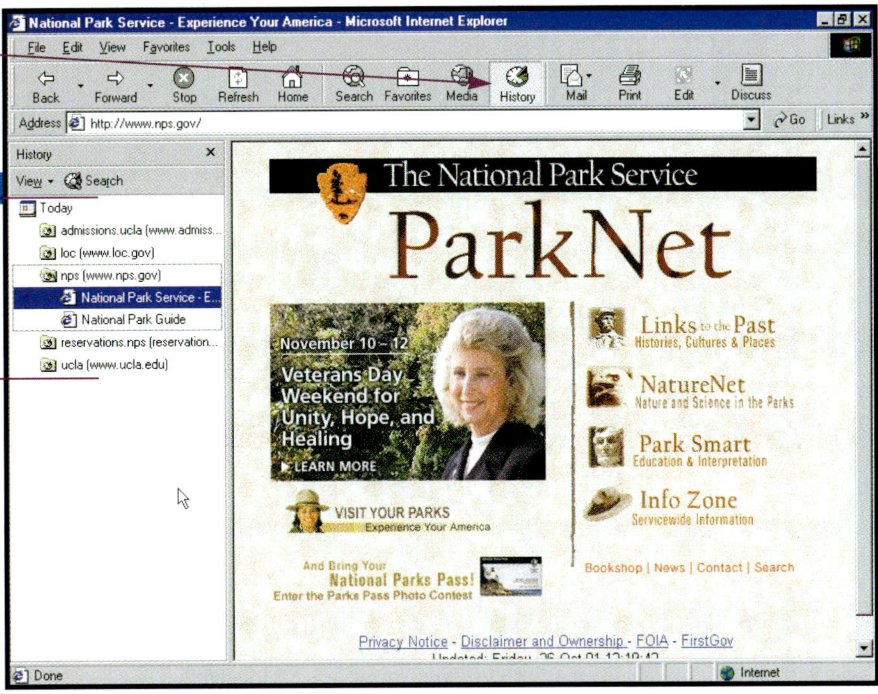

Figure 2-23 Web page displayed in the right panel

Library of Congress Home Page link selected on the History bar

Library of Congress Home Page in the right panel

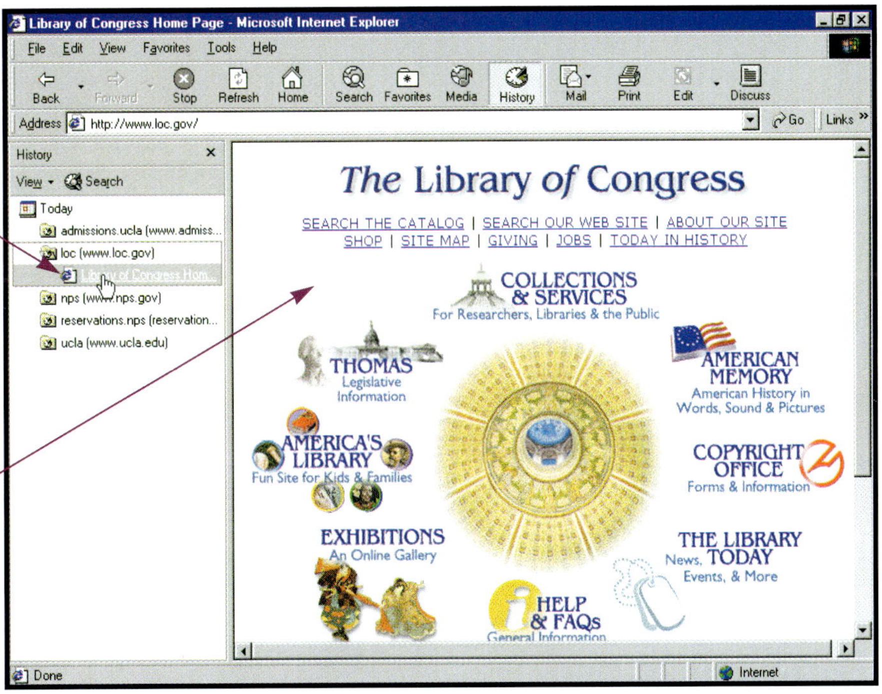

Practice

Use the History bar to locate the URL of the home page of your browser. Open the home page. Finally locate the URL of the page you have just left on the History bar and then open the page.

skill Modifying the History of Your Browser

concept

When you first use Internet Explorer, the History function is set to store the URLs of the Web pages you have visited in the last 10 days. However, you can reduce or increase this time. If other people have access to your computer, your History folder can allow them to see what sites you have visited. If this concerns you, you can use the History function as a safeguard for your privacy. You can remove an item from your history, or delete the entire record. When you do so, the items will be removed from the History bar and also from the drop-down menu under the Address bar.

do it!

Remove an individual page from the History list, change the duration of time Internet Explorer keeps pages in history, and clear the contents of the History folder.

1. Activate the History bar and locate the National Park Service Web page in the history of your browser. If necessary, click the appropriate day in your history list and then the folder labeled nps (www.nps.gov) to reveal National Park Service in the History bar.
2. Right-click the National Park Service hyperlink to display a pop-up menu, and then click the Delete command (Figure 2-24). A caution box will be displayed asking if you are sure you want to delete the history item.
3. Click Yes. The National Park Service entry will no longer be listed on the History bar.
4. Click Tools on the Menu bar and then click the Internet Options command. This displays the Internet Options dialog box.
5. Click inside the Days to keep pages in history spin box, in the History section of the General tab. By default, the Days to keep pages in history spin box displays the value 10 (Figure 2-25).
6. Type 5 to replace the selected value. You can also use the down and up arrows of the spin box to decrease and increase the value in the spin box, respectively.
7. Click Clear History in the History section. A caution box is displayed asking if you want to delete all the items in your History folder.
8. Click Yes to confirm that you wish to delete all items.
9. Click OK again in the Internet Options dialog box and close the History bar.

more

Because items in your History folder have an expiration date, you may not want to rely on this function for permanent storage of the links to the Web sites that you want to visit again. Note also that it takes more computer storage resources to keep a larger number of days in History. Therefore, limit your History to the lowest number of days you actually need for accessing previously visited Web sites.

Figure 2-24 Deleting a History item

Options available by right-clicking a link in the History bar

Figure 2-25 Change number of days for which to maintain History

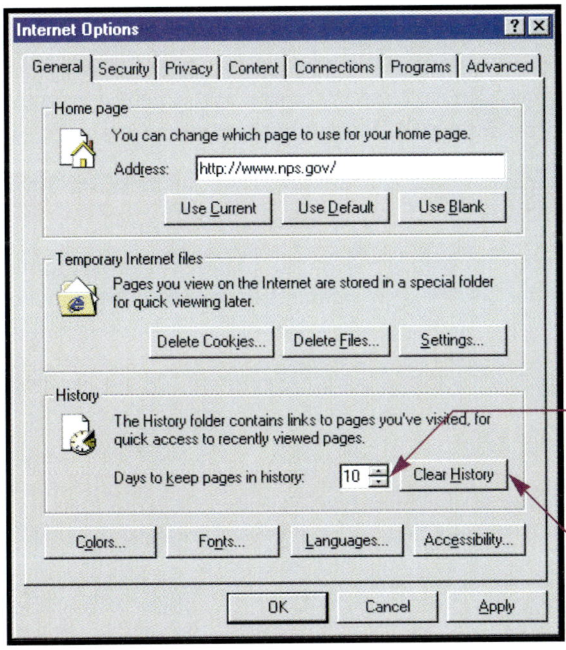

Spin box for specifying number of days to store in History function

Deletes all the items in the History folder

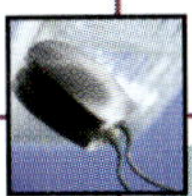

Practice

Readjust the History settings in your browser so that a history is maintained for ten days.

skill E-mailing a Web Page

concept

While viewing a Web page, you may wish to share it with someone else. For instance, a friend may be doing a project on network protocols. If you come across a Web page that has relevant information, you might want to send him or her the page, thereby saving your friend the trouble of looking for the relevant link. Internet Explorer enables you to use your default e-mail program to send a Web page as an e-mail message. Like many computing tasks, there is more than one way to complete this procedure. We will look at each of these methods in this skill.

do it!

Send a Web page as an e-mail message.

1. Click Tools on the Menu bar, and point to Mail and News. A submenu is displayed.
2. Click the Send Page command in the submenu. This command will launch a new message window from the e-mail program that you have selected on the Programs tab of the Internet Options dialog box (this example uses Microsoft Outlook Express).
3. When the message window opens, the page you were viewing will be displayed in the body section (Figure 2-26). In order for Web pages to be sent and received in this manner, both parties must be using mail programs that are capable of displaying HTML documents. Otherwise, you will have to save the Web page and e-mail it as an attached file. The Subject line in the addressing area will contain the name of the page.
4. Type the e-mail address of the recipient in the To text box and click Send on the toolbar of the e-mail program.
5. You can also e-mail a Web page by clicking Mail on the Standard Buttons toolbar (Figure 2-27) and then clicking the Send Page command in the drop-down menu, which is displayed.
6. Alternatively, a Web page can be e-mailed by clicking File on the Menu bar, pointing to Send, and clicking the Page by E-mail command in the submenu (Figure 2-28).

more

The different procedures for sending a page by e-mail also include an option for sending a link by e-mail. This option, called the Send a Link command, is available in the drop-down menu of the Mail button on the Standard Buttons toolbar (Figure 2-27). If you send someone a link, he or she will receive an e-mail message containing the URL of the page you are currently visiting. The URL you send will be an active hyperlink if your recipient has an Internet browser and a valid Internet connection. He or she will be able to access the page by clicking the URL in the body of the e-mail message. Before you send the message, you can type additional information along with the URL, just as you would type an ordinary e-mail message (such as "Hey, Jane, I thought you might enjoy this site! Love, Bob").

If you are trying to decide whether to send someone a whole page or just the link, consider whether that person has access to the Web or not. If not, you should send the whole page, which the person can access if both of you are on the local intranet. Also, if the page changes frequently and you want your recipient to see something that is on it right now, send the page. If you send the link, your recipient will see the page as it exists later and not necessarily what you saw.

Figure 2-26 E-mailing a Web page with Outlook Express

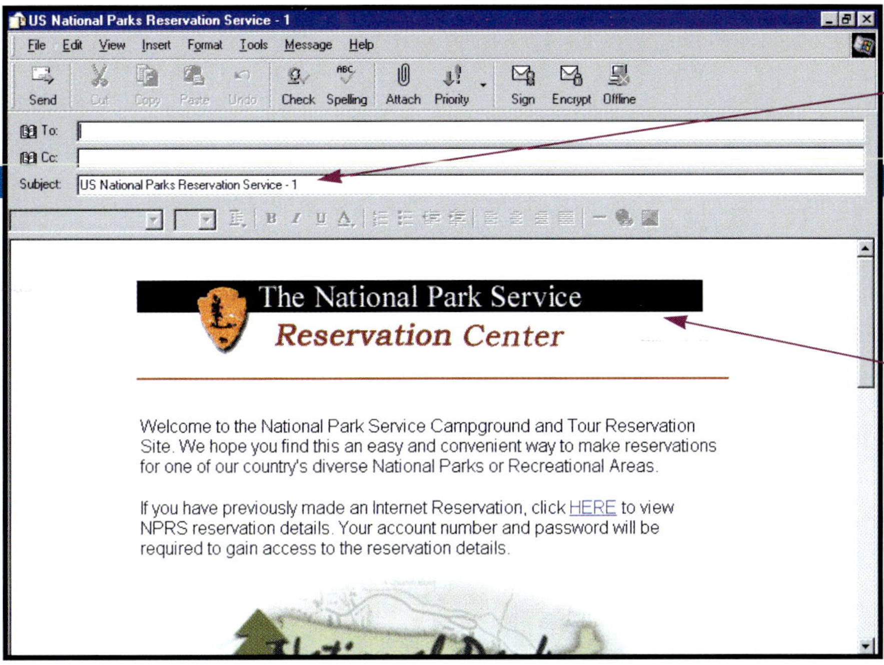

Figure 2-27 Using the Mail button

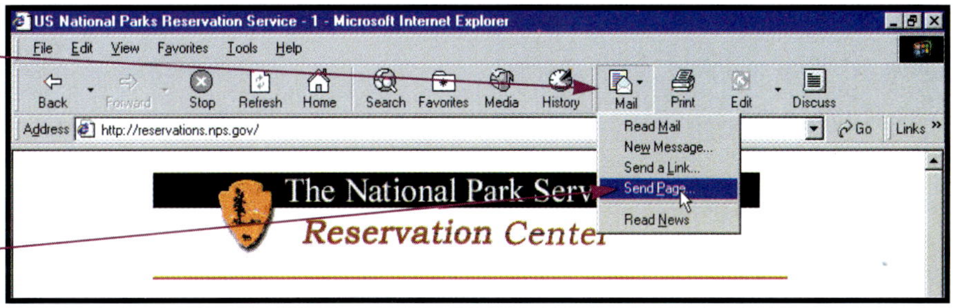

Figure 2-28 Using the File menu to e-mail a Web page

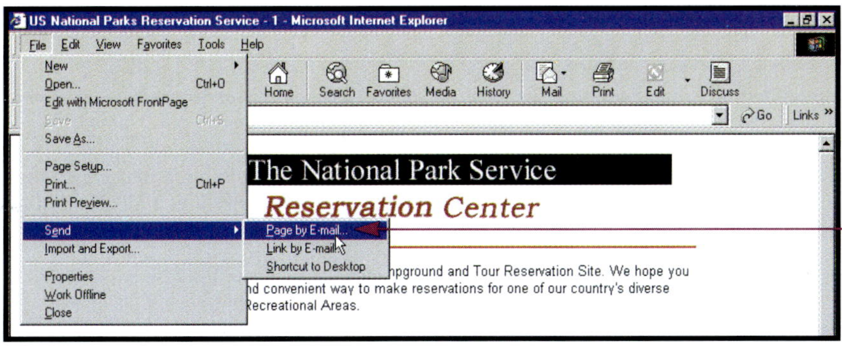

Practice

In the National Park Guide page, click the National Park Passes hyperlink and e-mail the National Park Passes page to your friend.

shortcuts

Function	Button/Mouse	Menu	Keyboard
Add www. before and .com after a site name in the Address bar			[Ctrl]+[Enter]
Select the current URL in the Address bar		Click inside the Address bar	[Alt]+[D]
Browse back to the previous page		Click View, point to Go To, then click Back	[Alt]+[Left Arrow]
Browse forward to the last page viewed		Click View, point at Go To, then click Forward	[Alt]+[Right Arrow]
Display the Address bar drop-down history menu		Double-click in the Address bar	[F4]
Stop downloading a page		Click View, then click Stop	[Esc]
Refresh the current page	Refresh	Click View, then click Refresh	[F5]
Copy selected text to Clipboard		Click Edit, then click Copy	[Ctrl]+[C]
Paste text from Clipboard		Click Edit, then click Paste	[Ctrl]+[V]
Select the entire content on a Web page		Click Edit, then click Select All	[Ctrl]+[A]
Activate the History Explorer bar		Click View, point to Explorer Bar, then click History	[Ctrl]+[H]

quiz

A. Identify Key Features

Name the items indicated by callouts in Figure 2-29.

Figure 2-29 Elements associated with Web browsing

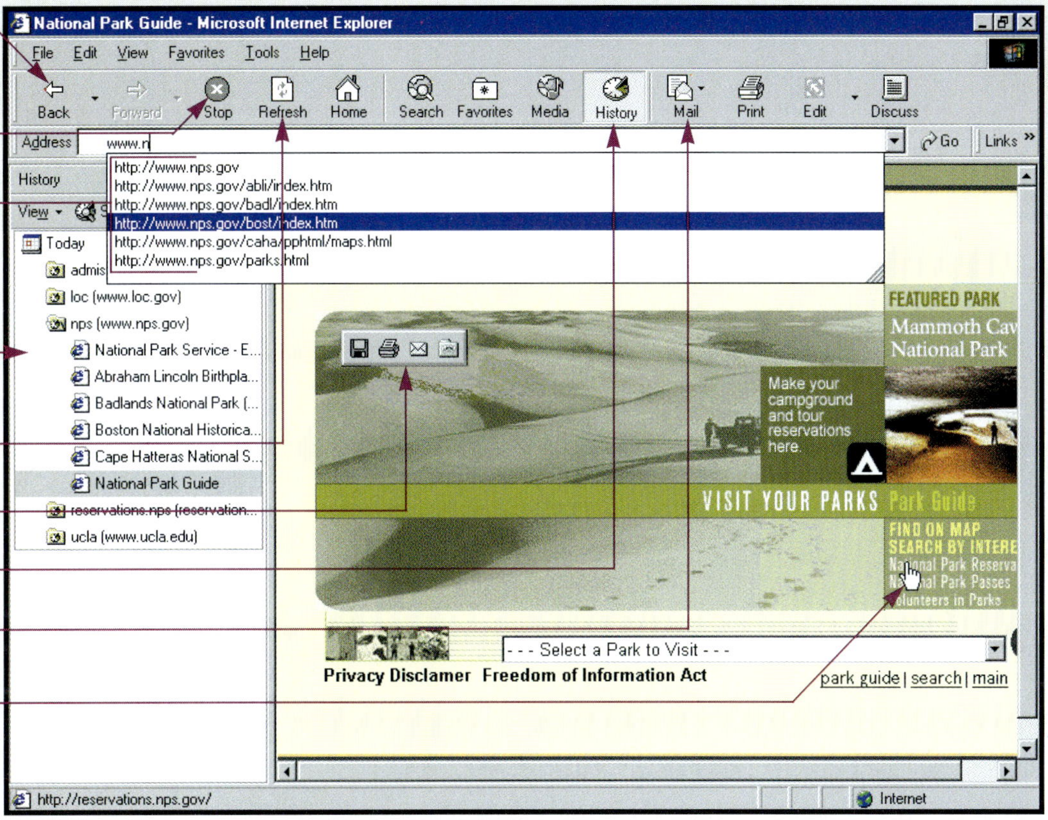

1. ____
2. ____
3. ____
4. ____
5. ____
6. ____
7. ____
8. ____
9. ____

B. Select the Best Answer

10. Saves the URLs that you have typed recently and completes them automatically in the Address bar

11. Creates an e-mail message that includes the contents of the current page

12. Brings up the most recently viewed page

13. An image you install as part of your desktop

14. Reloads the contents of the current page

15. An icon you create on your desktop to call up a Web page

16. Brings up the page that you visited after the current page

17. Creates an e-mail message that includes the URL of the current page

18. A pane that lists the pages you visited recently and helps you access them

19. Interrupts the loading of a page

a. Forward button

b. Shortcut

c. Refresh button

d. Wallpaper

e. Send Page command

f. Back button

g. AutoComplete

h. History bar

i. Send a Link command

j. Stop button

quiz (continued)

C. Complete the Statement

20. The mouse pointer changes to a hand with a pointing finger to indicate that:

a. The page you requested has finished loading

b. The link you are pointing to is a favorite

c. You must wait for a page to load

d. You are pointing to an active link

21. The Stop button:

a. Terminates your Internet connection

b. Terminates the loading of a page

c. Pauses the loading of a page

d. Prevents display of animations on the current page

22. By creating a desktop shortcut, you can:

a. Open a particular Web page directly without first starting Internet Explorer

b. View your desktop without exiting Internet Explorer

c. Copy items to your desktop from the History folder

d. Extend the AutoComplete feature to the desktop

23. When you save an image from a page, you can:

a. Put it in a folder on your hard drive

b. Print it

c. Set it as your desktop wallpaper

d. All of the above

24. If you think the contents of a Web page may have changed since you last accessed it, you should:

a. Check to see whether it is in your History folder

b. Type the current date in the Address bar

c. Reload the page using the Refresh button

d. E-mail the site to request an update

25. When viewing a page with Internet Explorer, you cannot directly e-mail:

a. The URL of the page

b. Selected text of the page

c. The full content of the page

d. The URL of the page with an explanatory message

26. When visiting a page for the first time, you are most likely to use:

a. AutoComplete

b. History

c. A hyperlink or the Address bar

d. The Forward button

27. AutoComplete:

a. Inserts characters in the Address bar that you have not yet typed

b. Makes a list of your recently viewed pages that you have shared with others on the Internet

c. Makes your personal information available to others on the Internet

d. Connects you to the Internet before you finish the dial-up procedure

interactivity

Build Your Skills

1. Visit and explore a Web site:
   a. Use the Address bar to visit the home page of the National Weather Service at http://www.nws.noaa.gov.
   b. Use the hyperlink on the National Weather Service home page to visit the Warnings page.
   c. Use the Address bar to visit the home page of msnbc at www.msnbc.com.
   d. Observe the Status bar flash its various messages as the msnbc home page downloads.
   e. Stop the msnbc home page just before it finishes loading.
   f. Navigate back to the National Weather Service home page.
   g. Go forward again to the msnbc home page and refresh it.

2. Create a shortcut for a Web page and mail the Web page:
   a. Create a desktop shortcut to the National Weather Service home page.
   b. Mail the Web page to your friend.
   c. Mail just the link to the Web page to your friend.

3. Save the text and image of a Web page:
   a. Open the National Park Service home page and navigate to a page that has several paragraphs of text.
   b. Click and hold the left mouse button, then drag to select a desired paragraph of text.
   c. Copy the selected text to the Clipboard.
   d. Open WordPad from the Start menu and paste the text you copied.
   e. Save the WordPad file as ie6skills2-1.doc.
   f. Save an image on the National Park Service home page as a separate file named ie6skills2-2.gif.

interactivity (continued)

Build Your Skills (continued)

4. Use AutoComplete and the History Explorer bar:

   a. Visit the following Web sites:

The Associated Writing Programs	www.awpwriter.org
About.com	www.about.com
The Altavista search engine	www.altavista.com

   b. Revisit the Associated Writing Programs home page by using AutoComplete.

   c. Activate the History Explorer bar, using it to go to the About.com home page.

   d. Set your History folder to retain pages for 5 days.

   e. Close the History Explorer bar.

5. Browsing Challenge: Use the Address Bar to go to www.msn.com. Follow hyperlinks on www.msn.com to navigate to the following Web sites. E-mail one site to yourself or another person:

   a. MSNBC News home page

   b. ESPN Sports home page

   c. A third link of your choosing

   d. Choose the smallest Web page of the three, and e-mail it to yourself or to a friend.

Problem Solving Exercises

1. You are scheduled to lead a tour of a construction site for your company's new building three days from now. Since much of the tour will be spent out in the open, you want to make sure that the weather forecast is good. Starting from www.msn.com, access a weather report for a major city that is closest to your current location. (You can enter the name of any major city in the world, or use U.S. ZIP Codes.) When you reach a page with the extended forecast, refresh it to make sure you have the most up-to-date information. Then create a desktop shortcut to the page. Finally, copy the text of the forecast and paste it into a WordPad document. Save the WordPad document using the file name ie6problem2-1.doc.

2. The director of marketing in your company has asked you to survey several Web sites to see what types of advertisements they include. Use a combination of the links and URLs you know to visit some of the commercial sites you have seen so far. Scan these pages for advertisements that include images. Save at least three of the images you see to your hard drive using the Image toolbar (or by right-clicking on the images). In addition, create desktop shortcuts to the pages on which the images are located. If you have an active e-mail account, send one of the pages you have discovered to a friend as an e-mail message.

3. You have just completed a research project and are now ready to move on to your next assignment. You have visited a great number of Web pages over the last week, and your History folder has become quite cluttered. It would probably be a good idea to clear the folder before beginning the new project, but first you should check to see if any of the pages you have visited would still be useful. Activate the History bar and review all the sites and pages you have visited since your history was last cleared. Delete the page you visited most recently from your history. Then, clear the contents of the History folder. Finally, reset the days to keep pages in the History folder to 10.

Searching the Web

skills

- Exploring the Search Assistant
- Finding Web Pages Using the Search bar
- Searching for Other Types of Information
- Removing a Search Category from the Search Assistant
- Customizing Search Engines in the Search Assistant
- Using Previous Search Results
- Accessing a Search Engine Directly
- Searching Using the Address Bar
- Searching on the Current Page

The WWW is a huge encyclopedia of information. It enables you to access Web pages easily at the click of a button. Accessing information on the Web is further enhanced by the Search feature in Internet Explorer.

When you have to make a project on American History, how do you start? If you were looking for the relevant information in an encyclopedia you would look for the section starting with the letter 'A' and then flip over to the relevant page. Similarly, you can access information pertaining to American History or, for that matter, any topic using the Search feature in Internet Explorer. In a search, you are prompted to enter the keyword to obtain the information you want to access. Then you are presented with a list of links to Web sites containing the information you require.

Web sites called search engines help you search for information on the Web based on key words. You may have heard of commercial sites such as Yahoo, Infoseek, Hot Bot, or Lycos. Microsoft has its own search engine for searching. You can use any search site, and many more are being added all the time. Search engines have huge databases of topics that are regularly updated.

With early Web browsers, people accessed search engines the same way they accessed any other page: by entering URLs. More recent browsers have featured a Search button that would take you directly to a particular search site. Internet Explorer has a comprehensive search function called the Search Assistant that enables you to use multiple search engines, organize which engines you use for different kinds of searches, and save the results of the searches. The Search Assistant's usefulness goes beyond finding Web sites; through the use of specialized search engines, it can help you find people, businesses, maps, newsgroup postings, or even entries in the Microsoft encyclopedia.

Internet Explorer also features a shortcut to search using the Address bar. And if you feel like it, you always can type in the address of your favorite search engine manually.

Lesson Goal:

In this lesson, you will learn about the Search Assistant in Internet Explorer 6.0 and explore the options available to customize the Search function.

skill Exploring the Search Assistant

concept

The Search Assistant is a feature of Internet Explorer that helps you conduct, customize, organize, and save searches on the Web. It functions through an Explorer bar, similar to the one you used for the History function. Accessing the engines and services of the Search Assistant is like accessing anything else on the Web. Your Internet connection must be active and valid before you proceed.

do it!

Activate the Search bar of the Internet Explorer.

1. Type www.msn.com in the Address bar and press [Enter] to open the Home page of the MSN Web site.
2. Click Search on the Standard Buttons toolbar.
3. The Search bar opens on the left side of the browser window and the other contents of the browser window slide to the right to make room for it, as shown in Figure 3-1.

more

As you can see in Figure 3-1, the Search bar includes several categories of searches, each of which is accompanied by an option button. Activate each of them and notice how the lower half of the Search bar changes, prompting you for different search information for each category.

Below the listed categories is a hyperlink for More, which, if clicked, will make two additional search categories available which are Look up a word and Find a Picture (Figure 3-2). Look up a word option allows you to search for a word in the Encyclopedia, Dictionary or Thesaurus. Find a Picture option finds a picture that matches a keyword.

Figure 3-1 Active Explorer bar

Figure 3-2 Search bar

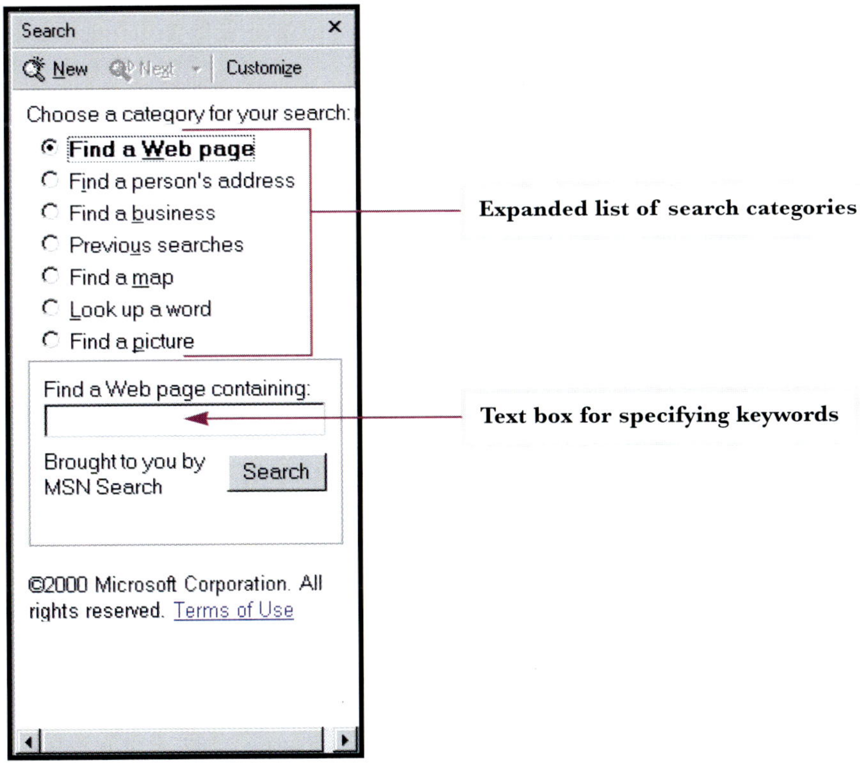

skill Finding Web Pages Using the Search Bar

concept

Finding a Web site on a selected topic using the Search Assistant is a simple matter of entering the necessary information in the Search bar and letting Internet Explorer do the work. The Search Assistant will look up your keyword in a variety of available online resources and present you with a list of links to Web pages containing the information you seek.

do it!

Find a Web site containing information about the early American explorers Lewis and Clark.

1. With the Search bar open, activate the Find a Web Page option button.
2. Type Lewis and Clark in the Find a Web page containing text box, as in Figure 3-3.
3. Click Search or press [Enter]. The message retrieving results... will appear near the top of the Search bar. After a brief wait, a list of search results from a search engine will appear in the Search bar, similar to the list in Figure 3-4. The Web is a dynamic place where new pages are added each day and old ones moved or deleted. Hence, search results of the same keyword yield different results over a period of time.
4. The results are displayed as hyperlinks. Click the Lewis and Clark National Historic Trail link to open that page in the browser window (Figure 3-5). The Search bar and its contents will remain intact, allowing you to check out several search results without having to redo the search or to return to a search page each time. Even if you close the Search bar, the results will still be there if you activate it again during your work session. As with links in other situations, search results you have already visited will appear in a different color in the Search bar.

more

You can search many sites by typing just a few words in the text box(es) on the Search bar. The cumulative list of links to relevant sites or pages is sometimes preceded by the number of matches found to the query you have posed to the search engine. Web pages are graded on the percentage of match found between the search criteria and the pages. This percentage represents the relevance of a search result to a search query. Designing your inquiries to get relevant returns (and learning how to deal with the irrelevant returns you will get anyway) is a skill you will develop over time. In Internet Explorer's Advanced Search mode, you can use logical operators such as "and" or "or" in your search string to refine Web searches. Also use "+" immediately before a word to include it in, or use "–" immediately before a word to exclude it from the search results.

Some search engines allow you to control how many results are displayed at a time. Most include a list of hyperlinked page numbers that enable you to view more results if the first set is not satisfactory. Other search engines let you expand each result so that it includes a description instead of just a one-line hyperlink. Since space in the Search bar is limited, you can point to a hyperlink to receive a ScreenTip containing a description of the page to which the result is linked.

Table 3-1 Using Logical Operators in Advanced Search mode

Example	Results
Hotels +Montreal	Will include "Montreal" as an essential word when searching for information on hotels
Hotels -Montreal	Will exclude "Montreal" when searching for information related to hotels
Hotels Vancouver OR Montreal	Will include "Vancouver" or "Montreal" when searching for information on hotels
Vancouver AND Montreal	Will include "Vancouver" and "Montreal" when searching for information on any topic

Figure 3-3 Entering a search string

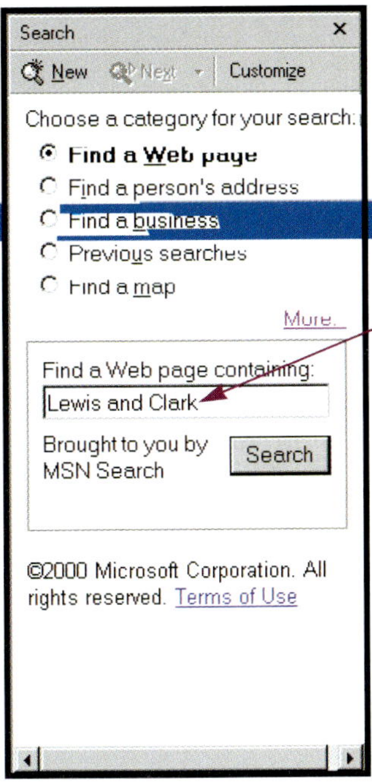

Figure 3-4 Search Results

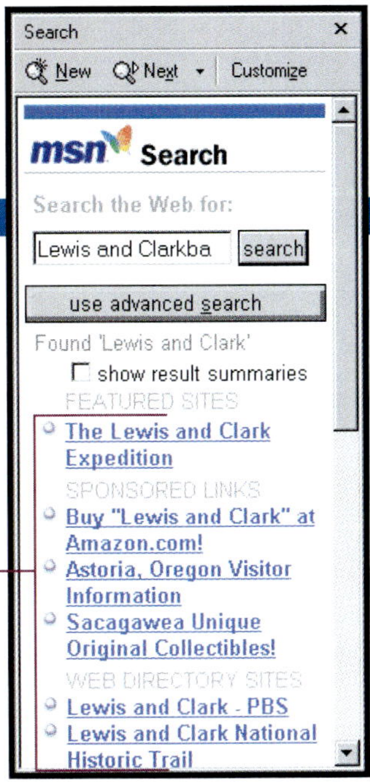

Figure 3-5 Viewing a search result

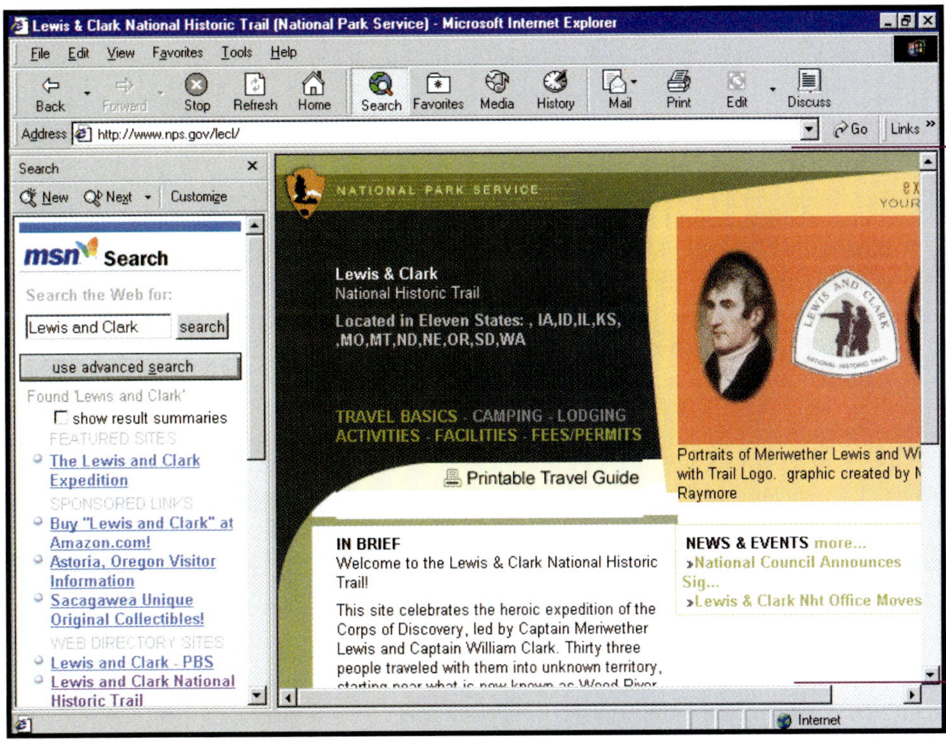

Practice

Follow several of the links produced by the Lewis and Clark search. Then conduct a search for Web pages that discuss the Louisiana Purchase.

skill Searching for Other Types of Information

concept

All Web searches technically involve finding Web pages. However, the contents of some Web sites are very specialized. Therefore, Internet Explorer categorizes them differently in the Search bar. You can search the Web for information pertaining to individuals, companies, and maps etc. Each of these searches has a separate screen suited to the particular kind of search.

do it!

Search for a map using the Search bar.

1. Click New on the Search bar, which displays search results for Lewis and Clark. The original Search Assistant options will reappear.
2. Activate the option button labeled Find a map. A new set of text boxes will be displayed.
3. Accept the default selection in the Search for text box.
4. Type 1600 Pennsylvania Avenue inside This Address text box.
5. Press the [Tab] key to move the insertion point to the City text box and type Washington.
6. Press [Tab] again and type DC in the State/province text box. Notice that, as in Figure 3-6, you do not have to enter data for every field in the form, but the more specific you are, the more accurate your results are likely to be.
7. Click Search to find a map for the requested address from Microsoft's proprietary database called Expedia Maps. The resulting map that appears in the right half of the browser window should be similar to the example shown in Figure 3-7. The Search Assistant options for finding people and businesses work very similarly. To try these out, click New in the Search bar, activate the appropriate option button and enter the required information.

more

You can close the Search bar by clicking the depressed Search button on the Standard Button toolbar. Closing the Search bar makes the Web page occupy the entire window as before. If you open the Search bar again before exiting Internet Explorer, your previous search results will be displayed.

Figure 3-6 Searching for a map

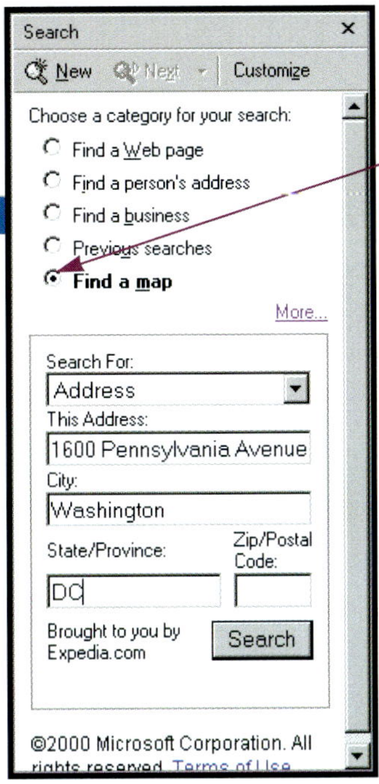

Figure 3-7 Search results

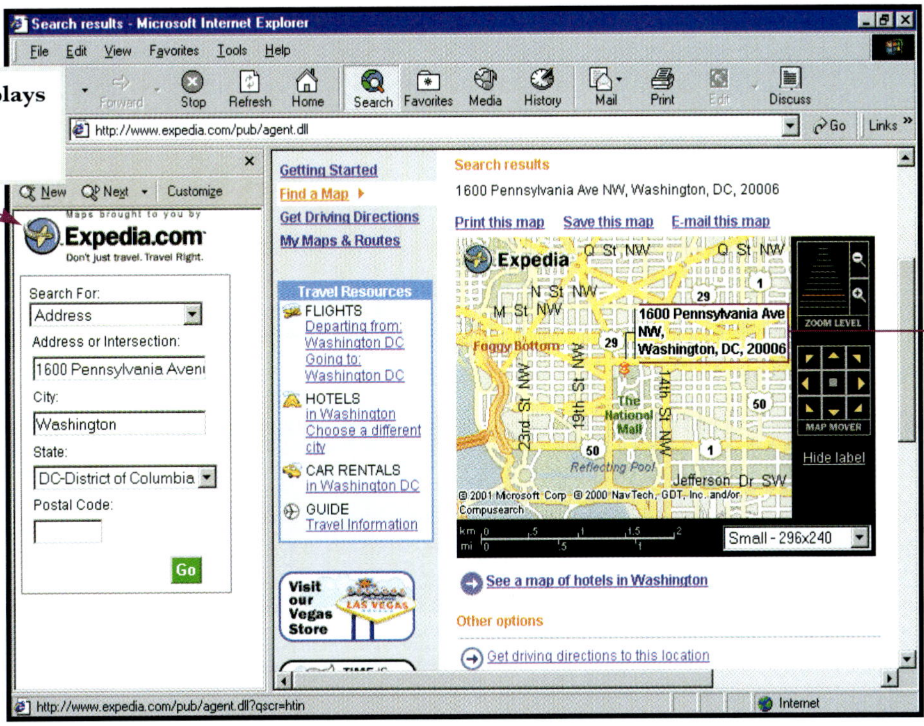

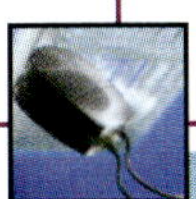

Practice

Search for a map using your home address.

skill Removing a Search Category from the Search Assistant

concept

The search categories available in the Search Assistant can be added or removed to suit your needs. Also the order in which these categories appear can be altered. This is particularly helpful for users whose search habits and needs are consistent. Each of the categories available in the Search bar caters to a particular search need, whether you wish to view Web pages or the address of a person, etc. Depending upon the category that you use the most, you can alter the order of these categories.

do it!

Remove a search category from the Search Assistant.

1. Click Customize at the top of the Search bar. The Customize Search Settings dialog box will appear (Figure 3-8). The dialog box is divided into categories for each of the different kinds of searches you can perform. Next to each main category is a check box that allows you to determine whether that category is to be included in the Search Assistant. Below the category heading is a list box that displays all of the search engines available for the category, in the order they will be used. Next to the list box is a series of check boxes. Search engines that are checked are currently active in your Search Assistant. Only a few categories are visible at once, but you can scroll down to view more.
2. Clear the Find a Business check box (Figure 3-9).
3. Click OK to close the dialog box. Close the browser Window. When you open Internet Explorer again, the Search bar will be reloaded without the Find a business option button, as in Figure 3-10. The browser window will return to the page you had been viewing before entering the customizing function.

Table 3-2 Modifying the Customize Search Settings dialog box

Desired Modification	Action to Take
Choose which search categories are available	Select the check box for each category that you want to display.
Choose search engines within a category	Within each category, select the check box for each search engine you want available.
Choose the main search engine to use within a category	Within each category, click the main search engine you want to use, then click the up arrow below the list to move the search engine to the top of the list.
Arrange the order in which to use search engines	Within each category, click a search engine in the list, then click the up or down arrows under the list to rearrange the list order. The search engine at the top of the list is the first one used within the category.
Arrange the order of search categories in the Search bar	Select the category in the category list, then click the up or down arrow under the category list to change its position.
Save previous searches	Select the **Previous searches** check box.
Use one search engine at a time	At the top of the Customize Search Settings dialog box, click the **Use one search service** option button, then click the desired search engine in the list.

Figure 3-8 Customize Search Settings dialog box

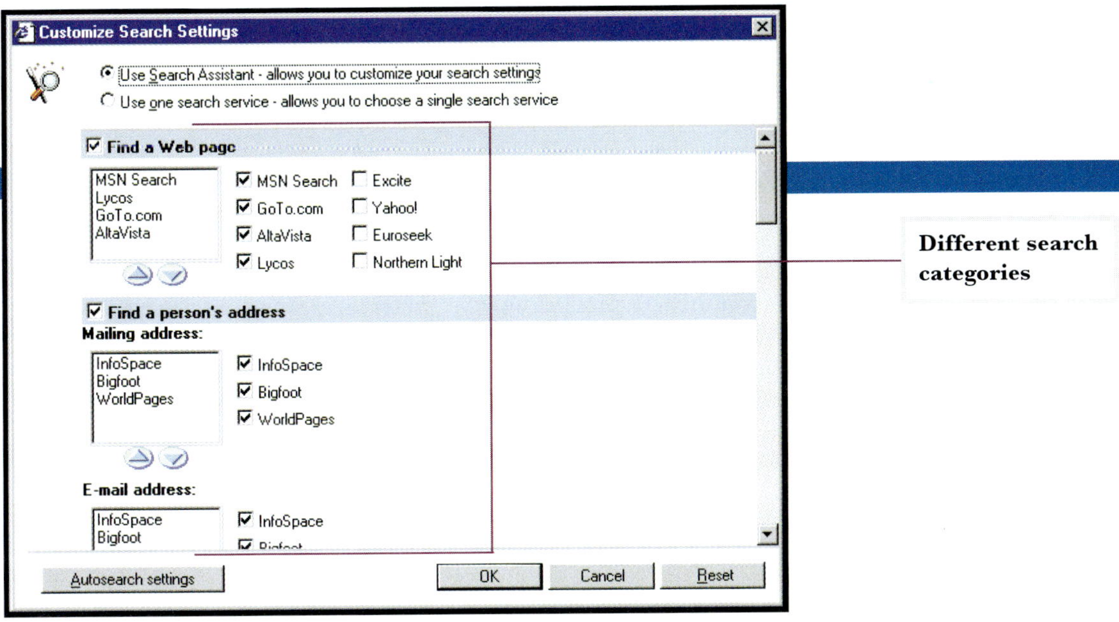

Figure 3-9 Removing a search category

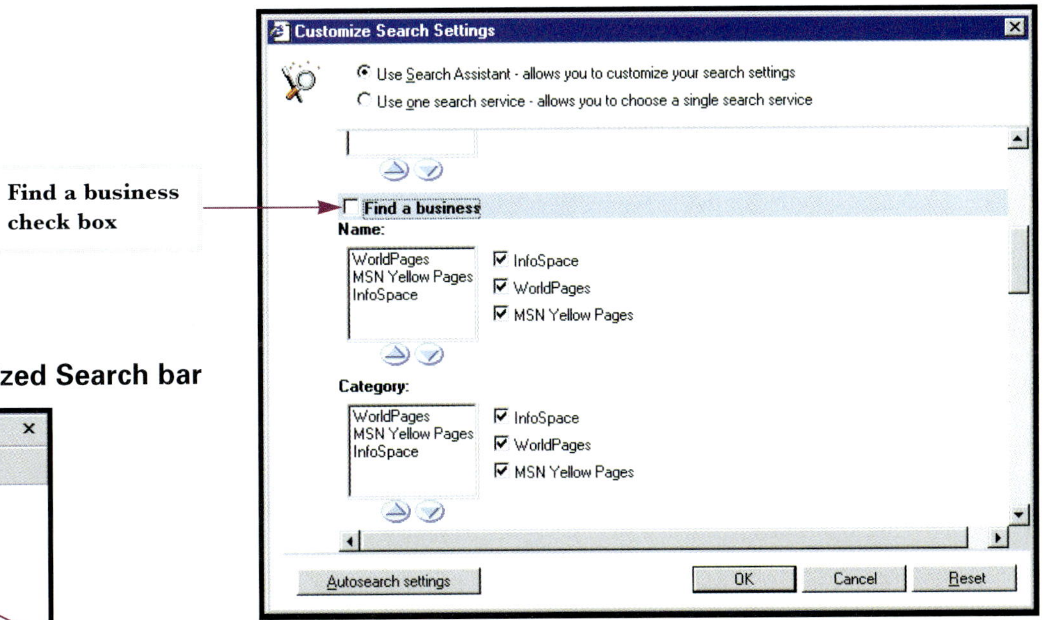

Figure 3-10 Customized Search bar

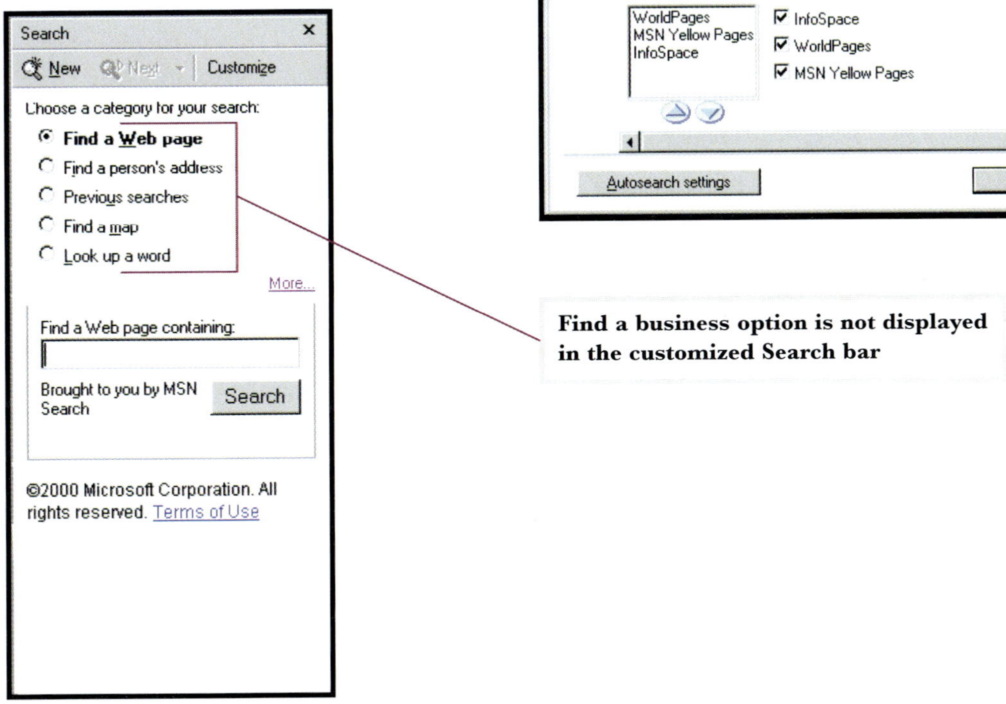

skill Customizing Search Engines in the Search Assistant

concept

There is usually more than one search engine available in the Search Assistant. However, you may choose to remove any of them depending on your preferences. In addition to removing a particular search engine, you can alter the order in which the search engines are to be used by the Search Assistant. Thus, you can customize the searches to suit your needs. If you have made several changes to the Search Assistant settings, later you may want to return to the default settings of the Internet Explorer. To do so, click [Reset] in the Customize Search Settings dialog box, then click [OK] to accept the defaults and to close the dialog box.

do it!

Remove AltaVista from the search engine categories list and alter the order of search engines.

1. Click [Customize] on the Search bar to display the Customize Search Settings dialog box.
2. In the Find a Web page category, clear the AltaVista check box (Figure 3-11). AltaVista is removed from the list of search engines to the left.
3. Click [OK] to accept the change to the Search Assistant. Any future searches for Web sites will not include the AltaVista search engine unless you restore it to active status.
4. Open the Customize Search Settings dialog box.
5. In the Find a Web page category, click MSN Search in the list box and click the Move-up button enough times so that MSN Search moves to the top of the list (Figure 3-12).
6. Click [OK] to close the Customize Search Settings dialog box and confirm the new search engine order. In any future searches for Web sites, MSN Search will be the first search engine accessed by the Search Assistant.

more

The customization window allows you to choose between the search engines that are to be used for all searches. If you would prefer to use a particular search engine all the time rather than the multifold resources offered by the Search Assistant, activate the Use one search service for all searches option button and follow the instruction to select a search engine. Examples are InfoSeek, Yahoo, Lycos, HotBot, and AltaVista. All of these are privately managed and for-profit businesses. You use them for free, but they sell the advertising that you see on their pages. Several of these named search engines are used in more than one category by the Search Assistant because these services are able to perform more than one function.

As with screen colors and fonts, the options of the Search Assistant are best left at their default settings until you have familiarized yourself with the search process and have established usage patterns of your own.

Figure 3-11 Deactivating a Search engine

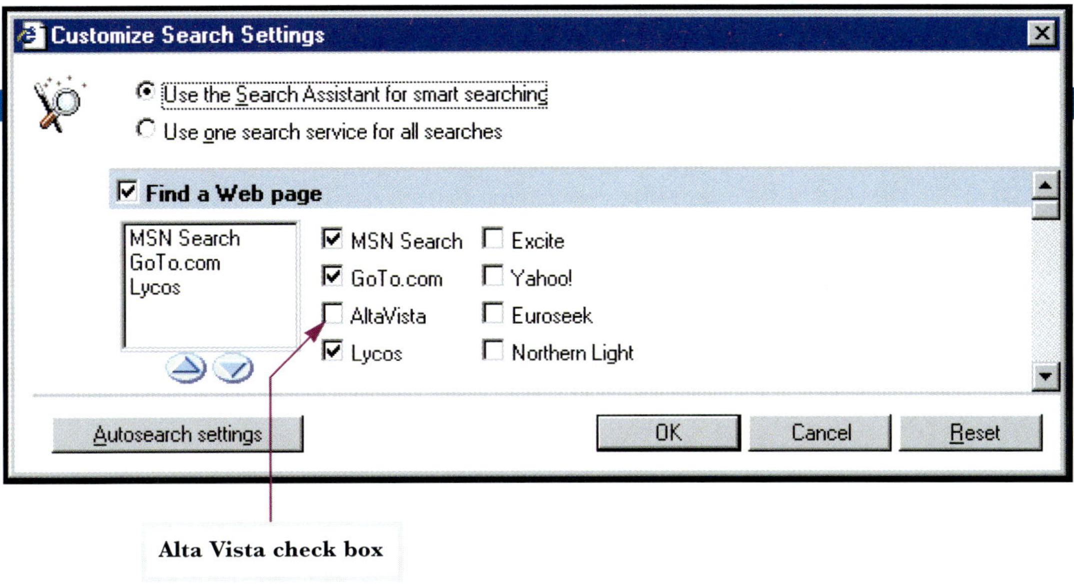

Figure 3-12 Changing the order of a search engine

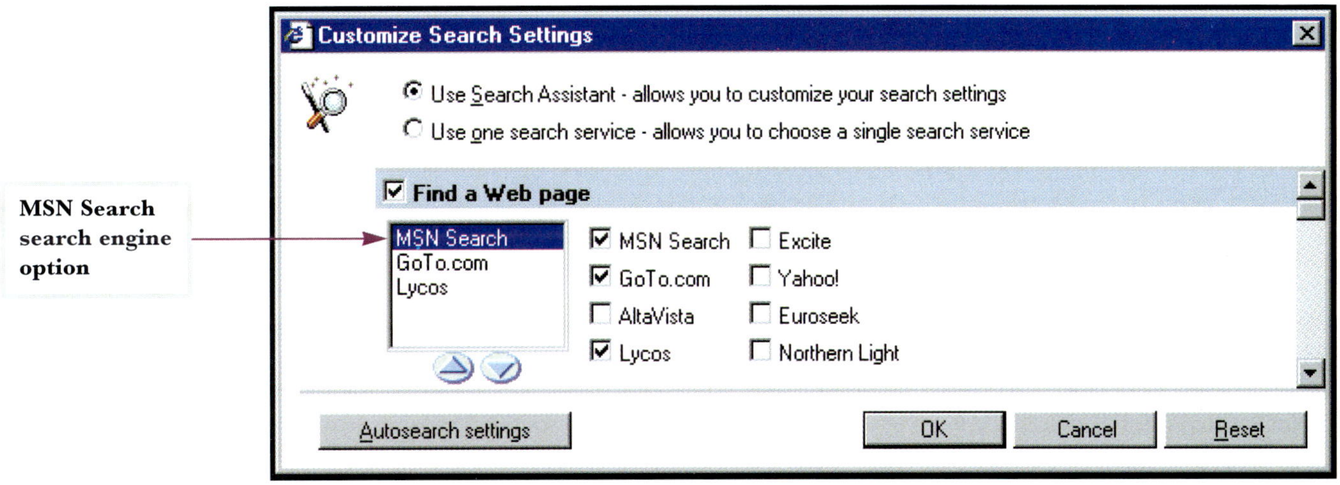

Practice

Restore the Find a business category to active status. Also restore the AltaVista search engine in the Find a Web site category, and move it to fourth place in the list of active search engines for that category.

skill Using Previous Search Results

concept

The Search Assistant in Internet Explorer enables you to save the results of previous searches. It also allows you to recall the saved searches. It is a time saving feature and is especially useful when you have to interrupt your Web browsing session. For instance, you will be able to recall the results of the search you had conducted some time back on the progress of Information Technology over the years.

do it!

View the saved results of previous searches.

1. With the Search bar open, click Customize. The Customize Search Settings dialog box will be displayed.
2. Scroll down to the category named Previous searches (Figure 3-13).
3. Select the Previous searches check box if not already selected.
4. Click OK to close the dialog box.
5. In the Search bar, activate the Previous searches option button. A section showing your recent searches will be displayed as a list of hyperlinks (Figure 3-14).
6. Click the hyperlink for the Lewis and Clark search and the results of that search will be displayed. You can utilize those search results in the same way that you did when you first conducted the search.
7. Close the Search bar by clicking the Close button ✕ on the top right corner of the Search

more

Search results are saved as files. The files containing the searched results are not searched for all over again when you recall them, so any changes that you have made to customize the Search Assistant since making the search will not be reflected in the saved search results. For example, if you conduct a search and receive results from the Infoseek search engine, then customize the Search Assistant so that Infoseek is no longer consulted, the Infoseek results will still be there when you recall the saved search results. This also means that if new information on your topic has become available on the Web since you originally made your search, it will not show up in the recalled search. The Search Assistant cannot save more than the last 10 searches. If you find a page you like in a search and want to save its location more permanently, the best way to do so is to use the Favorites function or to save the Web page displayed by the search result.

Figure 3-13 Previous Searches Category

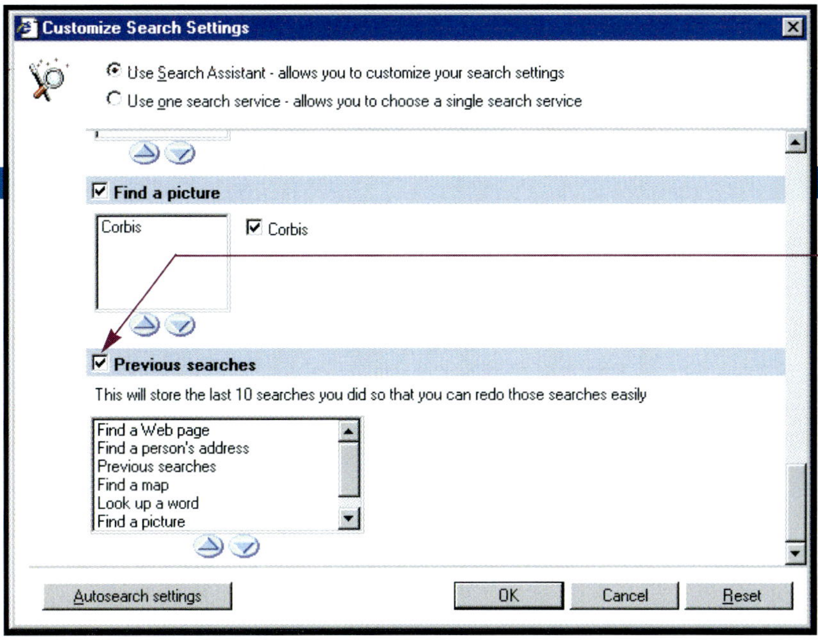

Previous searches option enabled

Figure 3-14 Viewing previous searches

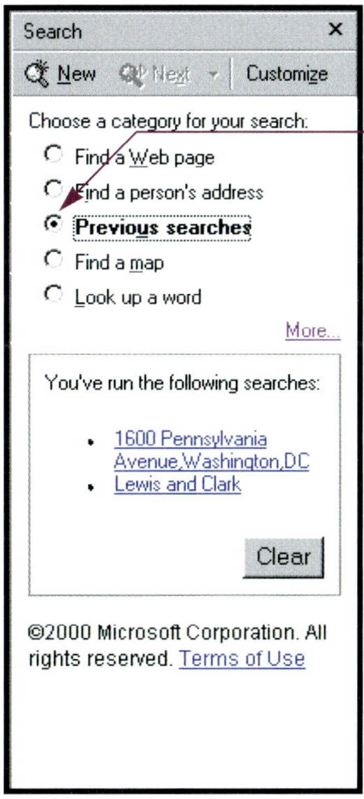

Previous searches option enabled in the Search bar

Practice

Access the map you found for your home address from the list of previous searches.

skill Accessing a Search Engine Directly

concept

There are many search engines and information services available on the Web. These are not the part of Internet Explorer, and most of them are private companies that have no connection with Microsoft. Each of them has its strengths and weaknesses, and each of them function a little differently. The Search Assistant uses many of them simultaneously for each of your searches. However, you can bypass the Search Assistant and go directly to one of these sites depending upon your area of interest. For instance, www.webopedia.com is a specialized search site for computer-related terms or definitions.

do it!

Access the Lycos search engine directly, without using the Search Assistant.

1. Click the current URL in the Address bar to select it and type the URL for Lycos, www.lycos.com.
2. Then click [Go]. You also can press the [Enter] key after typing the URL, to go to the site.
3. If your Internet connection is active, the Lycos page is displayed in your browser window like any other Web page, as in Figure 3-15.
4. Lycos is typical of many commercial search engines in that it offers a variety of "extras" such as news headlines, Internet tools, and direct links to specific kinds of information. But like all search engines, it is built around a general search function with a text box and an command button (in this case, [GO]).
5. Type Web browsers in the Search for text box (Figure 3-16) and click [GO]. In most search engines, the [Enter] key will work as well. Enclosing a search phrase in quotations instructs the search engine to return only those Web pages that contain the exact phrase.
6. A page of search results will appear that resembles the ones you have seen in the Search bar, except that the page will fill the whole browser window. You may have to scroll down the page to see all the results(Figure 3-17). You can click the links provided and access the pages in the same way as you did earlier.

more

When you use a search engine in this way, you will almost always find yourself in a commercial environment. Note the many ads, offers of services, and other "extras" pasted into the results page you just called up. On the other hand, many of the sites offer powerful search functions. The Lycos page is like many others in that the results page features a Search These Results option where you can enter more keywords and further define the search you already made rather than starting a new search from scratch.

Several of the advantages of the Search Assistant are not available when you search using this method. Your search results will not be saved automatically for later reference. Also, since a directly accessed search engine does not use the Search bar to split the screen, you will have to use the [Back] to return to the results list after having looked at one or more of the pages you find.

If you find a particular search engine you like so much you want to use it all the time, you can customize the Search Assistant so that clicking the Search button on the Standard Buttons toolbar will open the Search bar directly to that site instead of activating the traditional Search Assistant options.

Figure 3-15 Lycos Home Page

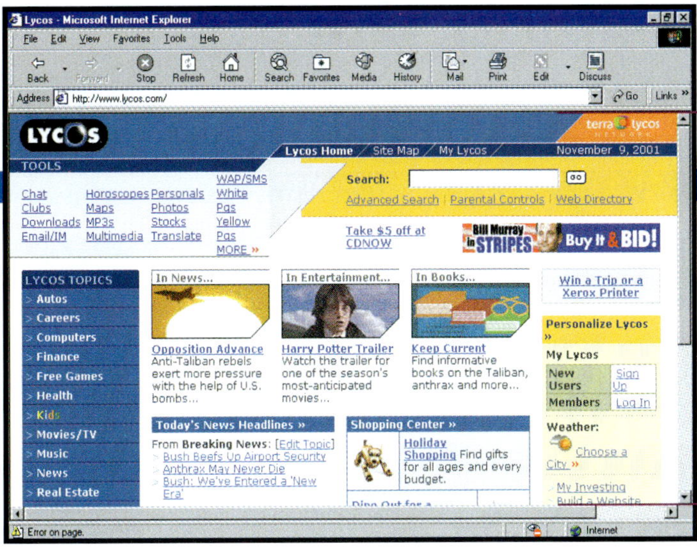

Contents of the Lycos Home page

Figure 3-16 Searching on Lycos Home Page

Search text box

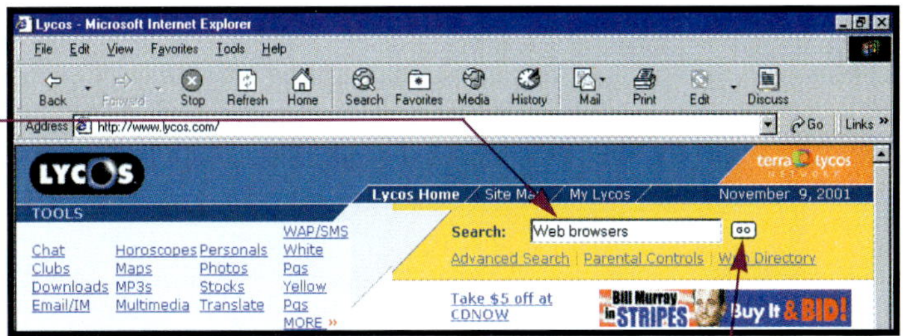

Click Go button to activate Lycos search

Figure 3-17 Lycos Search results

Numbered Search results

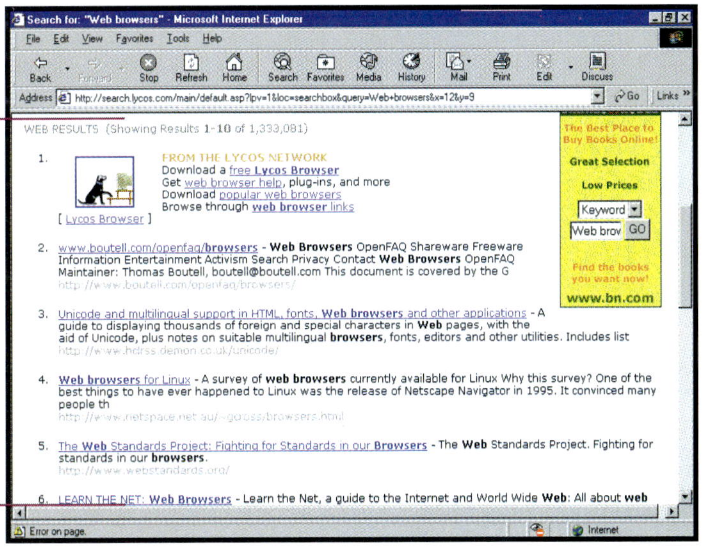

Practice

Visit the search sites at www.excite.com, www.yahoo.com, and www.hotbot.com, and search for Web browsers at each site. Compare and contrast the different search sites and the results they return.

skill Searching Using the Address Bar

concept

So far, we have only used the Address bar to access the Web pages whose URL is known to us. However, the Address bar can also be used as the Search bar. Here is a trick that even some veteran Web surfers do not know. For a quick, simple keyword search of the Web, you can enter your search criteria in the Address bar preceded by go, find, or ? and Internet Explorer will begin a search using its preset search service, MSN Autosearch.

do it!

Search the Web from the Address bar of the Internet Explorer.

1. Using your mouse, select the contents of the Address bar and delete them.
2. Type find NASA (Figure 3-18) and press the [Enter] key. This will display the NASA Home page at www.nasa.gov (Figure 3-19). The default setting for Autosearch is to load automatically into the browser window the most likely match from a search. If you do not get the results shown in Figure 3-19, you can change to the default setting in the Customize Autosearch Settings dialog box, as noted in the More section below.

more

Searching a Web page using the Address bar is a simple way to search the Web, which is great if you want to find something quickly, but not necessarily the best way to start a detailed search of a complicated topic. Another advantage of using the Address bar is that you can start your search without opening the Search Assistant or another page, which saves time.

You can control how the Autosearch feature operates from the Customize Search Settings dialog box. If you click the Autosearch Settings button [Autosearch settings] at the bottom of the dialog box, the Customize Autosearch Settings dialog box will be displayed (Figure 3-20). In this second dialog box, use the Choose a search provider for address bar searches list box to specify which search service to use for Address bar searches. Use the When searching list box to specify how the browser window will behave when a search is initiated. In the Customize Autosearch Settings dialog box, then click the OK button [OK] to accept the Autosearch changes and to return to the Customize Search Settings dialog box.

Figure 3-18 Entering an AutoSearch query

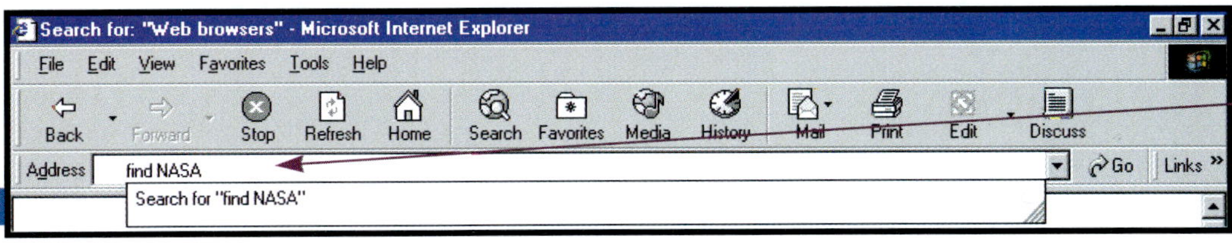

Figure 3-19 Results of search with MSN

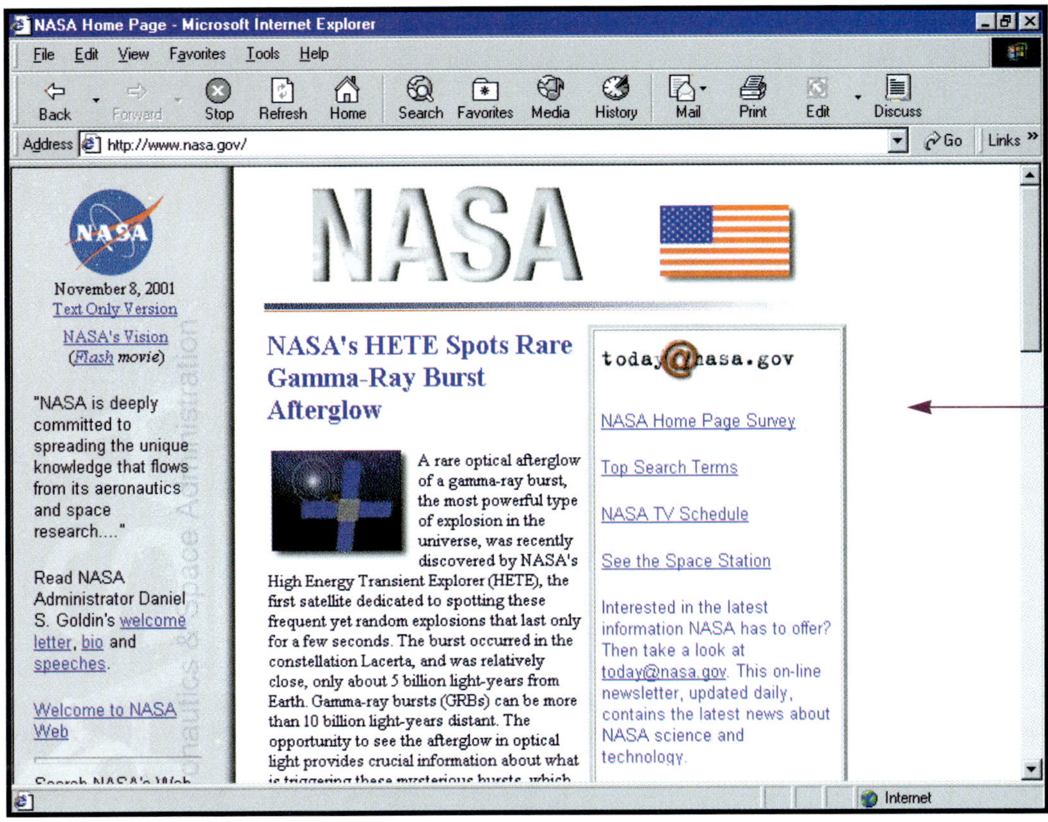

Figure 3-20 Customize Autosearch Settings dialog box

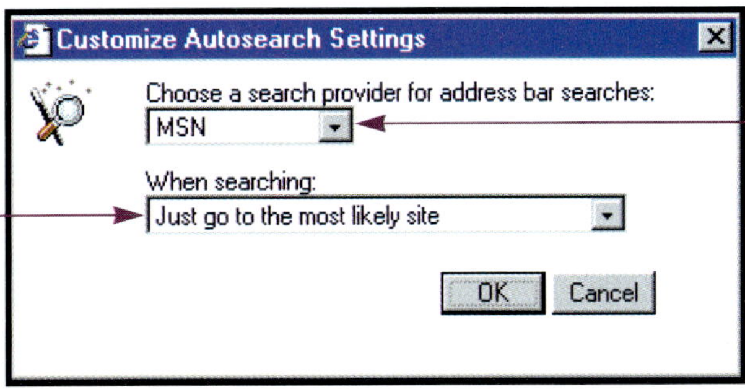

Practice

Use the Address bar to search information on major league baseball.

skill Searching on the Current Page

concept

By now you know how vast the Web is, and you have come to appreciate the value of search engines. But what about individual Web pages themselves? Some of them are pretty vast, too. Often, when you find the page that contains the information you are looking for, the page is so voluminous that your search hardly feels like it is over. Internet Explorer allows you to search for text within a displayed Web page, using the Find feature that will be familiar to the users of popular word processors.

do it!

Find a phrase in the journals of Lewis and Clark.

1. Type www.pbs.org/lewisandclark/archive/idx_jou.html in the Address bar to open the Lewis and Clark page.
2. Scroll to the end of the current page. Without changing any of the options, click Submit on the current page.
3. When the new page is displayed, click Edit on the Menu bar and then click Find (on This Page) command (Figure 3-21).
4. The Find dialog box is displayed (Figure 3-22). In the Find what text box, type the word human.
5. Click Find Next in the dialog box as shown in Figure 3-22.
6. Internet Explorer will find and select the word human on the page in Sergeant Patrick Gass's May 14, 1804 journal entry describing the unknown road ahead (Figure 3-23). The Find dialog box remains displayed, allowing you to click Find Next again if you want to search for later occurrences of the same text string in this document.
7. Close the Find dialog box.

more

The Find dialog box gives you a selection of useful options. By activating the appropriate option buttons you can select to search down, or forward, in a document (the default setting), or up (backward).

The search carried out through the Find dialog box is not case-sensitive by default. However, this setting can be changed to allow a case-sensitive search. Select the Match case check box to specify that Internet Explorer find only those instances that match the uppercase and lowercase usage in your search criterion.

Finally, Internet Explorer is normally set to find your search word as a whole word or as a word fragment: a search for "human" will turn up occurrences of "humanity" or "humane." You can select the Match whole word only check box also in the dialog box, to specify that only the exact word, with no additions, turns up in your search. The ideal way to search is to make the search words unique. If you are searching the Declaration of Independence and want to find the phrase "When in the course of human events" search for "course" not "the" since there are lots of "the's" in the document.

Figure 3-21 Activating the Find function

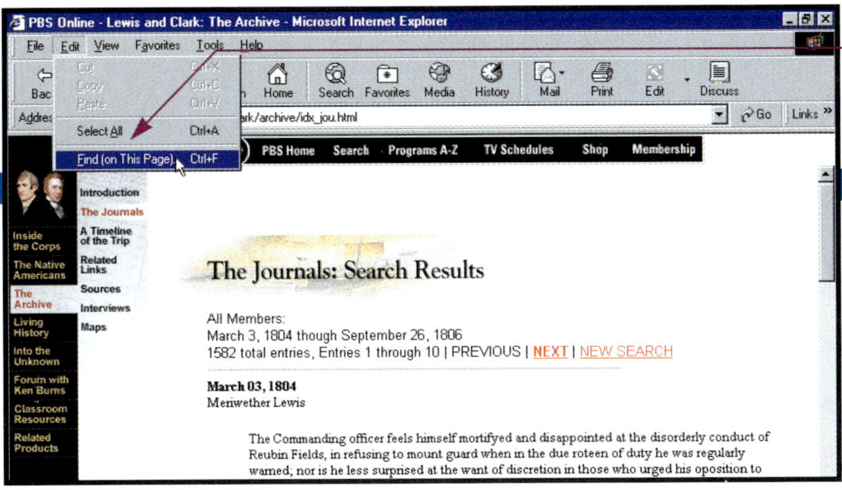

Activating the Find (on This Page) command

Figure 3-22 Find dialog box

Enter the text for which you want to search

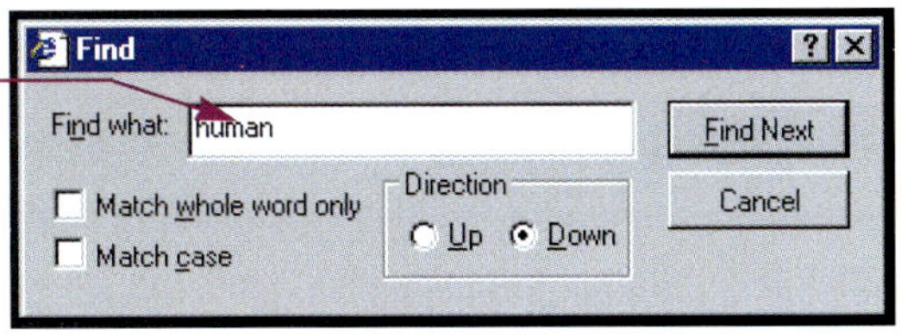

Figure 3-23 Search results

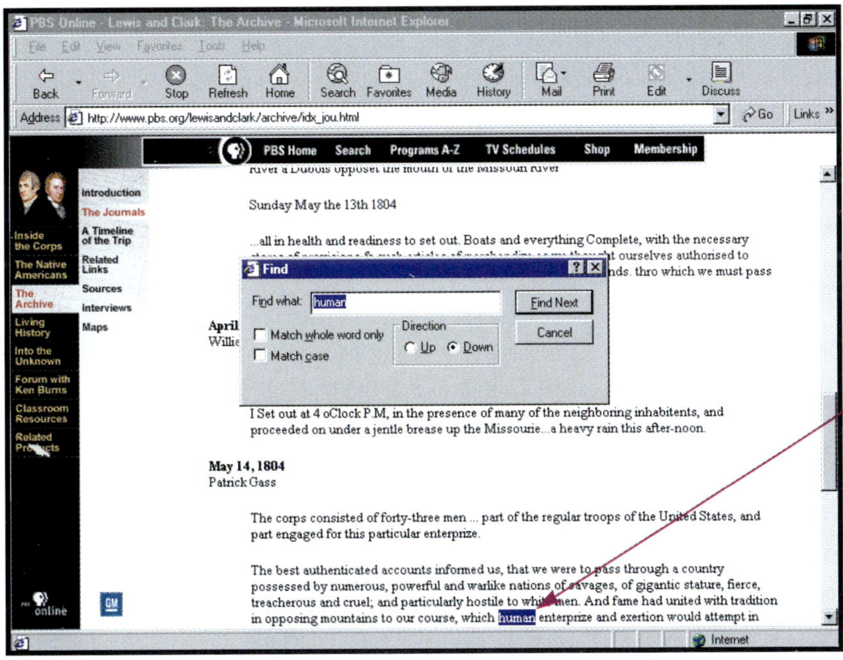

The first instance of Searched text found

Practice

Use the PBS site to find the Lewis and Clark expedition's journal entries for November 10, 1805. Then use the Find dialog box to find the word porpoises.

Internet Explorer 6.0

shortcuts

Function	Button/Mouse	Menu	Keyboard
Activate the Search bar		Click View, point to Explorer bar, then click Search	[Ctrl]+[E]
Find text on current page		Click Edit, then click Find (on This Page)	[Ctrl]+[F]
Begin new search in Search bar			[Alt]+[N]
Customize search settings			[Alt]+[Z]

quiz

A. Identify Key Features

State the names and, where applicable, the functions of the items indicated by callouts in Figure 3-24.

Figure 3-24 Elements in Internet Explorer that help in searching

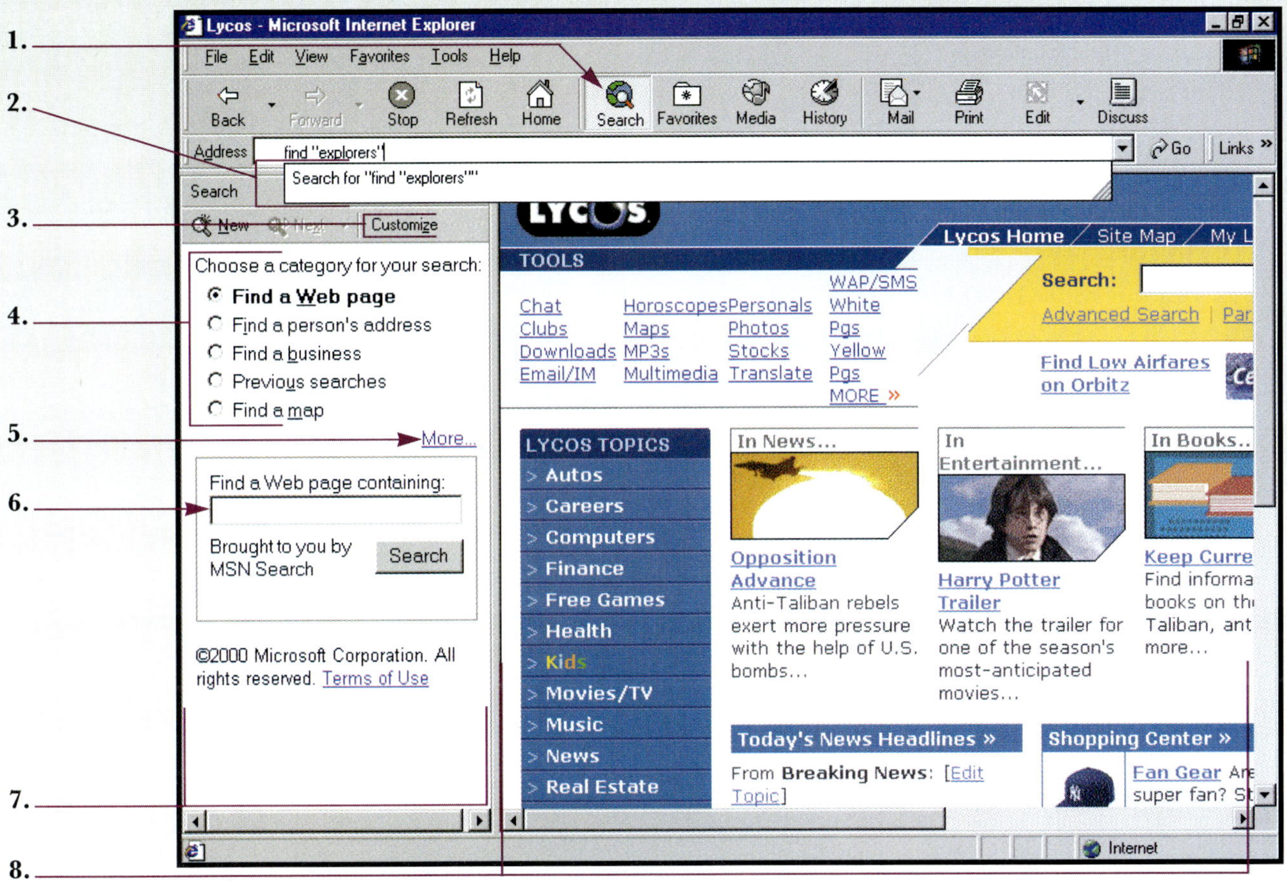

B. Select the Best Answer

9.	The process of finding Web pages based on keywords	**a.**	Category
10.	A Web site that lets you find other Web sites relevant to a topic or question	**b.**	Find
11.	The links to relevant pages that appear after a successful search	**c.**	?
12.	This can be used to search quickly from the Address bar	**d.**	Previous search
13.	A particular kind of search that is organized specially under the Search Assistant	**e.**	Results list
14.	A list of links from a search that you have recalled	**f.**	Search
15.	The menu item that lets you locate a word or text string on the current page	**g.**	Search Assistant
16.	A feature of Internet Explorer that organizes, manages, and saves your searches	**h.**	Search engine

quiz (continued)

C. Complete the Statement

17. A Web search cannot help you locate:

a. Web pages

b. Addresses of people

c. Your current location

d. A map of your current location

18. You can customize the Search Assistant in all of the following ways, except:

a. Always using your favorite search site

b. Deactivating the Find a business category

c. Always using your favorite search site first

d. Finding your search keyword only when it appears in all uppercase letters

19. Relevance of a search describes:

a. How closely a Web page relates to your search topic

b. How important the topic of your search is

c. How much the page you locate resembles the page you just left

d. How out-of-date the information is, on the page you have found

20. When you save the search results and recall them later, you can:

a. See if any new information on your topic has been added to the Web

b. Look at a Web page whose link you did not follow the first time

c. See how changes you have made to the Search Assistant altered the results

d. Check the results of a search you did 20 searches ago

21. To locate a word on the current Web page, use the

a. Search bar

b. Search Assistant

c. Address bar

d. Find (on This Page) command

22. You can access the Customize Autosearch Settings dialog box directly from the:

a. Autosearch command on the View menu

b. Customize Search Settings dialog box

c. Settings command on the Links bar

d. Customize button on the Standard Buttons toolbar

23. You can use all of the following terms to start a search from the Address bar, except:

a. Search

b. Go

c. Find

d. ?

24. You can change the order in which search engines are consulted by the Search Assistant from the:

a. Address bar

b. Customize Autosearch Settings window

c. Customize Search Settings dialog box

d. MSN AutoSearch Expedia guide

25. Logical operators:

a. Reduce your chances of finding Web pages that are relevant to your Search process

b. Work the same way on all search engines

c. Can include the words AND and OR, as well as the symbols "+" and "–"

d. Work only in the Address toolbar of Internet Explorer

interactivity

Build Your Skills

1. Open the Search Assistant and practice searching the Web:
   a. Find a Web page about your favorite sports team, music group or organization.
   b. Look up the address of a friend you have not seen in years.
   c. Find information on the company you work for, or a company you patronize.
   d. Locate a map of the town where you grew up, then print it out.

2. Customize the Search Assistant:
   a. Change the order of the search categories so that maps come first, then Web pages, then addresses of the people, then businesses.
   b. Change the available search engines for finding Web pages so that only your three favorite search engines are enabled.

3. Go back to a previous search and find a fact you did not know on a page you did not look at the first time. Copy the information into a word processor file.

4. Access five or six of the most popular search engines manually by typing their URLs into the Address bar (remember, nearly all use www.enginename.com):
   a. Conduct the same search on each of them and compare the results you receive.
   b. Note which advanced search options, "search within results" options and other features they all offer.
   c. Look up news headlines on the ones that offer them, and compare the news stories that appear via the different engines.

5. Find a Web site that offers:
   a. Job listings, and find listings for your profession.
   b. Apartment ads, and find vacancies in your community.
   c. Sports scores, and find all the references to your favorite player.
   d. Television listings, and find out what time "I Love Lucy" is on. It is always on somewhere.

interactivity (continued)

Build Your Skills (continued)

6. Modify your Search Assistant settings:

a. In the Find a Web page category, use the search engines in the order MSN Search, AltaVista, and Yahoo!, for searching.

b. In the Find a person's address category, use only Bigfoot for both Mailing address and E-mail address.

c. In the Find a Business category, use all available services, but put them in the same order for Name and Category.

d. Remove the Find a picture category.

Problem Solving Exercises

1. You are a Project Manager for a graphic design company. A friend has suggested that you give your team an afternoon off for a team picnic to increase camaraderie and morale. Use the Search Assistant to find a Web page that lists public parks in your county, state, or province. Find a map of the park you have chosen for the picnic, or the neighborhood in which it is located. Then visit the Web page of any search engine, and conduct a search to find out more details about the park.

2. The human resources department at your company recently hosted a seminar on stress relief for the businesspersons. Based on what you learned at the seminar, you have decided that you need to acquire a new hobby as a way of escaping the rigors of your work. Conduct an Autosearch from Internet Explorer's Address bar on hobbies. Explore the links that result from the search and select three different hobbies that interest you. Run searches on the three hobbies themselves.

3. The Internet has played a crucial role in the growth and technological progress of telecommuting. Your consulting firm has been hired by another consulting firm to gather data on the latest trends in telecommuting. You will start your research, appropriately, with the World Wide Web. Use the Search Assistant to find Web pages that discuss telecommuting. Visit each of the links returned in the first set of results. Then, since your research must be exhaustive, run the same search using each of the search engines that the Search Assistant makes available. Print one page of the three best sites that you find.

4. Make a list of your three favorite school subjects or three favorite personal activities. Using the Search bar, look up the history of a specific aspect of one subject or activity (e.g., For a school subject, enter history of geometry, not history of mathematics. For a personal activity, enter history of Olympic swimming, not history of sport). Find and read two or three Web sites that explain the history of the topic you chose. Make a list of two or three names of persons who are famous in that topic, and use the Search bar to find their biographies. Print the shortest history Web site and shortest biography that you find.

Exploring the Web

skills

- Using Favorites
- Creating Folders within Favorites
- Organizing Favorites
- Sharing Favorites
- Working in the Offline Mode
- Viewing Web Pages Offline
- Using the Links Toolbar
- Using Audio Files on the Web
- Viewing Video Files on the Web
- Exploring Privacy Features of IE 6.0
- Instant Messaging with MSN Messenger

The skills that you learned so far have been your passport into the Web—the tools you need to get in, look around, and find what you are looking for. Now, it is time to take off your shoes, get comfortable, and start living in the Web using its higher-level resources, take advantage of Web site properties to suit your security needs and ethical standards, and make Internet Explorer a personal reflection of the work you do and the places you go to every day.

The first thing we will do in this lesson is to explore Favorites, the feature that lets you keep a permanent record of the sites you want to revisit and organize them in categories that you specify. We will also examine a few other ways to keep frequently used URLs on hand.

Internet Explorer offers the offline feature that helps you cut down the time you spend viewing the Web pages online. You will learn about marking Web pages for offline viewing and then viewing them in the offline mode.

This lesson also introduces you to the Links toolbar, which is used for accessing selected Web pages.

The use of audio and video media on the Web has blossomed. Internet Explorer will let you find audio and video files on the Web, access them, and play them, but that is not all. With a fast enough Internet connection, you can actually see live video and hear live audio through a real-time process called "streaming."

This lesson will explore the privacy features of Internet Explorer that enable you to control the access of Web sites to your personal information.

Instant messaging is a useful feature that has become very popular recently. Microsoft has its own messenger service called MSN Messenger Service. You will be introduced to this messenger service in this lesson.

Lesson Goal:

In this lesson, you will learn about using the Favorites feature of Internet Explorer and viewing your favorite Web pages in the offline mode. In addition, you will learn about the security features of Internet Explorer and playing audio and video files from the Web. This lesson also introduces you to the Links toolbar in Internet Explorer. Finally, you will learn about the messenger service from Microsoft called MSN Messenger.

skill Using Favorites

concept

Internet Explorer can save the URLs of the Web sites that you wish to revisit in a permanent location called Favorites. Favorites are Internet shortcuts and work with an Explorer bar, similar to the History and Search functions. Using the Favorites bar, you can create folders to organize shortcuts to your favorite sites, export them to another application or computer, and even view sites when you are offline. Using Favorites prevents you from having to remember and enter long URLs each time you want to visit a particular site.

do it!

Add the National Park Service home page to your list of Favorites.

1. Type www.nps.gov in the Address bar of your browser window. Press [Enter] to open the National Park Service page.
2. Click Favorites on the Menu bar and then click the Add to Favorites command (Figure 4-1). The Add Favorite dialog box is displayed with the title of the current page in the Name text box.
3. Click OK to accept the favorite with its default settings and to close the dialog box (Figure 4-2).
4. Either click Home on the Standard Buttons toolbar to open the home page or go to any other Web site.
5. Click Favorites on the Standard Buttons toolbar. The Favorites bar is displayed on the left side of the browser window. The Favorites Explorer bar may include already existing folders and favorites, and should also display the favorite you just added.
6. Click the National Park Service favorite (Figure 4-3). The page will be displayed in the right panel of the browser window.

more

There are two principal advantages of the Favorites function over the History file and the previously saved searches. The most important one is that it is permanent: if you visit a lot of pages after the one you like, it will be dropped from your History file, and only 10 previous searches will remain on file. A site you have saved as a favorite is there until you decide to delete it.

The other advantage is that you can organize your favorites. For example, if you visit the National Park Service site and check out seven or eight different parks, you can create a folder within favorites called National Parks and save the individual page links in the National Parks folder. Then, if you visit a half-dozen sites about baseball, you can create a Baseball folder and save those links there. This makes it more convenient to look up a site you have saved. Your favorites are also listed in the Favorites menu on the Menu bar, so you can access them without activating the Favorites bar.

The Favorites folder has a few folders already established the first time you use it. These contain sites that the creators of Internet Explorer thought you might find useful. If you bought a new computer with Internet Explorer already loaded, you might find some sites preset in your Favorites folder that the computer maker and/or store want you to see.

Figure 4-1 Adding a Favorite

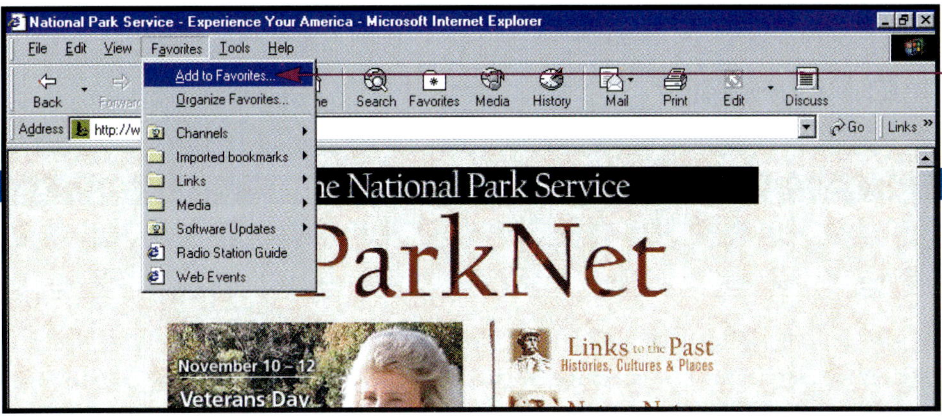

Click to open Add Favorite dialog box for adding to list of Favorites

Figure 4-2 Add Favorite dialog box

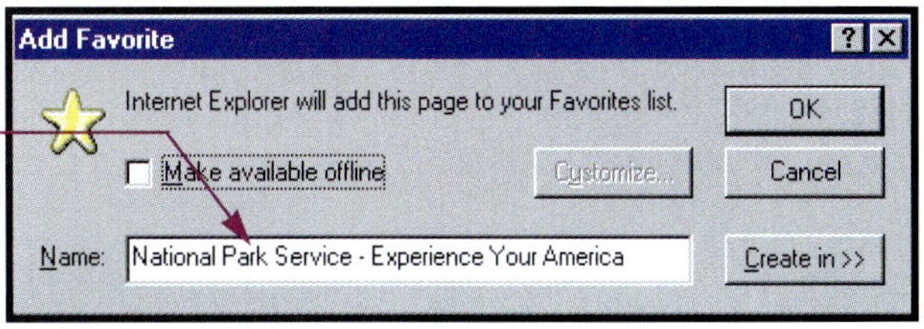

Title of the current Web page

Figure 4-3 Opening a favorite

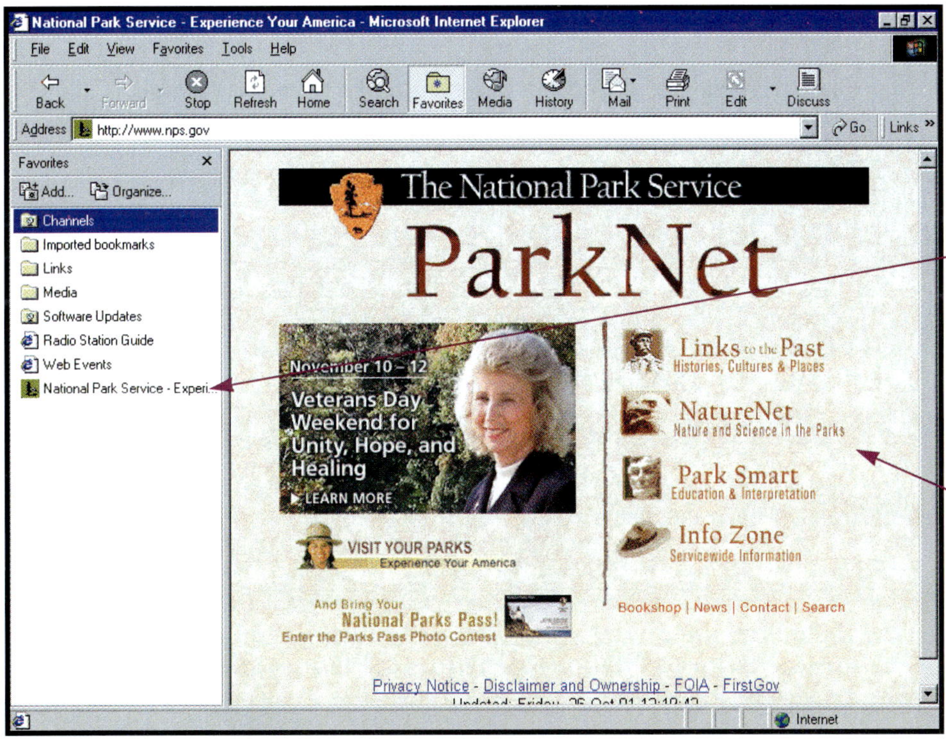

Title of the favorite displayed in the Favorite bar

Favorite page displayed in the right panel

Practice

Visit www.altavista.com and add the page to your Favorites list. Then, visit another page and return to AltaVista using the Favorite you just created.

skill Creating Folders within Favorites

concept

Your list of favorites can grow significantly since it does not expire with time (like files in the History folder) or use (like previously saved searches). Thus, you could have trouble keeping track of the topics you have information on unless you organize this information. For instance, you are headed for a ski weekend and you would like to save the Web site of the resort where you are going to stay. You also would like to view the snow report during the week by adding the URL of a weather forecast site to your favorites folder. The resort's Web page and the snow report Web page will remain there until you remove them. Suppose also that you are really interested in baseball, but you also like sailing, paintball, Delta blues music, theories about Sasquatch, and would also like to keep track of news and stock market forecasts. In this case, it would be a good idea to classify all of your information to have some semblance of order.

Internet Explorer allows you to create folders, delete folders, add and remove your individual favorites to the folders, and even have folders within folders.

do it!

Create a folder for National Park Service Web pages within Favorites.

1. Click Favorites on the Menu bar, then click the Organize Favorites command. The Organize Favorites dialog box is displayed, as shown in Figure 4-4.
2. Click [Create Folder] in the Organize Favorites dialog box. A new folder is added to the list to the right with a default name New Folder selected.
3. With the default name still selected, type the new name as National Parks. You can create a hierarchy of folders in the Favorites folder through the Organize Favorites dialog box, by creating a folder and then dragging it into another folder, giving you multiple layers of organization. For example, you could have folders inside the National Parks folder titled Rockies, Maritime, Appalachian, and so forth.
4. Press [Enter] to confirm the new folder name. The dialog box should now resemble Figure 4-5.
5. Click [Close] to close the dialog box.

more

You can also use the Add Favorites dialog box to create a folder under the Favorites folder. Click [Create in >>] in the Add Favorites dialog box. A list of favorites is displayed, where you can create the new folder. The double arrow on the Create in button faces left in the expanded Add Favorites dialog box, whereas it faces right in the truncated form of Add Favorites dialog box.

Figure 4-4 Organize Favorites dialog box

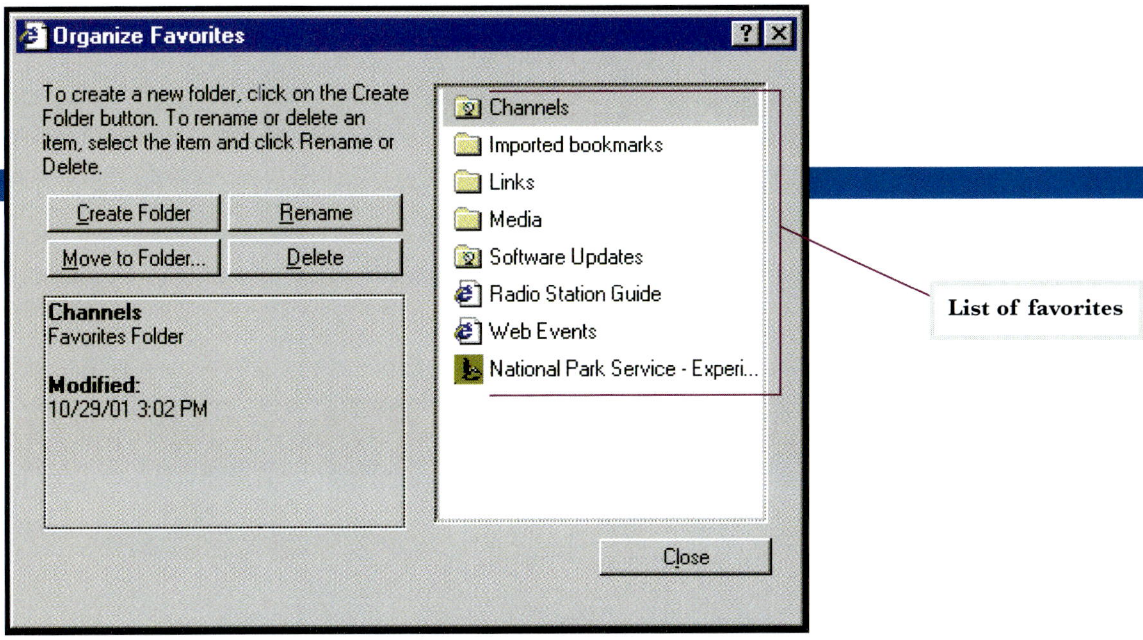

Figure 4-5 New folder added to the Favorites list

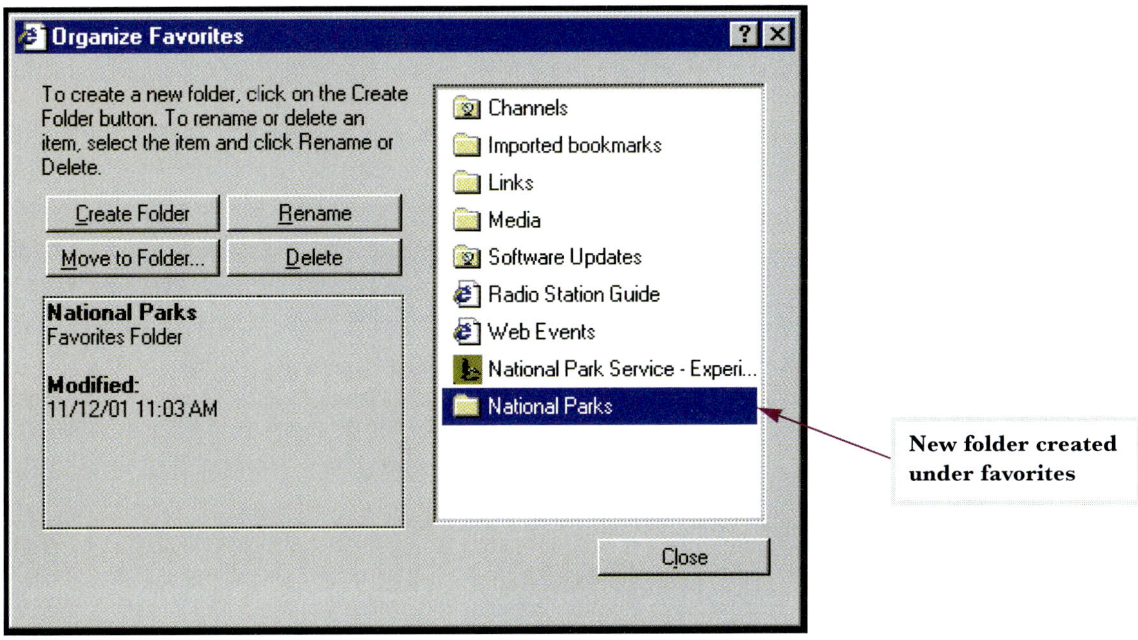

Practice

Create a new folder under Favorites called Congress. Go to the Library of Congress Home Page (www.loc.gov) and add it to favorites.

skill Organizing Favorites

concept

The importance of organizing information can never be over-emphasized and can be understood from the following example. You have been asked to prepare a project on operating systems. You would perhaps start by collecting general information pertaining to operating systems. At a certain point, however, you would feel the need for segregating this information into appropriate categories depending on the features of each operating system. Hence, if you follow some order while collecting information, your job in the following stages is made much simpler. The practice of organizing information logically can also be implemented in Favorites.

do it!

Organize Web pages into the folders created under Favorites.

1. Click Favorites on the Menu bar, then click the Organize Favorites command. The Organize Favorites dialog box is displayed.
2. Click the National Parks Service - Experience Your America favorite listed under the favorites and hold down the left mouse button, as you drag the mouse pointer toward the National Parks folder. A faint representation of the favorite name and icon will travel along with the mouse pointer as you drag it (Figure 4-6). The mouse pointer will appear as a circle with a line through it as long as it is not over a valid drop location for the favorite.
3. When the mouse pointer is over the National Parks folder (the folder will be selected), and the standard pointing arrow has reappeared, release the mouse button to drop the favorite into the folder. The National Park Service favorite is no longer displayed in the list, as it is now stored inside the National Parks folder.
4. Click [Close] to close the Organize Favorites dialog box. If you click the National Parks folder in the Favorites bar, the National Park Services favorite will appear below it. Both items are also available in the Favorites menu. See Figure 4-7 for a representation of the new items in both locations.

more

If dragging favorites in the Organize Favorites dialog box is proving to be difficult, click [Move to Folder...] in the Organize Favorites dialog box. This will display the Browse for Folder dialog box, which allows you to select a destination folder for the favorite you are moving and move the favorite with a series of simple clicks.

You can also add and organize favorites by clicking [Add...] and [Organize...] at the top of the Favorites Explorer bar.

Figure 4-6 Moving a favorite

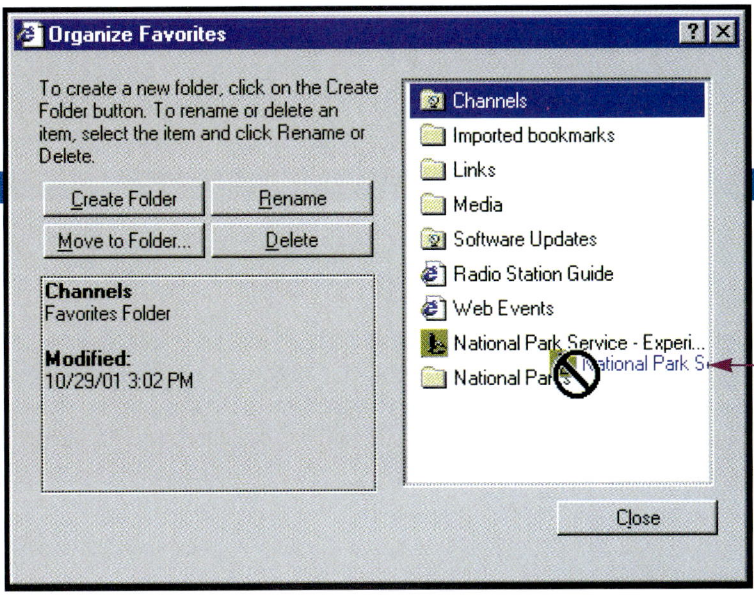

National Park Service favorite being moved

Internet Explorer 6.0

Figure 4-7 Updated Favorites bar and Favorites menu

Favorites bar and Favorites menu showing the newly created folder

National Park Service favorite in the National Parks folder

Practice

Create favorites folders for some of the other types of Web sites you have visited so far, such as Search engines. Then, move any favorites you have added into the appropriate folder.

skill Sharing Favorites

concept

Internet Explorer allows you to share the Web pages in your Favorites folder with others. You can also send or export the favorites to another file or application, such as a presentation you are creating on another Web browser. You may also e-mail your favorites to a friend or teammate if both of you are working on a common project. Computers on the Local Area Network (LAN), that are using Internet Explorer can easily share favorite items among them. Exported favorites are saved as a regular HTML file which has links to the exported favorites.

do it!

Export a Favorites folder for use in an e-mail message to a friend.

1. Click File on the Menu bar, then click the Import and Export command. This will launch the Import/Export Wizard, shown in Figure 4-8. A wizard is a series of dialog boxes designed to help you complete a task one step at a time.
2. Read the introductory screen and then click Next > to advance to the next screen.
3. Select the Export Favorites option from the Choose an action to perform list and then click Next >.
4. Click the National Parks folder to select it as the folder you want to export.
5. Click Next > to advance to the next screen (Figure 4-9). In this screen you can determine where to export the folder. Activate the Export to a File or Address option button . Click Next > to accept the default file location. Otherwise, click Browse... to select a different location. This action will open the Select Bookmark File dialog box.
6. To export Favorites to a hard drive, click the Save in box near the top of the dialog box and select the My Documents folder. To store Favorites on a floppy disk, insert a formatted disk in the floppy drive on your computer, and then click 3-1/2 Floppy (A:). Choose a third location if your instructor or trainer directs otherwise. Click the Save button Save to close the dialog box and to return to the Import/Export Wizard. Be sure to remember this location, as you will need to know it to access the Favorites file.
7. Click Finish to exit the Import/Export wizard and to confirm that you are ready to complete your task. Your folder of favorites will be saved in the indicated location as an HTML file with the default name, bookmark.htm. A small dialog box will appear to confirm that the operation was completed successfully. Click OK to confirm. You can attach the HTML file to which the favorites have been exported, to your e-mail message. You can use a similar process to bring the folder into a word processing document, a presentation creation application, or another Web browser.

more

The Export Favorites option in the Choose an action to perform list enables you to export the entire Favorites folder. The third screen of the Import/Export Wizard enables you to select the Favorites folder for exporting. This feature is extremely helpful if you have decided to change browsers but do not want to lose the shortcuts to your favorite sites. (Note that this feature does not move the folders and files, but only copies them to a different location.)

Figure 4-8 Import/Export Wizard

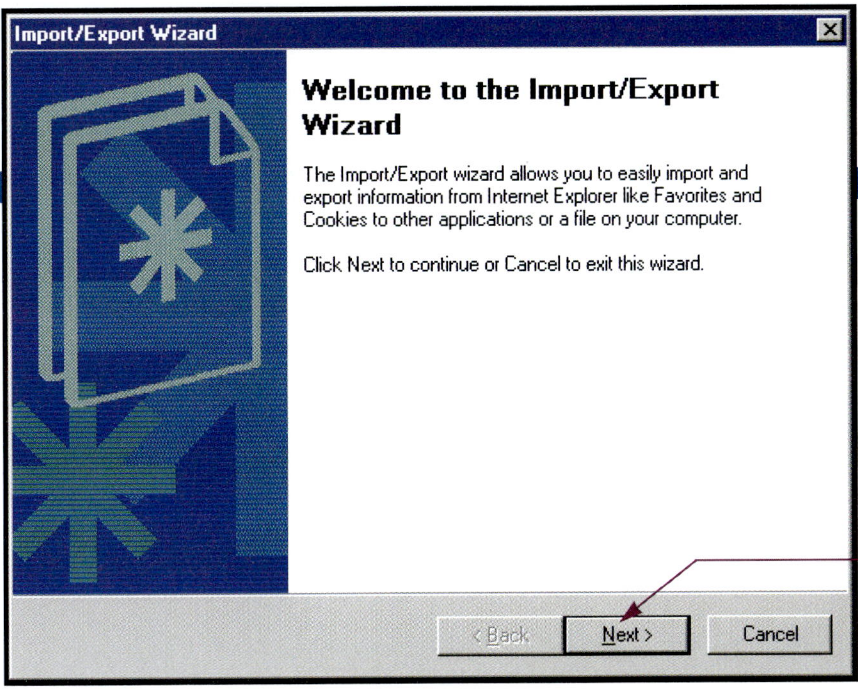

Click Next button to move to next screen of Wizard

Figure 4-9 Choose destination for exporting the favorites

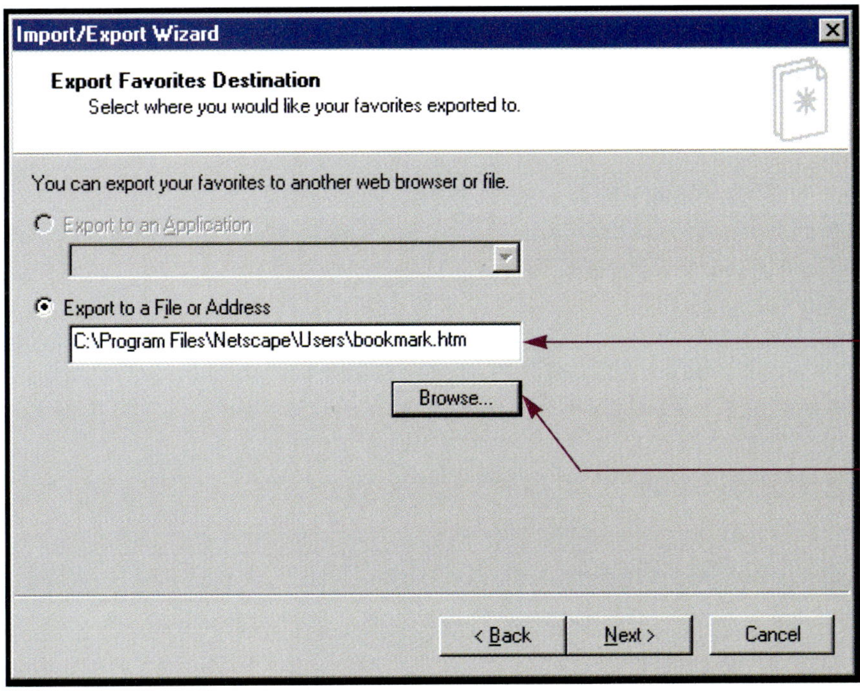

Destination folder for exporting the favorites

Click here to find and select a different file location

Practice

Export one of the Favorites folders you created to your hard drive.

skill Working in the Offline Mode

concept

Internet Explorer enables you to view and work with Web pages in the offline mode, which involves viewing Web pages even when you are not connected to the Internet. Offline viewing is possible because you have saved a Web page before closing your Internet connection. Viewing offline is something you might want to do so you can view Web pages on a laptop computer that does not have a network or Internet connection. You also may want to view pages offline to free up a telephone line or to cut connection costs if you pay for Internet access hourly or cannot access the Internet via a local call. In earlier versions of Internet Explorer, offline viewing was known as subscribing. Web pages that are Favorites can be viewed offline. You can even request to receive e-mail notification when the contents of a page have changed. In this skill, you will learn how to mark a particular Web page for

do it!

Make the National Park Service favorite available for offline viewing.

1. Click Favorites on the Menu bar, and then click the Organize Favorites command, the Organize Favorites dialog box is displayed.
2. Click the National Parks folder to view its contents, and then click the National Park Service - Experience Your America favorite. When a folder is selected, information related to the selected favorite is displayed in the bottom-left portion of the dialog box.
3. Select the Make available offline check box in the bottom-left portion of the Organize Favorites dialog box, as in Figure 4-10. This displays the Properties button, below the Make available offline check box.
4. Click [Properties] to display the Properties dialog box for the Web page. Click the Schedule tab to bring it forward, as shown in Figure 4-11.
5. Activate the Only when I choose Synchronize from the Tools menu option button so that you can synchronize the Web pages as and when you want rather than follow a pre-defined synchronization schedule. Simply defined, synchronization involves updating one set of data (in this case, the Web page you will view offline) based on a similar but more recent set of data (in this case, the source Web page).
6. Click [OK] to close the Properties dialog box.
7. Click [Close] to close the Organize Favorites dialog box. Depending on how your browser is configured, the Synchronizing dialog box may be displayed, and the Web page will be downloaded for the first time. This process may take several minutes. When the download is complete, close the dialog box.

more

Along with synchronizing by clicking on the Tools menu and then clicking Synchronize, you can schedule the synchronization for a given day and time. Set a schedule as follows: (1) Click the Favorites menu, click Organize Favorites to open the Organize Favorites dialog box, and click the desired Web page for downloading. (2) Add a check mark to the Make available offline check box, which displays the Properties button, then click the Properties button [Properties] to open a dialog box with the name of the previously selected Web page, followed by the word Properties. (3) In this second dialog box, click the Schedule tab to bring it forward. On the Schedule tab, click the Add button [Add...] to open the New Schedule dialog box, as shown in Figure 4-12. (4) In this third dialog box, set the interval of days for downloading, set a time of day, and specify a name for the download. This name will appear on the previously mentioned Schedule tab. (5) Close the New Schedule dialog box, close the Properties box, and close the Organize Favorites dialog box. Internet Explorer will perform the scheduled downloads only if your Internet connection is active at the time specified in the schedule.

Figure 4-10 Mark a favorite available for offline viewing

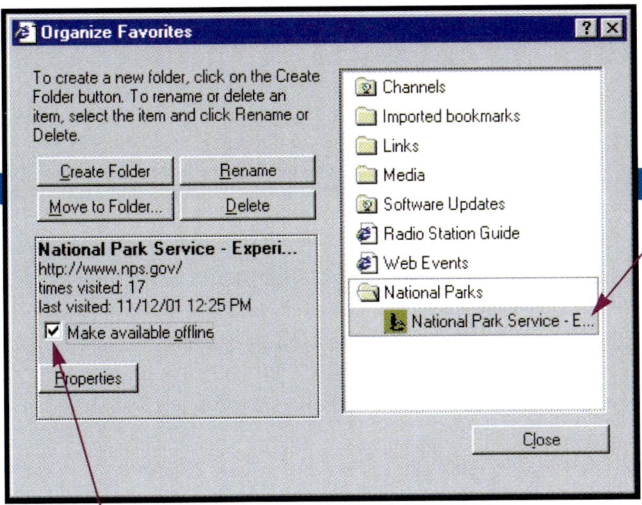

Figure 4-11 Schedule tab for the selected favorite

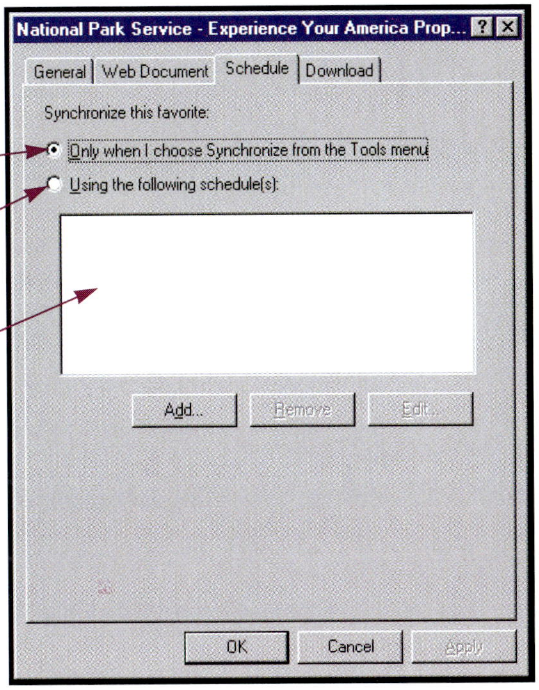

Figure 4-12 New Schedule dialog box

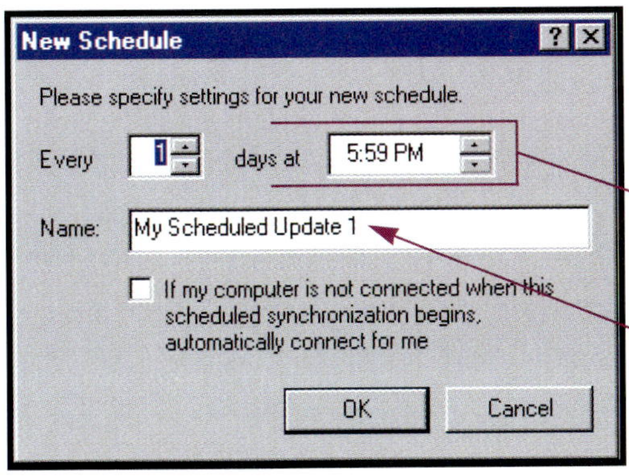

Practice

Make the Library of Congress Home Page a favorite and make it available for offline viewing.

skill Viewing Web Pages Offline

concept

Viewing a Web page in the offline mode reduces costs incurred for Internet connection. In the offline mode, you are only reading material from your own hard disk, and cannot receive new content unless you connect to the Web and reload the page. If you set a news page for offline viewing and synchronize it on Tuesday, and then view it on Friday, you will still see Tuesday's news. In this skill, we will view the Web pages that have been synchronized in the offline mode.

do it!

View Web pages in the offline mode.

1. Click Tools on the Menu bar and then click the Synchronize command while you are online. The Items to Synchronize dialog box is displayed (Figure 4-13). One of the entries in this dialog box is My Current Home Page. The synchronization of this page happens by default each time you initiate the synchronization process, and always precedes the synchronization of the other pages. The default page that is synchronized would vary depending on your system settings.
2. Make sure that the National Park Service - Experience check box is checked, then select the National Park Service - Experience entry. Click Synchronize in order to download the latest version of the Web page. The Synchronizing message box is displayed to indicate the progress of synchronization (Figure 4-14).
3. After the download process is completed (the completion is notified by a message box), disconnect from the Internet. Now you are ready to work in the offline mode.
4. Click File on the Menu bar, and then click the Work Offline command.
5. Type the URL of the synchronized National Park Service Web page (www.nps.gov) in the Address bar and press [Enter]. The requested page will be displayed in the browser window in the offline mode. You will know that you are working in the offline mode because (Working Offline) is displayed on the title bar alongside the name of the Web page. Opening the File menu on the Menu bar also will display a check mark next to the Work Offline command.
6. After you finish reviewing the Web page offline, click File, then click Work Offline to restore your Internet connection.

more

Each time you wish to view the Web page in the offline mode, you should synchronize it if you wish to view the latest version of the Web page. You need not synchronize it if you have specified a schedule for synchronization of the Web pages.

Figure 4-13 Preparing to synchronize

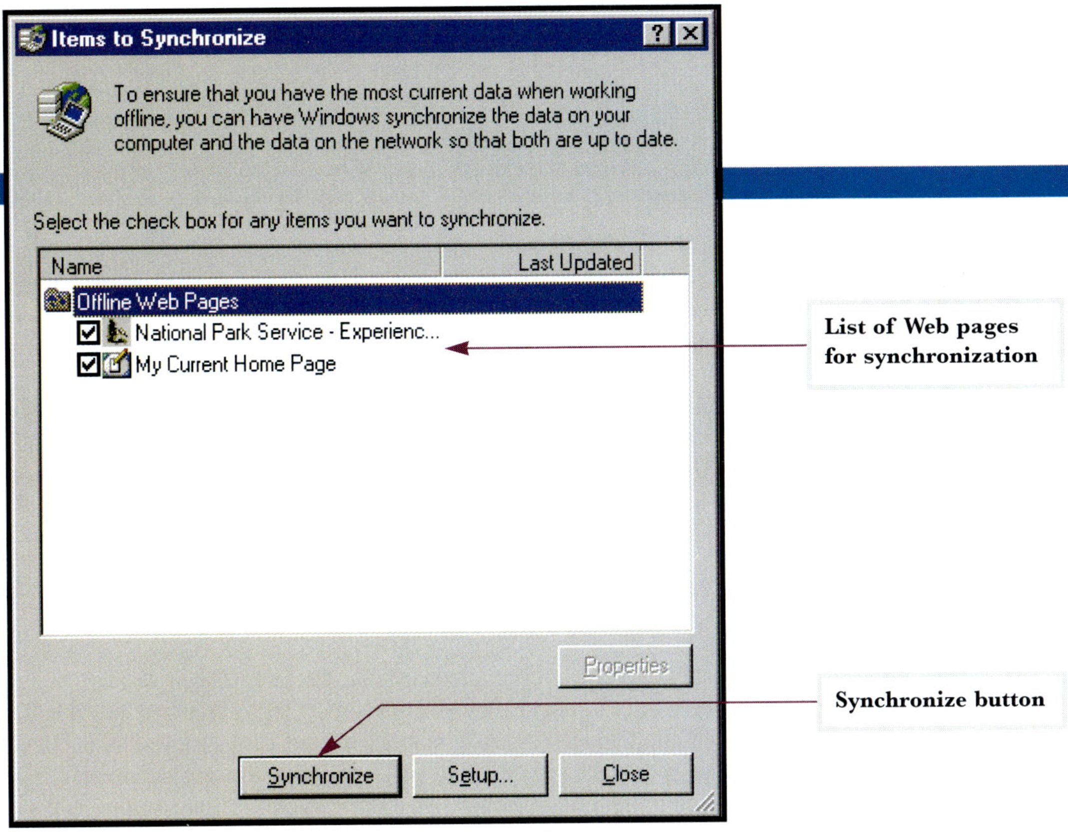

Figure 4-14 Synchronizing Web pages

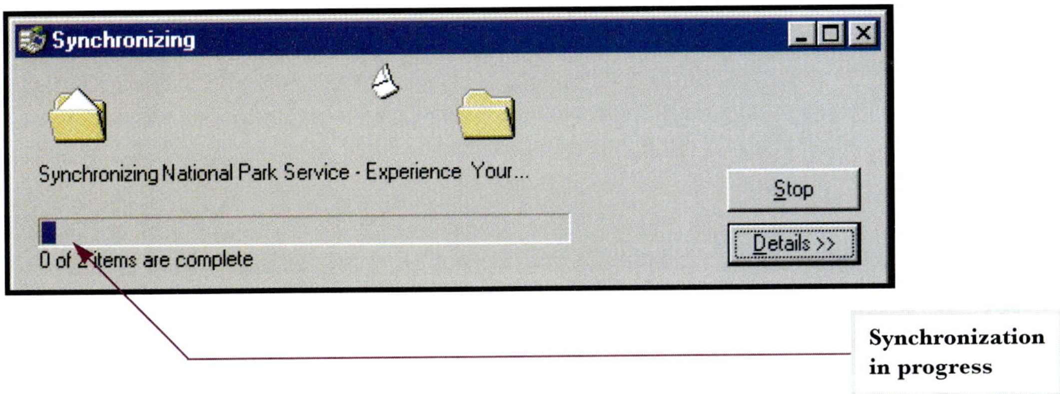

Practice

Synchronize the Library of Congress Home Page (www.loc.gov) for offline viewing using the Tools menu.

skill Using the Links Toolbar

concept

The Links toolbar is a component of the Favorites folder that has a unique display area. It is a place where you can store the URLs of the sites you visit frequently. This is a more direct link to the Web page than even the Favorites Explorer bar. There are a variety of very intuitive ways to add a site to your Links toolbar, and once you have done it, that site will appear as a button that gives you one-click access to the page it represents. Only the top few sites you use all the time should be added to the Links toolbar; if you include too many sites there, it will grow too big to be convenient. To use an analogy, think of favorites as your phone directory and the Links toolbar as your speed dial.

do it!

Create a button on the Links toolbar for a Web page that you visit frequently.

1. Make sure your Internet connection is restored if you were working offline in the previous Skill. If you do not see the Links toolbar, click View on the Menu bar, point to Toolbars and then click the Links command. If your Links toolbar is displayed only as a small tab at the end of the Address bar, place the mouse pointer over it, click and drag it downward, releasing the mouse button when the extended Links toolbar is displayed below the Address bar. As you can see, the Links toolbar comes with several buttons already added. Those that do not fit on the main bar appear on a menu that can be opened by clicking the double arrow at the right end of the toolbar.
2. Go to the National Park Service home page.
3. In the Address bar, click and hold your mouse button on the Internet Explorer icon next to the URL http://www.nps.gov. Drag the icon towards the Links toolbar. Notice that as you first begin to drag it, the mouse pointer will acquire a gray rectangle and a shortcut icon. Once you reach the Links toolbar, the pointer will appear either as a circle with a line through it (indicating you cannot drop the item there) or with a bold I-beam shaped marker (indicating where the item will go if you drop it), as in Figure 4-15.
4. Keep dragging the mouse pointer along the toolbar until the marker is displayed before the first link, in this case Best of the Web, and then release the mouse button. The new shortcut button will be displayed, as shown in Figure 4-16. From now on, you will be able to call up the National Park Service page merely by clicking the button you have created for it on the Links toolbar.

more

If you right-click a button on the Links toolbar, a pop-up menu is displayed that will let you perform operations such as sending the link to someone, setting it for offline viewing, printing it, or viewing its properties. You can also rename it or delete it. The way that you drag a URL from the Address bar is the same way you can drag a URL from the Favorites bar to the Links toolbar to create a new link. You can even drag a link from a Web page onto the Links toolbar to make it a Links button. Remember to depress your mouse button when dragging URLs around. If you give a URL, a favorite, or an online link the traditional "click and release," you won't drag the URL—you will just open the page.

If you prefer not to use the Links toolbar often, you may wish to drag it back to its former, reduced location next to the Address bar, or anywhere else you wish. You can also hide it from the menu as follows: Click View on the Menu bar point to Toolbars and click the Links command in the submenu. If the Links toolbar is already visible, it will now be hidden.

Figure 4-15 Creating a shortcut on the Links toolbar

URL being dragged onto Links toolbar

Figure 4-16 New shortcut on the Links toolbar

New shortcut on the Links toolbar

Practice

Visit the Web page of your favorite search engine and create a shortcut button for it on the Links toolbar.

skill Using Audio Files on the Web

concept

Just as Web pages can contain text, pictures, and links to other sites, they can also contain sound files. Some Web pages contain sounds or background music that play without any command. Most audio content on the Web, however, is in the form of files. You may or may not open these files depending upon your requirement. Thus, you save the time it takes to download the audio files if you do not want to hear the audio after all.

You can open and hear some sound files using software you already have as part of your Windows operating system. However, many sound files on the Web use formats prescribed by other applications not connected to Microsoft or Internet Explorer, which are usually available free (often alongside the sound files themselves). The most common of these applications is called RealPlayer. If a file you want to hear requires that you download and use this or a similar product, you will find the instructions easy to follow and the controls simple and intuitive. Of course, your computer must have properly connected speakers, either built in or peripheral, for you to hear sound files on the Web. Sometimes, Internet Explorer will ask whether you want to save a file to disk or simply open it (load it into your computer's memory without writing it to a storage device). If you have any doubts about the safety of the site you are visiting, you may wish to select the latter.

do it!

Access and listen to a sound file you receive over the Web.

1. Open the National Public Radio (NPR) Web site, www.npr.org (Figure 4-17).
2. In the listen now area at the left side of the Web page, click the Windows Media hyperlink under the NPR Hourly News category. The Windows Media feature will appear in the browser window
3. When you click the Windows Media hyperlink, the Media bar automatically will display on the left side of the screen (Figure 4-18). Since audio files are often large, they may take a few moments to open.
4. The audio will play over the speakers attached to your computer. You can use the buttons on the Media bar to control the playback. There is also a sliding volume control you may use instead of any manual volume control on your computer's speakers.
5. To stop the playback, click the Stop button at the bottom of the Media bar. To close the Media bar, click the Close button in the upper right corner of the Media bar.

more

To activate the Media bar, click View on the Menu bar and point to Explorer Bar. Click the Media command from the drop-down menu. If Media bar is not already displayed on the browser window, it will now display. On the other hand, if the Media bar is already active, it will no longer display. Alternately, you can click the Media button on the Standard Buttons toolbar to open or close it.

Figure 4-17 www.npr.org

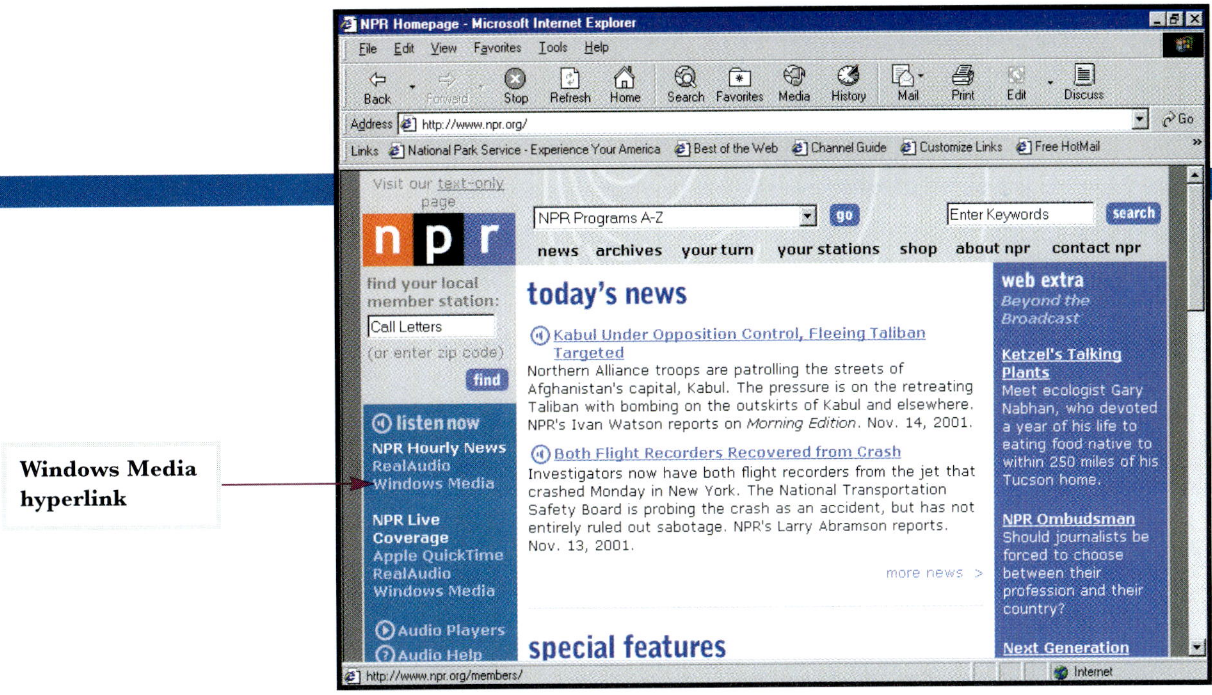

Figure 4-18 www.npr.org showing media bar for playing audio files

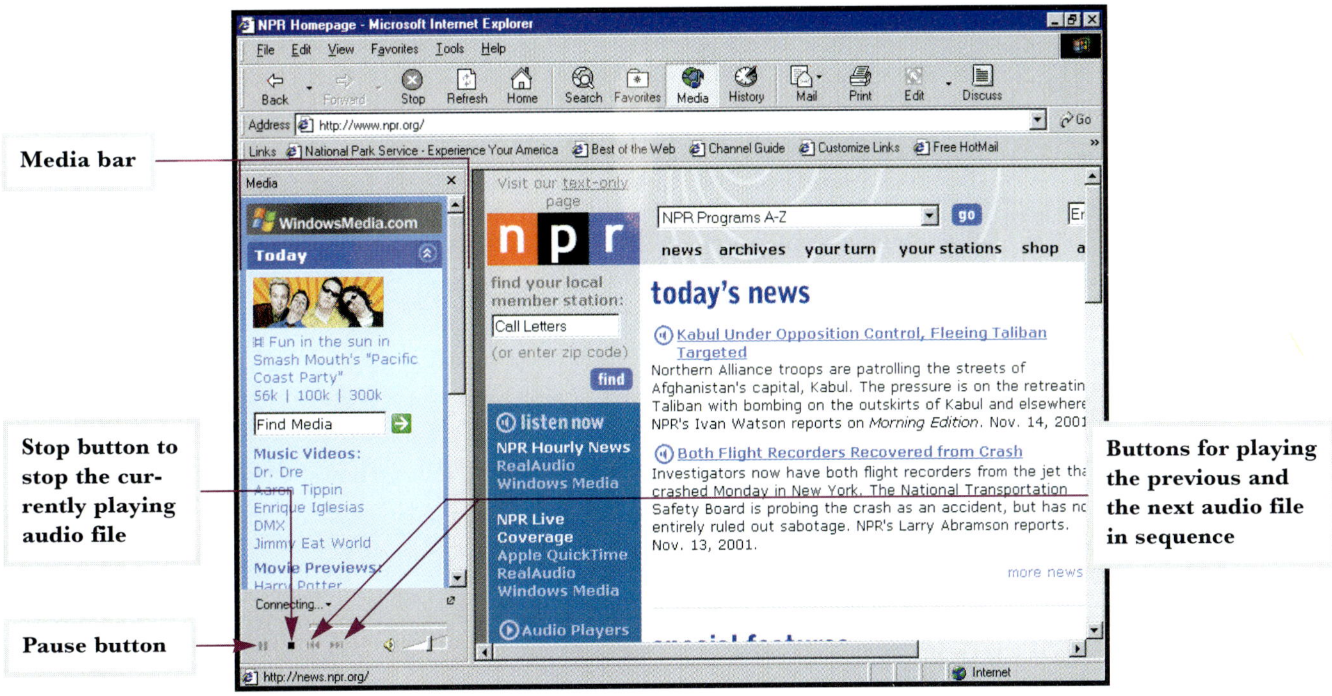

Practice

Go back to the NPR home page and listen to other available audio files.

skill Viewing Video Files on the Web

concept

Now you are getting to the exciting parts of the Web. Chances are you have tried this already, possibly within the first five minutes after you launched Internet Explorer for the first time. One of the most popular and rapidly growing abilities of the Web is to bring full-motion video, with sound, onto your computer screen. Like audio, watching video over the Web requires a special program such as Windows Media Player. If you attempt to play a video without having such a program, you will usually be prompted to download it.

Downloading video files from the Web demands a lot of bandwidth or transmission capacity. Before you start playing video, you may want to make sure any other applications operating over your Internet connection are idle as the video files are huge and take a long time to download.

do it!

View a video file you receive over the Web.

1. Make sure that you have closed the Media bar at the end of the previous Skill. Go to www.cnn.com and scroll down to the Video link.
2. Click the link to open a page, which has links to all stories that have a corresponding video file.
3. A page is displayed, which gives you the option of viewing the video with Windows Media video or Real video (Figure 4-19). Click the Windows Media option from the Choose your player drop-down list.
4. Select the appropriate speed that corresponds to the connection speed provided by your Internet Services Provider (ISP) from the Choose your connection drop-down list. After you have selected your viewer and speed, click the SET button.
5. Click the link for any story on the page. In this example, Windows Media Player does not open as a separate window; rather, it is launched as a built-in part of the page you are viewing.
6. After what may be a significant download time, the video newscast begins to play (Figure 4-20).

more

As you can see, the excitement of online video can wear off pretty soon after you view your first small, slow, grainy offering. However, this is one area of the Web that is rapidly improving in quality. Remember that a video file almost always means audio and video, so make sure you have speakers properly connected to your computer.

Large audio and video files sometimes download in chunks by a process known as buffering. With buffering, part of the file is transmitted and played, another part is transmitted and played, and so on. If everything goes well, your file runs all the way to the end with no interruptions. Streaming audio and video work this way, allowing you to receive large media files without waiting for entire file loads. Streaming also allows for live Web broadcasts, provided that your computer has enough memory to support such large files. This process has become especially popular as a way to tune in distant radio stations, which usually are not available over networks as television shows are, and since audio data is less voluminous than full video. But streaming video is a reality too, and advances in the Web's transmission ability are certain to make both more commonplace.

more Listening to radio stations in this way can be one of the most enjoyable experiences on the Web, especially since the broadcast can be left running in the background while you do other work. Make sure you know the bandwidth of your Internet connection, especially if you are at work and sharing a connection. Without knowing it, you may take up so much of the bandwidth with your streaming broadcast that no one else can get any work done.Most streaming content can be played over the Web using either RealPlayer or Windows Media Player.

Figure 4-19 Choose your settings

Drop-down list box to choose the software for playing the video file

Drop-down list to choose the connection speed

Figure 4-20 CNN - Live Video/Audio page

Built-in window playing the video clip

Practice

Check out video offerings at popular sites like cnn.com, c-span.org, and msnbc.com.

skill Exploring Privacy Features of IE 6.0

concept

Internet Explorer divides the Internet world into security zones, so that you can assign a Web site to a zone with a suitable security level. There are four different zones, as shown in Table 4-1 on IE 4.23. The different levels of security that can be assigned to the zones include High, Medium, Medium-low and Low. In addition, you can control the way Web sites use your personal information by using Internet Explorer 6.0, which implements the Platform for Privacy Preferences (P3P) standard. The P3P is a standard under development by the World Wide Web Consortium (W3C). Internet Explorer 6.0 provides simple tools to allow users to control the information Web sites collect about them, and notifies users when sites contain third-party content with cookies. This standard helps to protect the privacy of personal information of the user on the Internet by simplifying the process for deciding whether and under what circumstances personal information is disclosed to Web sites.

Microsoft continues to aid consumers in protecting privacy on the Internet by building on the current Web privacy features and providing additional control with future Internet Explorer releases. Privacy can be implemented in Internet Explorer by using security certificates. A security certificate ensures secure transaction of information over the Internet. There are two types of security certificates that are used by Internet Explorer:

- A personal certificate is a kind of guarantee that validates your identity. The information in a personal certificate is used when you send personal information over the Internet to a Web site that requires a certificate verifying your identity.
- A Web site certificate states that a specific Web site is secure and genuine. It ensures that no other Web site can assume the identity of the original secure site.

do it!

Implementing security in Internet Explorer.

1. Click Tools on the Menu bar, and then click the Internet Options command to display the Internet Options dialog box.
2. Click the Security tab, and then select the Internet zone icon from the list of zones displayed at the top of the dialog box (Figure 4-21).
3. Under the Security level for this zone section, click Custom Level... to open the Security Settings dialog box.
4. Select High from the Reset to drop-down list (Figure 4-22).

(continued on IE 4.22)

Figure 4-21 Internet Options dialog box showing the Security tab

Internet zone icon

List of zones available for setting up security options

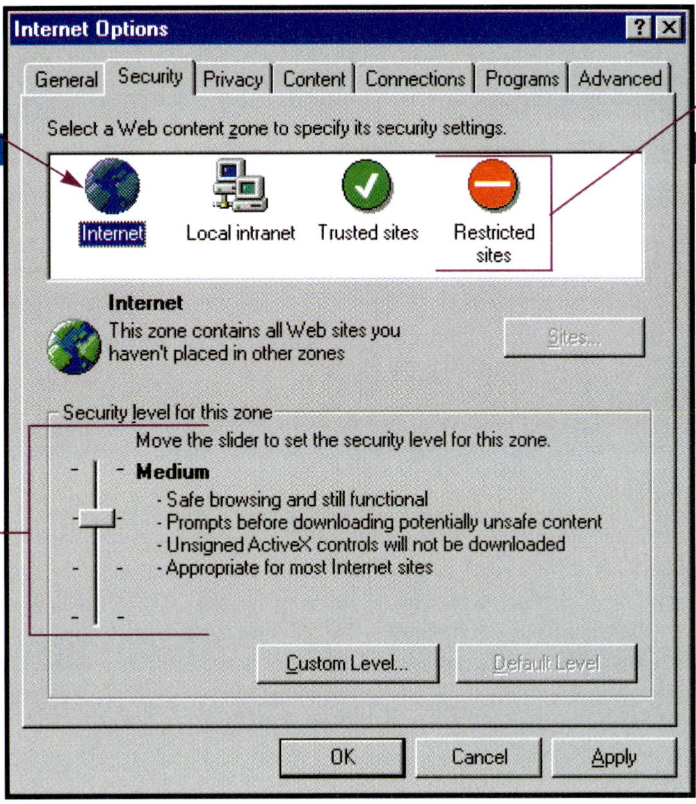

Slider and text indicate that selected zone is set at default level

Figure 4-22 Security Settings dialog box

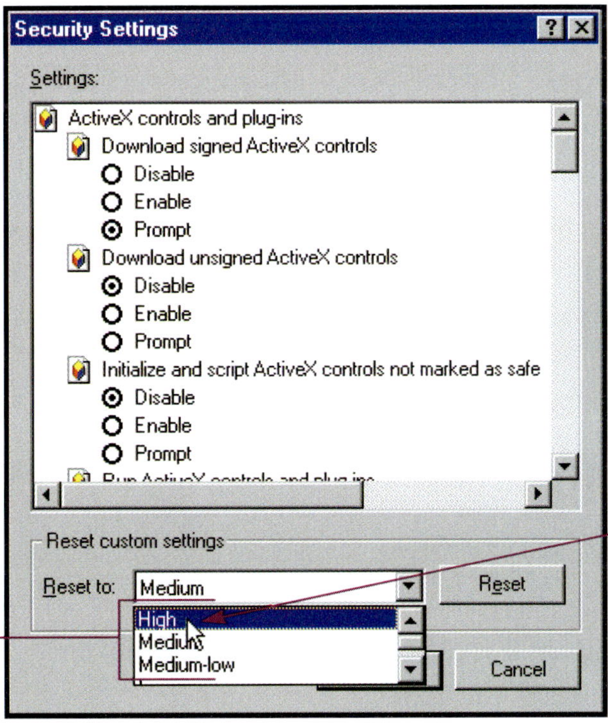

Click High setting to change from Medium setting

Security levels that can be assigned to the different zones

skill Exploring Privacy Features of IE 6.0 (continued)

do it!

5. Click to exit the Security Settings dialog box. To return the Internet zone to its default setting (Medium), be sure you have selected that zone on the Security tab in the Internet Options dialog box, then click the Default Level button, and click the OK button to accept the default and to close the dialog box.
6. Click in the Security tab to confirm the settings and exit the Internet Options dialog box.

more

A security certificate, whether it is a personal certificate or a Web site certificate, associates an identity with a "public key." Only the owner knows the corresponding "private key" that allows the owner to "decrypt" or make a "digital signature." When you send your certificate to other people, you are actually giving them your public key, so they can send you encrypted information, which only you can decrypt and read with your private key. The digital signature component of a security certificate is your electronic identity card. The digital signature tells the recipient that the information actually came from you and has not been forged or tampered with. Before you can start sending encrypted or digitally signed information, you must obtain a certificate and set up Internet Explorer to use it. When you visit a secure Web site (one that starts with https), the site automatically sends you its certificate.

Public key cryptography is a process of implementing information security through digital signatures. It employs an algorithm using two different but mathematically related keys. One key is for creating a digital signature which means transforming data into a seemingly unintelligible form. This is known as the private key and is known only to the person who creates the digital signature. The other key called the public key is used for decrypting a digital signature which means returning the message to its original form. The public key is usually more widely known than the private key.

Table 4-1 Security zones recognized by Internet Explorer

Zone	Description
Internet zone	By default, this zone contains anything that is not on your computer or an intranet, or assigned to any other zone. The default security level for the Internet zone is Medium.
Local Intranet zone	This zone typically contains any addresses that don't require a proxy server. A proxy server is the server that is located between a Web browser, and the Internet server. The Local Intranet zone includes sites specified on the Connections tab, network paths (such as \\computername\foldername), and local intranet sites (typically addresses that do not contain periods, such as http://internal). You can also add sites to this zone. The default security level for the Local intranet zone is Medium.
Trusted sites zone	This zone contains sites that you believe you can download or run files from without worrying about damage to your computer or data. You can assign sites to this zone. The default security level for the Trusted sites zone is Low. Files already on your local computer are assumed to be very safe, so minimal security settings are assigned to them.
Restricted sites zone	This zone contains the sites that you are not sure whether you can download or run files from without damage to your computer or data. You can assign sites to this zone. The default security level for the Restricted sites zone is High.

skill Instant Messaging with MSN Messenger

concept

MSN Messenger Service is an instant messaging program from Microsoft. You can download and install this software from the Microsoft site (www.msn.com). You must have a Hotmail account to use MSN Messenger Service. This service tells you when your friends are online so that you can send an instant message to a friend or chat with several friends at once. You can also invite someone in your contacts list to meet over the Internet using NetMeeting or to play an Internet game. You are notified by MSN Messenger, when contacts are online and you can instantly communicate with them over the Internet. In addition, MSN Messenger notifies you when you receive a new mail in your Hotmail account. Instant messages and e-mail are ways to send messages over the Internet, but they differ in the following respects:

- MSN Messenger Service sends instant messages in real time just like a telephone conversation. E-mail collects messages for you and lets you look at them later; this is somewhat like receiving mails through the post office.
- Instant messages in MSN Messenger Service are temporary and are not saved unless you save them, they are gone when you close the message window. E-mail messages remain until they are deleted.

You can use MSN Messenger Service for a host of other purposes other than sending or receiving instant messages; you can also use it to set up an online meeting or an Internet game, as well as to receive other notifications, such as the arrival of mail.You can even use it to send e-mail. See Table 4-2 for a detailed description for additional features of MSN Messenger Service. In the instant message window, you can type certain characters that are converted to graphic images, called emoticons, once they are sent. Emoticons are graphic images that represent the different states of the human mind.

do it!

Sign on to the MSN Messenger service. Then add a contact to your list in MSN Messenger and send an instant message to the contact.

1. Be sure that MSN Messenger is installed on your computer. Double-click the MSN Messenger icon on the Windows taskbar. The MSN Messenger dialog box will display (Figure 4-23).
2. Click the hyperlink that reads Click here to sign in, which will display the Sign in to .NET Messenger Service dialog box. In the Sign-in name text box, type the full e-mail address you normally use in Microsoft's Hotmail service. In the Password text box, type the password you normally use in Hotmail (Figure 4-24).
3. Click the OK button OK to accept your e-mail address and password, to close the dialog box, and to return you to the MSN Messenger dialog box. This dialog box now will read Signing In, and images will blink in various places near the top of the dialog box. Once you are signed in, information concerning your e-mail messages and your contact list will appear near the top of the dialog box. Additionally, near the bottom of the dialog box, a list of tasks you can perform will appear in the section entitled I want to (Figure 4-25).

(continued on IE 4.26)

Figure 4-23 MSN Messenger dialog box before sign-in

Figure 4-24 Sign in to NET Messenger dialog box

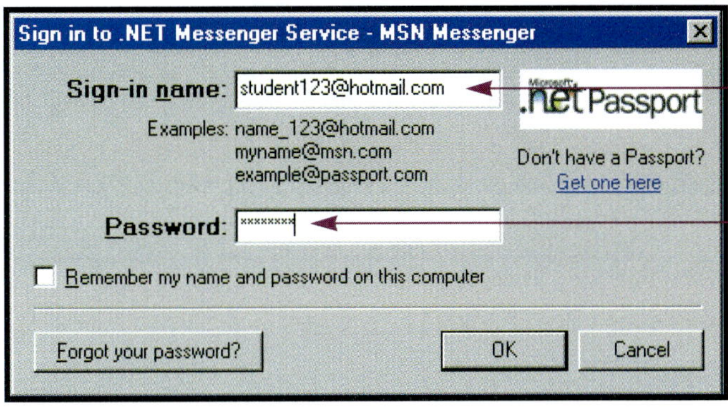

Figure 4-25 MSN Messenger dialog box after sign-in

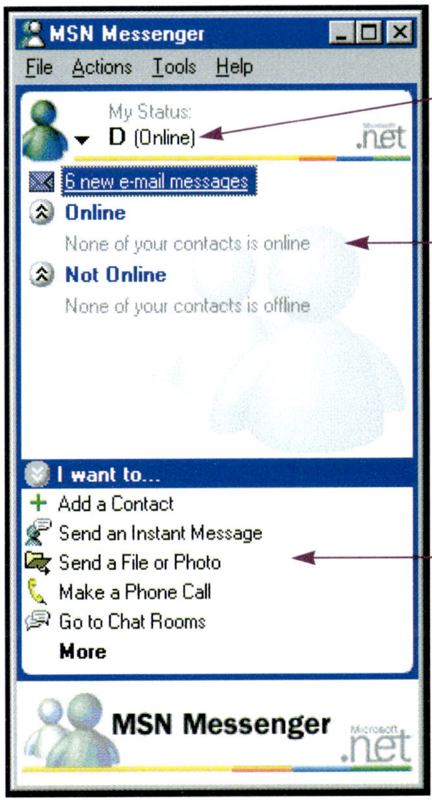

skill Instant Messaging with MSN Messenger (continued)

do it!

4. Under the I want to section, click the Add a Contact option to display the Add a Contact wizard. (Figure 4-26). Alternately, you can click the Tools menu at the top of the dialog box, then click the Add a Contact command on the drop-down menu.
5. The first screen in the Add a Contact wizard enables you to select a method for adding a contact to your list of contacts (Figure 4-26). Activate the By e-mail address or sign-in name option button.
6. Click Next >. This will display the second screen, where you can specify the e-mail address of the contact.
7. Click Next >. The wizard validates the e-mail address of the contact. If the e-mail address of the contact is valid, the wizard reports success, otherwise it reports failure (Figure 4-27). You can add up to 75 contacts to your list. However, remember that you can send an instant message to anyone who uses MSN Messenger Service.
8. Click Finish to confirm the settings and to exit the wizard.

more

Additionally, the Add a Contact wizard allows you to search for a contact mentioned in the address book in your computer or Hotmail Member directory. When you search for a contact, you cannot use wildcards or asterisks when you enter the name.

Figure 4-26 Add a Contact wizard

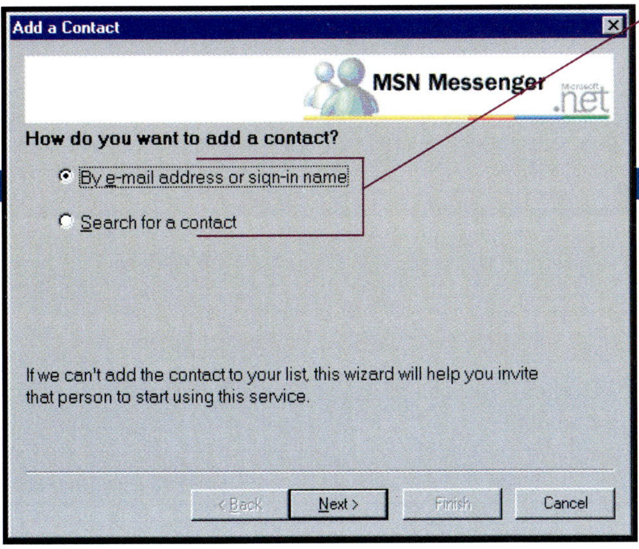

Options for adding a contact to Contacts bar

Figure 4-27 Wizard reports success

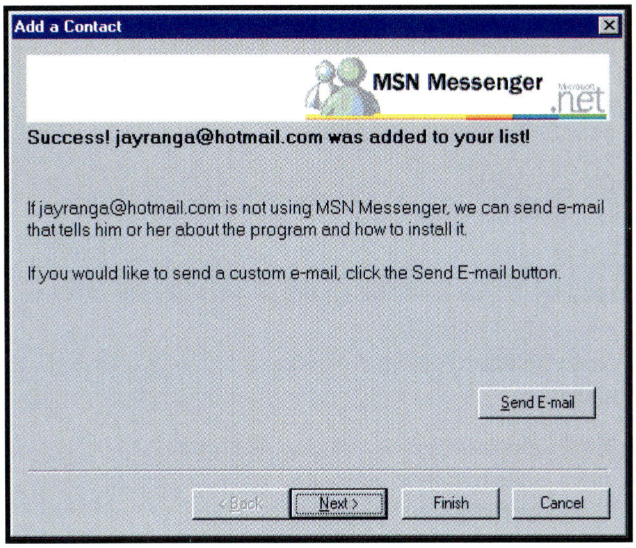

Table 4-2 Additional Functions of MSN Messenger Service

Function	Description
Worldwide phone calls	You can call anywhere in the world for a very low rate.
Easier connecting	If your computer is behind a firewall, you will now be able to connect automatically.
Voice conversations	You can have conversations with your friends from your PC—anywhere in the world.
Paging	You can send text messages to cell phones and pagers.
Share your files	Trade pictures, music, documents, or other files using MSN Messenger Service.
Easy access to Hotmail	You can see how many new Hotmail e-mail messages you have and get notified whenever you receive a new Hotmail e-mail message.
Automatic typing indicator	MSN Messenger Service lets you know when one of your friends is typing a response.
Rich customization	You can change the formatting of text and use special sounds that play when you receive an instant message or when a friend comes online.
Change your display name	You can frequently change your display name.
Control over your information	You control who can send you instant messages. You can also control who adds you to their contact list.

shortcuts

Function	Button/Mouse	Menu	Keyboard
Open Favorites Explorer bar		Click View, point to Explorer Bar, then click Favorites	[Ctrl]+[I]
Add current page to Favorites		Click Favorites, then click Add to Favorites	[Ctrl]+[D]
Open Organize Favorites dialog box		Click Favorites, then click Organize Favorites	[Ctrl]+[B]
Move selected item up in the Favorites list in Organize Favorites dialog box	Click and drag item		[Alt]+[Up Arrow]
Move selected item down in the Favorites list in Organize Favorites dialog box	Click and drag item		[Alt]+[Down Arrow]

quiz

A. Identify Key Features

Name the items indicated by callouts in Figure 4-28.

Figure 4-28 Tools used to explore the Web

1.

2.

3.

4.

5.

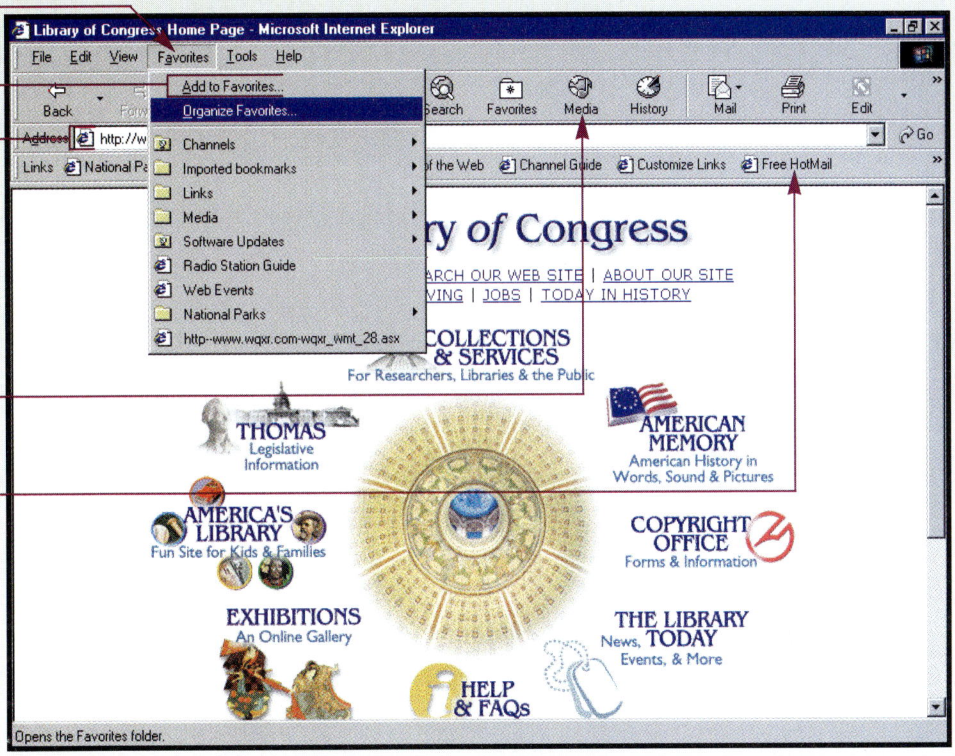

B. Select the Best Answer

6. Updating one set of data with a similar, but more recent set of data
7. An application that allows you to download audio and video material from the Web
8. A way to look at Web pages when your Internet connection is not active
9. The process of retrieving an audio file from the Web and then playing it
10. A feature that lets you save and categorize the Web sites that you visit frequently
11. A prerequisite for installing MSN Messenger Service
12. The Security Settings dialog box is accessed within this dialog box
13. Microsoft's instant messaging program
14. The default security level for the Local Intranet zone
15. The default security level for the Restricted sites zone

a. Downloading
b. Windows Media Player
c. Synchronization
d. Favorites
e. Offline viewing
f. Internet Options
g. Hotmail account
h. High
i. Medium
j. MSN Messenger

quiz (continued)

C. Complete the Statement

16. If you visit a particular Web page every day, you might want to convert it to:

a. A Favorite

b. A Links toolbar button

c. Your home page

d. All of the above

17. The folders you create in favorites are organized by:

a. How much you trust the validity of a site

b. Any distinctions you want to create

c. How appropriate you feel the site is for kids

d. How often you view each site in the folder

18. The most accurate description of viewing sites offline is that:

a. It lets you get the latest news updates when you cannot get to your Internet connection

b. It lets you save a page for later use so you can follow links from it to the rest of the Web

c. It is automatically available for any page you viewed during your last online browsing session

d. It provides a snapshot of contents of the Web page as of the last time you were online

19. The Links toolbar is:

a. A permanent fixture on the screen

b. Located under the Start menu

c. Part of your Favorites hierarchy

d. An Explorer bar

20. When you send Favorites to another person, the recipient can view them without:

a. Typing a URL

b. An Internet connection

c. A Web browser

d. Worrying about security

21. A Favorite can be created in:

a. A new folder that you create

b. The main level Favorites folder

c. An existing Favorites folder

d. All of the above

22. The process of downloading a favorite for offline viewing is called:

a. Synchronicity

b. Syncopation

c. Synchronization

d. Organization

23. The Explorer bar that helps you to play audio files:

a. History

b. Media

c. Favorites

d. Contacts

24. Security zones recognized by Internet Explorer 6.0 include the:

a. Internet zone

b. Local Intranet zone

c. Trusted Sites zone

d. All of the above

25. A Web site certificate:

a. Qualifies you for a job at an Internet company

b. States that a specific Web site is secure and genuine

c. Is a kind of guarantee that validates your identity on the World Wide Web

d. None of the above

interactivity

Build Your Skills

1. Pick three general topics that interest you. For each topic, perform an Internet search:
   a. Save at least five Web pages on each topic as favorites. If appropriate, make one of your selections a page whose content changes frequently, such as a news, sports, financial, or weather page.
   b. For at least one of the pages you save in each topic, give a name different from the default name the Web author gave it.
   c. Create a folder in the Favorites folder for each of your search topics.
   d. Move each of the pages you have saved into the appropriate folder.
   e. After you have ended your browsing session and exited Internet Explorer, launch it again and use Favorites to revisit the topics you researched.

2. Play an audio file on a Web site you consider trustworthy:
   a. Open the Public Broadcasting System Web site at www.pbs.org.
   b. On the left side of the screen, under the NEWSROOM area of the Web site, click the NPR Hourly newscast hyperlink.
   c. Record the name of the playback program that appears in the pop-up window. Try to record the names of the phases that the program goes through before it starts playing (e.g., Connecting, etc.).
   d. Listen to part or all of the broadcast, which normally runs about five minutes. Click the Close button on the pop-up window when you finish listening.

3. Look through Internet Explorer's Menu bar and find a function we did not discuss anywhere in this lesson. Experiment with it and try to learn how it works and what it does!

interactivity (continued)

Problem Solving Exercises

1. As a sales representative, you fit the title of "business traveler" perfectly. Fortunately, the World Wide Web can do wonders for your travel expenses. Various Web sites can now assist you in finding the cheapest air fares and hotel rooms available. Use the skills you have learned so far to find at least three of these sites on the Web. Add each site you find to your Favorites list. Then, create a new Favorites folder named Travel Savings and move the favorites you have added into the new folder. Finally, export the new folder to a file on your hard drive and name it as ie6problem4-1.htm.

2. As the director of Human Resources division at a large accounting firm, it is important for you to stay on top of the issues that affect the workforce. Chief among these is health insurance. Your approach to this topic is twofold. You like to keep one eye on what the insurance companies are saying about themselves and also on what the watchdogs are saying about the insurance companies. Use your Web skills to find the Web sites of major health care providers. Store the main pages of these sites in a Favorites folder named Health Care Providers. Then focus your Web search on pages that provide reviews of, or news about, particular health care companies. Organize these pages in a favorites folder named Health Care Reviews. Select two pages from each folder and set them for offline viewing. Synchronize the pages, close your browser and Internet connection, and read the pages offline.

3. Your department is in the market for a new color laser printer. You have been chosen to research the purchase and recommend a printer to your boss. Use your Web skills to find out as much as you can about four top of the line color laser printers. You should search for the Web sites of companies that actually manufacture and sell the printers as well as independent reviews of printers. When you find a page on a manufacturer's site, save it as a favorite in a folder named Printers. When you find a page that reviews the performance of a particular printer or printers, save it as a favorite in a folder named Printer Reviews. After studying the four candidates you have found, select the printer that you think will best suit your department's needs (a high output rate, low maintenance, network ready, reliable service program). Create a button for the Web page of the printer you have chosen on the Links toolbar.

4. Go to www.cnn.com and scroll to the Video links near the bottom of the page. Use Windows Media Player to watch video clips of the current top news stories. Then return to CNN's home page and click the Audio link. On the AudioSelect page, listen to a streaming broadcast of CNN's live news coverage.

5. You wish to chat securely with your friend and confidante. Activate MSN Messenger Service to do so. Note to Student: Remember that using MSN Messenger Service requires that you have a Hotmail account. To obtain a Hotmail account:

   a. Open the Hotmail Web site at www.hotmail.com, and click the Sign Up for FREE E-Mail Account! hyperlink near the top of the page to open the Registration page.

   b. On the Registration page, fill in the text boxes with the required information, then click the Sign Up button near the bottom of the page. If you fill in any required text box incorrectly or choose a sign-in name that already is taken, Hotmail will display a Registration Error page instructing you to correct your information.

   c. When you successfully complete the sign-in process, the Sign Up Successful! Web page will appear. Click the Continue at Hotmail button to display the Please re-enter your password Web page. Type in your newly created password, then press [Enter] or click the Sign In button. Click the OK button in the first Security Alert dialog box that appears, then click Yes in the second one to display a Terms of Use Web page.

   d. Read the Terms of Use, then click the I Accept button at the bottom of the page to display the WebCourier Web page. If desired, select only those free subscription services that you absolutely wish to send you e-mail. Click the Continue button near the bottom of the page to display the Special Offer Newsletters Web page. Again, if desired, select only those newsletters you wish to receive, then click the Continue to E-mail button at the bottom of the page.

   e. You will be returned to the second page of the main Hotmail Web site. Review the options available on that page, then click the Inbox tab or the Inbox hyperlink near the top of the page to display the Inbox. Your first e-mail will be a welcoming message from the Hotmail Staff. If you wish to open and read the e-mail, click on the Hotmail Staff hyperlink under the From column. (To send e-mail to friends announcing your e-mail account, click the Compose tab near the top of the page, fill in the required mailing information and your text, then Send the e-mail.)

glossary

a

Accessibility

The degree to which people with disabilities can make use of material on the Web, which Internet Explorer addresses by allowing changes in colors, text sizes and certain controls.

Active

Term used to describe the window in which you are currently working, especially if more than one window is open.

Address

The characters that tell a browser such as Internet Explorer where a particular resource resides on the World Wide Web, including a root, domain, path and filename. Also called a URL (Uniform Resource Locator).

Address Bar

The area in the browser window where you type in a Web site's address or URL, and where the address of the current page is displayed.

AltaVista

A popular commercial search engine.

Animations

Objects that are part of a Web page and which change or move once loaded, often in a continuous loop.

Application

Also known as a program, a piece of software that contains instructions for your computer and allows you to perform tasks. Internet Explorer is an application.

Archie

Developed in the late 1980s, one of the first indexes to the World Wide Web.

ARPAnet

An acronym for the U.S. Department of Defense's Advanced Research Projects Agency net, the earliest version (circa late 1960s) of what would become known as the Internet.

Audio files

Files in a particular format (such as .wav) that your computer interprets as sounds using a media player application.

Author

The person or agency who created a Web page.

AutoComplete

A feature of Internet Explorer that remembers entries you have made previously in the Address Bar or other locations and finishes your typing for you when you begin to make the same entry again.

AutoScan

Part of the way in which Internet Explorer can search the Web after a URL you enter has failed; it looks for sites that have the same root you entered but different common domains (such as ".org" or ".edu").

b

Back

A Standard Buttons toolbar button that takes you directly to the last page you viewed before coming to the current page.

Background

(1) The area in the browser window "behind" all the text and graphics on a Web page; it can appear blank, or colored, or in a pattern. (2) The part of your computer's memory where open applications or folders reside when others are open and being used.

Bandwidth

A term used to describe the capacity of an Internet connection, usually expressed in kilobytes (K) per second.

Browser

Any application that interprets HyperText Markup Language (HTML) to display Web pages. Internet Explorer is a browser.

Browser window

The segment of Internet Explorer's display where material from the World Wide Web appears for you to read.

Browsing

A common term for reading material on the Web.

Button

A graphical interface feature that functions like a real-life mechanical button when you click on it with your mouse.

C

Cancel

To halt the loading of a page from the Web before it is completed using the Stop button on the Standard Buttons toolbar.

Case-sensitive

Susceptible to mistakes when uppercase or lowercase letters are used in the wrong places. A case-sensitive application will not interpret "Hello" in the same way it interprets "hello."

Category

A certain kind of Web search – for people, for businesses, for maps, etc. – that you can perform using the Search Assistant.

Certificates

Documents appended to Web pages that help verify their authenticity and authorship for security purposes.

Channels

(1) A term for Web pages that you have set for automatic updating and offline viewing. (2) A feature of the popular RealPlayer application that facilitates access to different sources of audio and video material.

Click

To depress the button on your mouse while the mouse pointer is located over a desired item on the screen. Depending on the function, you may click and hold the button, click it and release it, or click and release it twice ("double-clicking").

Client

A computer which is receiving data or running software from another computer.

Client-server model

A way of arranging computer networks in which data or applications reside on one computer, the host, and one or more other computers, the clients, access these resources via a connection to the host.

Clipboard

The part of your computer's memory where items reside after you have cut or copied them for later use.

Close

To shut down a file, application or window so that it is no longer active and no longer appears on your screen.

Content Advisor

A feature of Internet Explorer that uses ratings standards to help users control access to Web pages which contain potentially objectionable material.

Cookie

An HTTP header that consists of a text-only string that gets entered into the memory of a Web browser; this string contains the domain, path, lifetime, and value of a variable that a Web site sets and is used to track a user's visits to Web sites.

Copy

To capture information, often a segment of text, to the Clipboard so it can be used in another place or in a different application.

Current page

The Web page you are viewing at the moment.

Cursor

A mark on your screen, usually a blinking vertical line, that indicates where the next character you type will appear. The mouse pointer is also sometimes called a cursor.

Customize

To alter the appearance or function of one of Internet Explorer's features to your own liking.

d

Default settings

The way in which certain options are set when Internet Explorer is first used and you haven't changed them—for example, your default home page is probably msn.com.

Delphi

Developed in the early 1990s, the first commercial online service provider, which offered full Internet access to its subscribers.

Desktop

The interactive display that fills your whole screen when you're running Windows and there are no folders or applications open.

Desktop icon

An object on the desktop that you can double-click to open a file, folder or application.

Desktop shortcut

A desktop icon you have created for a particular file, folder or application.

Dialog box

A box that opens when an application requires you to make a decision or enter data.

Disk

A mechanical device for storing data. It can be a removable floppy disk, but in current common usage it usually refers to your computer's hard drive.

Document

In Web terminology, a collection of text, graphics, links and layout information that is saved as a file and makes up a Web page. More generally, any file, especially a text or word processing file.

Domain

The three-letter portion of a URL such as .com, .gov, .org, or .edu that indicates what type of entity created the Web page.

Double-clicking

Depressing and releasing your mouse button twice in rapid succession, usually to open a file or application from its icon. You can modify the speed of your double-clicks on the Windows control panel.

Download

To transfer data from a server or host computer to a client computer.

Drive

Any device that stores data in a mechanical medium, including floppy disk drives, CD-ROM drives, but most commonly used as shorthand for a computer's internal hard disk drive.

e

Electronic mail

Commonly shortened to "e-mail." Messages sent from one computer user to another via the Internet.

Emoticon

A combination of characters that represents a graphic image (e.g., a smiley face) that indicate a state of the human mind; often used in e-mail messages to add emotional context to ambiguous comments to avoid misunderstanding by e-mail recipients.

Excite!

A popular commercial search engine.

Exit

To shut down an application.

Explorer Bar

An area containing commands and options that appears on the left-hand side of the browser window when using the History, Favorites or Search Assistant features.

Export
To make a file or folder available for use (or "importing") by another application.

f

Favorites
A feature of Internet Explorer that allows you to maintain organized groups of shortcuts to pages you have viewed in the past.

File
Any information stored as a unit on a computer and accessible by one name. A word processing document, a picture or a Web page are examples of items stored as files.

File tab
Part of the graphical arrangement in certain control boxes, such as "Internet Options," that resembles the cut tabs on a manila file folder and allows you to select from among several "pages" of command screens that appear to be piled on top of one another.

Find
(1) In Internet Explorer, a function that allows you to search the current page for a particular string of text. (2) In Windows, a function that allows you to search a drive or network for a certain file, application or folder.

Find a Picture option
A Search bar feature that enables you to search for pictures on the Web that match keywords; access this feature in the Customize Search Settings dialog box.

Folder
A subdivision of a storage disk that works like a filing system to help you organize and store files.

Formatting
The instructions that determine where text, pictures and other elements appear on a Web page.

Forms
Areas on a Web page in which you enter data that will be reported back to the server; for example, the space in which you enter your credit card number when making a purchase online.

Forward
A Standard Buttons toolbar button that sends you to a page that you have viewed previously but "retreated" from using the Back button.

Frames
A way in which certain Web pages are arranged that divides the browser window into distinct areas that can be scrolled or changed separately from one another.

FTP (File Transfer Protocol)
A method of transferring data files from one computer to another over the Internet.

g

Go
A button next to the Address Bar that instructs Internet Explorer to access the Web page whose URL you have typed.

Gopher
Developed by the University of Minnesota (whose school mascot is the gopher) in the early 1990s, a simple menu system for accessing Web files.

Graphic
Any photo, image, drawing or other picture included in a Web page.

h

Help
A feature of Internet Explorer that gives you instructions and advice on using the application.

Highlight

To select a segment of text for a particular use by dragging your mouse over it with the button depressed.

History

A feature of Internet Explorer that automatically saves the addresses of pages you've viewed recently so that you can return to them more easily.

Home

A Standard Buttons toolbar button that returns you to your selected home page.

Home page

(1) The Web site you've selected to be the one that appears when you open Internet Explorer. (2) A common term for the main or opening page of a Web site that contains many pages.

HotBot

A popular commercial search engine.

Hover

To position your mouse pointer over an object. Some hyperlinks and other objects will change color or animate when you hover over them, even though the mouse button is not depressed.

HTML (HyperText Markup Language)

The source code, or programming language, used to create and reproduce Web pages. A browser, such as Internet Explorer, interprets HTML to create the displays you see.

HTTP (HyperText Transfer Protocol)

The standard by which most Web data (pages and otherwise) is transferred between the server and the client computer.

Hyperlink

An object or text segment that has been made into an active "button" which will take you to another Web page when you click on it.

Hypermedia

Words and pictures that are linked to other sites on the Web and will transport you there when you click on them.

Hypertext

Hypermedia that appears as text.

i

Icon

An object on the Windows desktop that represents a file, folder or application. Also, a loosely used term for some objects displayed in Web pages.

IEAK 6 (Internet Explorer Administration Kit)

An Internet Explorer feature that facilitates deployment and support of Internet Explorer technologies; version 6 adds control over new features such as the Media bar and auto-image resize.

Image

A photo, drawing or other graphical representation that is saved as a file and can be included in a Web page.

Image toolbar

A toolbar with buttons that enable you to e-mail, save, or print images; the toolbar appears when you place the mouse pointer over an image at least 200 x 200 pixels in size on a Web page.

Infoseek

A popular commercial search engine.

Internet

An extended world-wide computer network that is composed of numerous smaller networks. The World Wide Web is part of the Internet.

Internet connection

The means by which your computer (the client) is connected to a Web or e-mail server, either through a network or by the use of a modem.

Internet Explorer 6

The latest version of Microsoft's Internet Explorer browser application, introduced in 2001. The subject of this book.

Internet Explorer icon

(1) A desktop icon that represents the Internet Explorer application and allows you to open the application with a double-click. (2) The image of the Internet Explorer symbol that appears in the upper right-hand corner of the browser window; when it is animated, the browser is busy seeking or transferring data.

Internet Options

A very useful group of controls, available under Tools on the Menu Bar, that allows you to alter the appearance and function of Internet Explorer in many ways.

Internet ratings

Graded descriptions of certain types of content (e.g. violence, foul language) used by the Content Advisor to control access to certain Web sites.

Internet Zone

A Security Zone that includes all material that is not on your own computer and which you have not previously assigned to a different Security Zone.

IP (Internet Protocol)

The most basic set of rules for communicating among computers that is used in the Internet; these rules help to identify the sending and receiving computers, how to break up transmitted Internet documents into packets, and so on.

ISP (Internet Service Provider)

A company, school or other entity that provides access to an Internet server, often for a fee.

k

Keyword

A term used as the basis for an Internet search.

l

LAN (Local Area Network)

An interconnected group of computers set up within a limited area such as a business, a school campus, a government department, or so on.

launch

To open an application such as Internet Explorer.

Layout

The spatial arrangement of text, pictures and other objects within a Web page.

Link

(1) Noun, a shortened version of the term hyperlink (see hyperlink). (2) Verb, to connect one element of hypermedia to a particular Web address so that it can serve as a hyperlink.

Links Toolbar

A portion of the browser window that you can set up to contain one-click shortcuts to a few Web sites you view very often.

Load

To download, or transfer data from a server computer to a client computer. When you access a Web page, you are loading it.

Local Intranet Zone

A Security Zone reserved for material that resides on your local network but not on your own computer.

Log off

To terminate your Internet connection, sometimes by sending the server a specific command, often by simply hanging up the phone.

Log on

To establish a connection to an Internet server, often through the use of a password.

Look Up a Word option

A Search bar feature that enables you to search for words in the Encyclopedia, Dictionary, or Thesaurus.

Lycos

A popular commercial search engine.

m

Mail

Another term for e-mail.

Maximize

To display a window across your entire screen.

Media bar

An Explorer bar that helps you play the media files available online.

Media Player

A Microsoft application, commonly included along with Windows or available over the Internet, that interprets sound and audio files so that your computer can play them.

Menu

Any grouped list of commands or options.

Menu Bar

The topmost portion of the browser window, containing a list of categories (File, Edit, View, etc.) that you can click on to view a menu of command options.

Microsoft Outlook

An application from Microsoft that handles e-mail, among other functions.

Minimize

To remove a window (containing an active file, folder or application) from the desktop without closing or exiting it. A minimized window is represented as a button on the status bar at the bottom of the Windows display.

Mouse

A pointing device that converts the movement of your hand into movements of a pointer or cursor on the screen, and includes one or more buttons used to actuate graphical controls.

Mouse pointer

The graphical object that indicates what location on the screen the mouse is covering. Typically a small arrow, in many applications it changes to other shapes to indicate available functions in different locations.

MSN Autosearch

The Microsoft service used for searches from the Address Bar.

MSN Messenger

An instant messaging program from Microsoft; downloadable for free from the Internet, this program tells you when friends are online, enables you to invite someone in your contacts list to meet over the Internet, enables you to play games live with other messaging partners, and so on.

n

Navigate

To move among the resources World Wide Web by using the controls on your browser.

Netscape

A popular browser application that has the same basic purpose as Internet Explorer.

Network

A group of computers linked together to share data.

Newsgroup

A portion of the Internet apart from e-mail and the Web, consisting of many separate "bulletin boards" on almost any topic imaginable.

Node

One computer on a network.

NSFnet

An intermediate step in the development of the Internet, created by the National Science Foundation in the early 1980s.

O

Object

Any distinct item on a Web page, such as a picture, an icon, or a block of text.

Offline

Not connected to a server computer.

Online

Connected to a server computer.

Open

To launch or activate an application, or to access the contents of a folder or file.

Operating system

The program that determines how your computer receives commands, handles files and applications, and arranges its display. Windows 98 and Windows XP are operating systems.

Organize

An option available with many of Internet Explorer's features, allowing you to alter the way they appear or operate.

Outlook Express

A simple e-mail program from Microsoft for e-mailing other computer users, participating in Internet newsgroups, and so on; downloadable on the Internet, this program requires use of Internet Explorer.

P

P3P (Platform for Privacy Preferences)

A standard under development by the World Wide Web Consortium (W3C) that helps users control the information that Web sites collect about them and notifies users when sites contain third-party content with cookies.

Packet

A "bundle" of information sent electronically from one computer to another; the basis of most networking schemes.

Page

(1) The data that fits on your display all at once without scrolling. (2) A single Web document made up of text, pictures, links, and layout information. (3) Casually, an entire Web site, which in fact may be made up of many pages.

Paste

To insert data from the Clipboard into a new location.

Path

The list of folder names that designates where a particular file resides on a drive or server; frequently part of a URL.

Personal certificates

Security documents you can create to substantiate your identity for use in Internet transactions.

(PICS) Platform for Internet Content Selection

A standard for ratings labels attached to Web content.

Picture

An image stored as a file and included as part of a Web page.

Pop-up menu

A group of command options that appears, if available, when the user clicks the right mouse button. This menu usually pertains directly to the object that was clicked.

Previous searches

A category on the Search Assistant that allows you to view the results of searches you have performed recently.

Print

To send a file, picture or other data to a properly connected printer device so that it will be reproduced on paper.

Print Range

A setting in the Print dialog box that determines what portion of a document will be printed.

Printer

A peripheral device that reproduces data from the computer onto paper.

Private Key

A key, or long character string, that is known to only the person who creates it; less widely known than a public key, it is used for decoding encrypted documents and messages.

Program

Another term for application, a piece of software that contains instructions for your computer and allows you to perform tasks. Internet Explorer is a program.

Prompt

A message or dialog box that appears when your operating system, an application or a Web site requires you to enter data.

Properties

Taken as a set, the various qualities of a Web page: its name, size, date of creation and other information. You can view a page's properties under the File menu.

Protocol

A scheme for transferring data from one computer to another, such as HTTP (HyperText Transfer Protocol) or FTP (File Transfer Protocol).

Public Key

A key, or long character string, that is more widely known than a private key; it is used for encoding or encrypting documents and messages to be decoded later by a private key.

q

Quick Launch toolbar

A feature available on Windows 98 and later Windows versions that enables you to create buttons at the bottom of your screen to launch applications with a single mouse click.

Quicktime

A popular format for encoding video files that requires a commercially available application to view them.

r

Radio button

A small, circular area you can click to activate options in many dialog boxes. When a radio button has a dot in it, the option it represents is active.

Ratings

Standardized descriptions, made available by private organizations and readable by Internet Explorer's Content Advisor, of the degree of objectionable content in Web pages.

RealAudio Player

A popular, commercially available application that interprets sound and audio files so that your computer can play them.

Recreational Software Advisory Council (RSAC)

The default rating service that Internet Explorer's Content Advisor is set to use.

Refresh

A Standard Buttons toolbar button that loads the contents of the current page again from scratch, useful in correcting transmission errors or viewing updated content.

Relevance

A statistical description of how closely a Web page found in a search matches the criteria you entered for the search. Many search engines rank their findings in order of relevance.

Reload

Another term for Refresh.

Restricted Sites Zone

A Security Zone to which you can assign sites you do not trust.

Results

A list of Web pages that a search engine produces in response to a search topic you've entered.

Right-clicking

Depressing the right-hand button on a mouse that is equipped with one (not all are), often to bring up a menu of options that pertains to the object you have clicked.

S

Save

To write data, such as a file or Web page, on to a disk for storage and later use.

ScreenTip

A brief explanation of a button, text box, list box, or other object that appears when the mouse pointer hovers over it.

Scroll

To manipulate the display, using scroll bars, arrow keys or a wheel mouse, so that the information moves up and down the screen or side to side, and information in the current page or document that was hidden comes into view.

Search

To use a specially designed Web site to locate Web resources on a particular topic or keyword.

Search Assistant

A feature of Internet Explorer that allows you to organize how you search for different kinds of information on the Web, which search resources you use, and in what order.

Search engine

A special Web site, typically a commercial entity, that is used for searching for Web pages that conform to keywords you enter.

Security Zones

Categories you can assign Web pages to based upon where they reside or how much you trust the validity of their content. Each Security Zone can be set with different safeguards against the downloading of material.

Send Link

To create an e-mail message that contains the URL of the current page for the recipient to use. Available under the File menu.

Send Page

To create an e-mail message that contains the entire contents of the current page for the recipient to view. Available under the File menu.

Server

The computer where Web pages and other data reside so that your computer, the client, can access them via the Internet or a local network.

Session

The time you spend connected to a Web server and working on the Internet.

Show Picture

A command, available by right-clicking, that enables you to display a particular image even though you've set Internet Explorer not to display pictures in general.

Site

A group of Web pages that relate to one another and all reside on the same server under the same root and domain.

Snap

A popular commercial search engine.

Socket

One end of a two-way computer connection; composed of the IP address of the server computer and its port number.

Software

A blanket term that describes all applications.

Standard Buttons toolbar

A portion of the browser window that contains several large buttons (Back, Forward, Stop, etc.) that activate Internet Explorer's principal functions.

Start Menu

In Windows 98 and later Windows versions, the principal menu you use to control the operating system. Accessible by clicking the Start button in the lower- left corner of the display.

Status bar

The bottom portion of the browser window, which displays which Security Zone the current page is in, the status of your Internet connection, and the function the browser is currently performing (such as "Finding page" or "Done").

Stop

A Standard Buttons toolbar button that halts the download of a page in progress.

Streaming

A way to send audio and video files in a continuous "stream" of small segments. If your Internet connection and your computer are fast enough, the result is an uninterrupted display of the audio or video material.

Submenu

A menu that appears when a menu item is highlighted; for example, on the Start Menu, you can highlight "Programs" to bring up a submenu of available applications.

Subscriptions

The term used to describe offline viewing of Web pages in earlier versions of Internet Explorer.

Supervisor Password

The code word you can establish to limit other people's ability to change your Content Advisor settings.

Surfing

A common term for browsing the Web, especially used to describe extended sessions in which the user follows links wherever his or her interest takes him with no particular plan in mind.

Synchronize

To download the content of pages you've set for offline viewing, an operation usually performed just before disconnecting from the Internet.

t

Target

The Web document that is connected to a particular hyperlink.

TCP/IP (Transmission Control Protocol/Internet Protocol)

A set of rules used on the Internet to provide reliable connections among computers on the overall network; these rules help coordinate which data has been sent and received, identify delays on Internet networks, manage the flow of data, and so on.

Telnet

One of the oldest Internet programs for connecting to remote computers; based on a text rather than graphic interface like Windows, users generally must log in to access the network in order to do e-mail, download programs, or chat with other Telnet users.

Temporary Internet Files

A location in which Internet Explorer saves the content of pages you have visited recently so that they will load more quickly when you return to them.

Text

Any set of alphanumeric characters.

Text string

A particular set of alphanumeric characters that you enter as the basis for a search.

Tip of the Day

An optional feature available through Internet Explorer's Help function that will greet you with a new piece of advice every time you launch the application.

Toggle

(1) To switch back and forth between two open windows or applications. (2) To alter the state of a command option which has only two possible states, such as "on" or "off."

Toolbar

A graphical segment of the Internet Explorer browser window, or of any application, that contains a selection of buttons you can use to activate functions with the click of a mouse.

Trusted Sites Zone

A Security Zone to which you can assign Web sites whose content you trust.

U

URL (Uniform Resource Locator)

The characters that tell a browser such as Internet Explorer where a particular resource resides on the World Wide Web, including a root, domain, path, and file name. It is also called an Address.

Usenet

Developed around 1980, a distributed computer-based bulletin board system supported mainly by IBM-based computers; often referred to just as newsgroups.

V

Virus

A program or piece of computer code that loads onto a disk or computer without the user's knowledge and operates against the user's wishes, often to consume memory or to damage or shut down normal computer operations.

W

W3C (World Wide Web Consortium)

An international group of industry and university representatives that monitors the development of Web technology.

WAIS (Wide Area Information Server)

Developed in the late 1980s, one of the first indexes to the World Wide Web.

Wallpaper

In Windows, an image you set up to be displayed as the background on your desktop. You can capture images from the Web and use them as wallpaper by right-clicking on them.

Web Site Certificate

A document appended to a Web page that states that a specific Web site is secure and genuine; it ensures that no other Web site can assume the identify of the original secure site.

Webcam

A still or video camera that produces images a Web author sends out over the Internet, often in real time, 24 hours a day.

Webcast

An event such as a concert or press conference that is made available as streaming video or audio over the Web.

Window

The graphical representation of a particular file, folder or application when it is active on the Windows desktop.

Windows

A popular operating system for PC-based computers, produced by Microsoft. Different versions of Windows include Windows 98, Windows Me, and Windows XP.

Windows Media Player

A Microsoft application, downloadable for free on the Internet, that enables users to watch video over the Web.

Wizard

In Windows, a program that guides you through a complex process. Internet Explorer uses a Wizard to help you export folders of Favorites for another user to receive.

WordPad

The built-in word processor on the Windows operating system; this program contrasts with advanced word processors such as Microsoft Word or Corel WordPerfect by providing only basic typing and formatting features.

World Wide Web (WWW, or the Web)

An enormous array of linked hypertext documents that reside on computers around the world, all of which can be viewed using a browser application such as Internet Explorer.

Y

Yahoo

A popular commercial search engine.

index